A WOMAN OF TWO WORLDS

Elizabeth Patterson Bonaparte

A WOMAN OF TWO WORLDS

ELIZABETH PATTERSON BONAPARTE

ALEXANDRA DEUTSCH

Maryland Historical Society

BALTIMORE, MARYLAND

2016

Library of Congress Cataloging-in-Publication Data

Names: Deutsch, Alexandra, 1971–

Title: A woman of two worlds : Elizabeth Patterson Bonaparte / Alexandra
  Deutsch.

Description: Baltimore : Maryland Historical Society, 2016. | Includes
  bibliographical references and index.

Identifiers: LCCN 2016008313| ISBN 9780996594424 (cloth : alkaline paper) |
  ISBN 9780996594431 (paper : alkaline paper)

Subjects: LCSH: Bonaparte, Elizabeth Patterson, 1785–1879. | Bonaparte,
  Elizabeth Patterson, 1785–1879 — Marriage. | Bonaparte, Elizabeth
  Patterson, 1785–1879 — Family. | Jérôme Bonaparte, King of Westphalia,
  1784–1860 — Marriage. | Napoleon I, Emperor of the French,
  1769–1821 — Family. | France — History — 1789–1900 — Biography. |
  Women — Maryland — Baltimore — Biography. | Baltimore (Md.) — Biography.

Classification: LCC DC216.95.B629 D48 2016 | DDC 943/.5506092 — dc23

LC record available at http://lccn.loc.gov/2016008313

Copyright © 2016

Maryland Historical Society

CLOTHBOUND: ISBN 9780996594424
PAPERBACK: ISBN   9780996594431

DESIGNED BY JAMES F. BRISSON

"To Dress for Admiration"

Elizabeth Patterson Bonaparte (1785–1879), Gilbert Stuart (1755–1879), 1804, oil on canvas, Private collection
Gilbert Stuart was so captivated by Elizabeth's beauty that he chose to paint her in this triple portrait, the only one of this type ever done by an American artist. Annoyed by Jérôme's critique of his work, Stuart refused to complete the painting, leaving it as an oil sketch. In 1807, Stuart brought the painting to his studio in Boston and placed it in his garret with other discarded canvases. Stuart's daughter Jane remembered "this beautiful sketch of Madame Bonaparte was the idol I worshipped." Although Elizabeth's friend Robert Gilmor Jr. retrieved Stuart's portrait of Jérôme in 1807, Stuart would not part with the triple portrait. In 1820, William Patterson finally succeeded in obtaining the portrait and hung it in his South Street house. He left it to Elizabeth in his will. Elizabeth regarded the portrait as the "only true likeness that has ever been made of me. My other pictures are quite like anyone else as me." Carrie Rebora Barratt and Ellen G. Miles, *Gilbert Stuart* (New York: Metropolitan Museum of Art, 2004), 249.

DEDICATION

To my father
CHARLES DEUTSCH
*who taught me
to love history*

and my mother
GAIL COOPER DEUTSCH
*who taught me
to love art*

and to
VERNE FOWLER KREISEL
*who taught me to
love old things*

❧

IN APPRECIATION

This book was made possible by
the generous support of

Barbara P. Katz

and additional support from
the Friends of the Press,
Maryland Historical Society
and

Furthermore:
a program of the J. M. Kaplan Fund

CONTENTS

CHAPTER 3
"O, for celebrity . . ."
71

CHAPTER 4
"Mésalliances are Fatal in Most Families"
103

A MESSAGE FROM
THE DIRECTOR

She belongs to history; she lived with kings and princes, philosophers and artists; there is about her a perpetual curiosity and romance.

— LADY SYDNEY MORGAN, CA. 1855

ELIZABETH PATTERSON BONAPARTE. Her name conjures up myriad thoughts and faint recognition, although many today have never heard of her or know that she was once extremely famous in Europe and America. She has been gone for over 130 years, yet she seems so present. Perhaps she is timeless as was suggested by her friend Lady Sydney Morgan, the famous Irish novelist. Or maybe some think she was one of the great Napoleon's wives. In Baltimore those who recognize her name have grave misconceptions about her. She is the subject of legends. Fictionalized stories of her walking the streets with her red carpetbag and an umbrella collecting ground rents and returning to her boarding house rooms in the Mount Vernon neighborhood are still numerous.

She was indeed a mystery. Once considered a most extraordinary beauty, she weathered storms of her own making. One need only look at the ethereal portrait painted by Gilbert Stuart of her three faces looking out at the viewer with an inviting gaze. Who was this enigmatic woman? Almost a century before wealthy American Consuelo Vanderbilt married the Duke of Marlborough in 1895, she was the most talked about American woman in Europe, the original dollar princess. She married the brother of the emperor of Europe and was at home in the grandest salons of the nineteenth century. She was a mother and a grandmother. Imperious creature, recalcitrant aristocrat. All of these characteristics were embodied by this once very famous woman, one ahead of her time but impatient in it. She tormented her son and grandsons expecting them to achieve what she was unable to achieve and most longed for—imperial status. She lived frugally in boarding houses, her possessions were few, she amassed a great fortune, she wrote copious notes of her pains and sufferings and of her loves and hates. She was above all resilient, and she is buried alone away from all family members. Books were written about her years before she died in 1879. Fictional novels, plays, and silent movies based on her life have all tried to convey her celebrity. And now this current work will encapsulate the life of Elizabeth Patterson Bonaparte in a way that has not been approached before.

In 1921, more than 600 items comprising portraits, porcelain, silver, jewelry, sculpture, textiles, journals, and books belonging to Elizabeth Patterson Bonaparte and her family were given to the Maryland Historical Society by Elizabeth's grandson's wife. It was this gift that enabled the society to become the official repository for both families. This unrivaled collection has in turn allowed Alexandra Deutsch as chief curator of the society to unravel the full life of this character from birth to death. Not concentrating solely on her marriage to Jérôme Bonaparte as her greatest accomplishment, but trying to understand the complexity and achievements of a woman ahead of her times in the nineteenth century. Deutsch's work will join the pantheon of great biographies in the field of women's history as well as American and European alliances. This is the story of an extraordinary woman in extraordinary times.

MARK B. LETZER
President & CEO
Maryland Historical Society

A MESSAGE FROM
THE FAMILY

OVER THE YEARS MANY BOOKS have been written about Elizabeth Patterson Bonaparte's extraordinary life. She appears to have invariably differed from the "normal" woman of her time, intriguing and fascinating many including our family in Denmark. In 2013, the Maryland Historical Society launched the first-ever exhibition dedicated entirely to the life of Elizabeth Patterson Bonaparte and her descendants. An impressive exhibition was the result! Alexandra Deutsch, Chief Curator at the Maryland Historical Society, responsible for archival research at the museum, has discovered new and interesting information about her, which is being published for the first time in this book.

Elizabeth had two great-grandchildren—Jerome Bonaparte and Louise Eugenie Bonaparte. Jerome had no children, thus ending the American line of the Bonaparte family. It would probably have pleased Elizabeth to know that a third-generation American Bonaparte had finally married into European nobility—my grandmother, Louise Eugenie Bonaparte, married my grandfather, Count Adam Moltke-Huitfeldt, in 1896. He was the owner of Glorup Estate in Funen, Denmark. My grandparents had five children, two of whom had their own children and today, thanks to them, Elizabeth Patterson Bonaparte's living descendants in Denmark total twenty-nine. Without doubt this exhibition, together with all the new information discovered in the archives of the Maryland Historical Society, is an enormous achievement, benefiting not only our Danish family but the history of Baltimore and American history in general.

COUNT ADAM MOLTKE-HUITFELDT

FOREWORD

"My words are severe, and designed to be severe."

— Elizabeth Bonaparte, 1857

There is little doubt that Elizabeth Patterson Bonaparte (1785–1879) was perpetually unhappy. Throughout her long life, she set frustrating, difficult goals for herself, always reaching for places that she was told were unattainable. As her own wealthy father, William Patterson, all but wrote her out of his will, he commented that Elizabeth was more trouble than his many other children combined.

Madame Bonaparte was beautiful, imperious, focused, fascinating, driven, and a great story that spanned almost a century. Her "severe" words, recorded over many decades and scribbled in account books, journals, letters, often in the margins of books, paint a lonely search for the opulent halls and smoke-filled back rooms of power that remained the havens of men. By her ninety-first year, she was priding herself on being one of America's rare self-made women. This American original was an odd combination of early feminism and old-fashioned political views favoring monarchy. Those views put her at odds with the "Great Democratic Experiment" that spawned her and made her family wealthy.

One quick look at Gilbert Stuart's engaging 1804 three-faced portrait of the captivating Baltimore-bred Elizabeth sets off a flurry of speculations. Nineteen years old, rich, smart, and ready to turn heads wherever she went, she was out to leave her mark from the start. Her appearances at Washington gatherings sporting the revealing new French fashion set tongues wagging and garnered everyone's attention.

At the same time, an 1803 American visit from French Emperor Napoleon Bonaparte's youngest brother, Jérôme, began a chain of events that would define the still teen-aged Elizabeth's life. Their meeting sent young sparks flying, and a doomed international courtship and marriage that produced a child became the fodder of Hollywood movies (two films were produced a century and a quarter later). The oft-told story took only a handful of years at the beginning of a long, eventful life, but Elizabeth's quest to obtain an "Imperial Legacy" for her son "Bo" became a relentless obsession. The tale of an American belle caught up in the family politics of the Napoleonic Era is beguiling. The object here, however, is to tell the rest of the story as well.

During seven decades after her dramatic episode with the Bonaparte family, Elizabeth Patterson Bonaparte traveled to Europe frequently, met scores of notable people on both sides of the Atlantic, and grew a small annuity from Napoleon into a fortune. Born just after the American Revolution, Elizabeth set her own course in a society with few opportunities for women. In 1879, when her grandson telegraphed the news to the family that "the Madame has expired" at ninety-four, the United States was in its "Gilded Age." Madame Bonaparte, the self-made entrepreneur, took full advantage of the times to become a highly successful business woman. In the process, she both witnessed and made history.

The Maryland Historical Society became a part of the Bonaparte story in 1921. By 1919, the Society had moved into philanthropist Enoch Pratt's house at the corner of Monument Street and Park Avenue in Baltimore's posh Mt. Vernon neighborhood. Not even a block down Park, Charles Joseph Bonaparte, a grandson of Madame Bonaparte, died in his townhouse that featured a "Bonaparte Room," filled with notable mementoes of the previous century. His widow, Ellen Channing Day, graciously decided to donate the hundreds of artifacts and thousands of documents that chronicled the Baltimore Bonaparte legacy over four generations. With this generous gift, the Society received one of the most important legacies and stories in its long history.

Almost a century later, the Bonaparte story, told and retold, has a new focus. The Maryland Historical Society has been mining its Bonaparte Collection as never before. The Bicentennial of the War of 1812 provided an opportunity to feature a familiar figure from that era. Chief Curator Alexandra Deutsch led the staff in constructing an exhibit devoted to the lady who lived in both Europe and America during her lifelong quest, seeking a French Imperial Legacy for herself and her descendants. A timeline that stretches down a wall at the exhibit entrance follows the whole intricate story from Elizabeth's birth in 1785 to her great-granddaughter's marriage to a Danish count in 1896 and beyond. Elizabeth would have been pleased that all of her direct descendants are now Europeans.

Walking into the jewel box of an exhibit, gazing at the finely rendered portraits and miniatures, the exquisite ceramics, the fashionable dresses, and the many small domestic items collected over a lifetime, a visitor is struck by two items. One is a decorated traveling trunk featured at the room's center. After decades of accompanying Madame Bonaparte on her numerous trips back and forth across the Atlantic, the trunk is a little worse for wear. It is stamped with various versions of Elizabeth's identity from Elizabeth Patterson to Madame Bonaparte. It is the tangible symbol of her peripatetic life, always seeking, always restless.

The other is high on the walls around the exhibit. A quick survey of the quotes recorded from journals, letters, and jottings cuts to the heart of Elizabeth Bonaparte's frustration with her lot in life, her unhappy relationship with her family, her business acumen, her fascination with fashionable frugality, and her never-ending attraction to the politics and customs of the Old World. Alexandra Deutsch's discoveries in this vast collection of artifacts and documents cried out for an investigation of the complete story of Elizabeth Bonaparte and her family.

This book is the result of that investigation. It is a time capsule of an eventful century. It is an engaging, image-laden catalogue of the many things, important and insignificant, that Elizabeth held near and dear and passed on to her descendants. Most of all, it is a narrative of a busy, self-absorbed life as well as a self-styled Bonaparte legacy embraced by the grandchildren and great-grandchildren. Never before has the story of this intriguing woman been so thoroughly explored.

Although Madame Bonaparte paid close attention to the political and intellectual life over several generations, she remained focused on growing her money and getting her son and grandsons the status they deserved as children of French nobility. She witnessed tumultuous times: steam power and the telegraph, signatures of a titanic Industrial Revolution, the wars of Napoleon, an 1814 British invasion of the young United States, frayed monarchies that created unrest, even revolutions in Europe, and the American Civil War, which brought an occupying Union army to her native Baltimore.

Yet her valuable account books, journals, and letters reveal appointments, purchases, and expenses, the minutiae of everyday life. Personal opinions about the often fractious world around her are absent.

With this handsome and substantive book, we are privileged to discover a nineteenth-century original as never before. Always striving, always present, Elizabeth Patterson Bonaparte mixed the past and future in ways that made her unique to her day and age. Enjoy this brand new look at one of Maryland's most fascinating daughters.

BURTON KUMMEROW
Historian in Residence
Maryland Historical Society
February, 2016

PREFACE

"MADAME BONAPARTE SAYS SHE PRIDES HERSELF on being a self made woman," observed Martha Custis Williams, Elizabeth Patterson Bonaparte's friend.[1] In her ninety-first year, Elizabeth reflected on her life with pride. Although to a public intrigued by her celebrity, her greatest accomplishment was her brief marriage in 1803 to Jérôme Bonaparte, Napoléon's youngest brother, which catapulted her into the public eye and laid the groundwork for her imperial legacy, far more noteworthy was that as a single woman she had managed to build a fortune of over one million dollars through astute investments. A "shrewd Baltimore banker" remarked that he knew "no man more capable of creating legitimately with so small a capital the large fortune she amassed."[2] In addition, her determination to create an independent life that did not conform to social norms based upon marriage and domesticity was a remarkable achievement for a woman of the nineteenth century. Until recently, those aspects of Elizabeth's story went largely ignored in favor of more romantic and tragic accounts of her Bonaparte *"mésalliance."*

Born in 1785, just two years after the United States achieved nationhood, Elizabeth was a revolutionary in many ways. Just as her country defied disbelievers and triumphed over a world power to make itself into something wholly unique, Elizabeth pushed aside the American disdain for monarchy and embraced her own unique, royal destiny, one that included her son and grandsons and left a legacy that still touches her descendants today. Not surprisingly, her self-determination, scorn for American culture, and open defiance of American social norms prescribed for women drew considerable criticism during her lifetime. A celebrity for much of her life as well as a curiosity in America because she preferred to live in Europe, Elizabeth was often maligned for her revealing fashions, love of aristocracy, and unwillingness to conform to the role of wife and mother. She lived with constant disapproval from her American peers, but European aristocrats and intellectuals admired her mind and strong will.

Her greatest critic and the person who, in many ways, inflicted the most emotional pain was not her estranged husband or the emperor who ended her marriage but her father, the wealthy Baltimore merchant, William Patterson. Although she referred to him as "her blast from the Desert" and spent decades trying to prove to him that she was not a failure, ironically, Elizabeth was more like her father than anyone else. In matters of finance, Patterson guided his daughter toward sound investments and helped her dodge the new American republic's savage economic cycles, and, like him, she was judgmental, shrewd, calculating, and slow to forgive. A prominent French nobleman observed, "She charms with her eyes while she slays with her tongue."[3] Severe though Elizabeth could be, she could also be charming, sentimental, generous, and prone to melancholy, all qualities that have remained largely ignored despite being prominent in her writings. Patterson's continual criticism of his daughter's life left Elizabeth feeling that no matter how respected, admired, or wealthy she became, she would forever be a failure. When Patterson died in 1835 and left little to her in his will, Elizabeth feared that, even from the grave, her father would disapprove of her for eternity. Although books continued to be written about Elizabeth long after her death, the neglect of her accomplishments in these works has made that fear into a reality. She simply has not been "seen" for the woman she was.

Even before her death in 1879, books were published about Elizabeth's unusual and intriguing story, a brush with European royalty. The first, a collection of letters assembled by W. T. R. Saffell and entitled, *The Bonaparte-Patterson Marriage in 1803 and the Secret Correspondence on the Subject Never Before Made Public*, revealed far more than its title suggests. In fact, Saffell's work uncovers more than the drama of Elizabeth's marriage; it sheds light on aspects of Elizabeth's complex relationship with her father and documents the national and international complexity associated with Elizabeth's union and its subsequent dissolution. In selecting his title, Saffell knew that her marriage was "the" story that would sell his book. In 1879, after Elizabeth's death, Eugene L. Didier published an expanded version of Saffell's work, including additional letters that date beyond 1806 and document Elizabeth's European social life, her relationship with her son Bo, and sketch an even clearer portrait of the troubled relationship she maintained with her father.[4]

Although writers continued to explore her story for decades after her death, their focus remained fixed on the marriage and their versions of the story bear little resemblance to the facts. It was during this period that many of the "romantic' and often repeated stories of Elizabeth take hold. For instance, an article published in the *Baltimore Sun* in 1900 contains the first fictitious account of Elizabeth's seeing Jérôme at the Pitti Palace decades after their estrangement. The author recalled, "One day Jerome was walking with his new wife in the gallery of the Pitti Palace, at Florence, when Madame Bonaparte came upon the scene. When he recognized her Jerome hurriedly whispered to his Catherine, as Elizabeth silently walked on, 'That lady is my former wife.' He took care not to tarry in the gallery, and the next morning left the city."[5] Subsequent authors embellished the story, claiming that Elizabeth opened her cloak to reveal her beautiful figure to Jérôme and remind him of his loss. This story, unsubstantiated in the Bonaparte papers, caught the public's attention and to this day is retold. In 1906, a play entitled, "Glorious Betsy," written by Mrs. Rida J. Young of Baltimore, was performed at the Academy of Music (now Peabody Institute). It featured an upbeat ending in which Elizabeth and Jérôme remained happily married despite Napoléon's protestations. Young's version of the story departs from the facts in almost every aspect of the telling and, in the original play, includes a scene between Elizabeth and Napoléon in which the emperor implores Elizabeth to give up Jérôme because, as an American woman, she owes a debt to France and the memory of the Marquis de Lafayette's role in the American Revolution.[6] According to the *Sun*, Charles Bonaparte, Elizabeth's grandson, attended the performance. His observations about the play do not survive, but it is interesting to imagine what he thought of this fanciful and inaccurate version of his grandmother's life. In 1928, Hollywood transformed "Glorious Betsy" into a silent film featuring a blonde Elizabeth and a Hollywood-style happy ending.

While these tall tales of Elizabeth's romantic life were keeping her celebrity more or less intact, decades passed before historians attempted to extricate fact from fiction. Stories about everything from how Elizabeth and Jérôme met to her puttering about Baltimore with a carpetbag of money gained a firm hold on a story that deserved more accuracy. The notion that Elizabeth was known as Betsy persists to this day despite the fact that she never referred to herself by that name. In her case, romance made the facts, well documented in her papers, far less interesting than charming tidbits. Fiction dominated biography.

Elizabeth's marriage lasted two years, but she lived more than seven decades after it ended. The history of her marriage can, in fact, be told very quickly, and yet it often became the focus of subsequent works about her life. Her whirlwind romance with Jérôme trumped all else and left a record of a beautiful, ambitious, shallow woman who craved an international stage and aristocracy. That Talleyrand once said of her, "If she were a queen with what grace would she reign?" remained forgotten.[7] For more than a century, no author ever spoke of her as a "self-made" woman, a figure in American history to be admired for her intellect and determination as much as her financial acumen. She was condemned by many as nothing more than an ambitious gold-digger, a royal wanna-be. Unlike her friend Dolley Madison, who is celebrated for her spirit, her wit, and her will to make America's first lady a significant political force, Elizabeth remained that intriguing, scandalous figure whose ambition was worthy of attention but not praise.

If we analyze the rest of Elizabeth's long life, her biography becomes a window into nineteenth-century American and European culture and politics. A monarchist to her dying day, Elizabeth was both modern and archaic in her views of society and culture. She believed women should control their own destinies—from the choice of a husband, and the decision to have children to the ability to manage (and make) money. In a new country where self-made men like Benjamin Franklin would become icons, Elizabeth was the original self-made woman. Yet, despite these thoroughly modern ideas, Elizabeth held onto the belief that society needed order, and that democracy left individuals without defined roles in society. The great irony is that America and the freedoms it offered her, made her rich. To trace the outline of her life is to discover moments in history that she witnessed and the historical figures she met. If a complete address book for Elizabeth survived it would boast an international list of the "who's who" of nineteenth-century Europe and the United States. Addresses for Madame Récamier, Pauline Borghese, the Duke of Marlborough, and Lady Sydney Morgan would appear together with James and Dolley Madison, Robert Gilmor, John Jacob Astor, and Robert E. Lee. Her letters and journals read like cinematic glimpses into the nineteenth century.

Although engaged in the politics and intellectual life of her time, she possessed a monocular vision of her world, her lens always focused on her money and the imperial legacy of her son and later her grandsons. She paid close attention to events that shaped the European and American economies and scrutinized the rise and fall of political power abroad, thus providing modern readers with a window into the complexities of the century. Unencumbered by the responsibilities of a permanent residence and the typical domestic duties of a nineteenth-century woman, Elizabeth wrote little about the minutiae of everyday life, but her account books and journals shed light on a life very different from that lived by her peers in America. Her expenses and purchases in Europe, well documented in her papers, reveal what it cost to live among nobility without being noble herself. They record with whom she socialized, where she traveled, and by what means. Elizabeth's expenses and purchases in Baltimore reveal much, not only about trends in fashion but about the burgeoning city. The records of her stock purchases and real estate investments document how Baltimore grew to be America's third-largest city by mid-century. Moreover, it is in the annotations found in her books, journals, and letters that the inner Elizabeth emerges and where her human side and emotions can be found. In the margins, Elizabeth's celebrity falls away, leaving the record of a woman far more complex than previous histories have suggested.

This book, both an exhibition catalogue and historical biography, represents the first attempt to examine the material culture associated with Elizabeth and her descendants. What began as an outgrowth of the Maryland Historical Society's 2013 exhibition, "Woman of Two Worlds: Elizabeth Patterson Bonaparte and Her Quest for an Imperial Legacy," became a thematic exploration of Elizabeth's journey from daughter of a wealthy Baltimore merchant to self-made millionaire. It also allowed for an in-depth analysis of the Bonaparte decorative arts collection, from grand pieces of furniture and portraits to the smallest fragment of lace. The Maryland Historical Society's collection of more than six hundred objects related to the Patterson-Bonaparte story, coupled with the boxes and boxes of documents written by Patterson and Bonaparte family members, particularly Elizabeth, made this scholarly exploration possible.

Bringing the objects together with the documents revealed new stories and rewrote often repeated, but inaccurate, tales regarding some of Elizabeth's possessions. For example, the carpetbag she allegedly used to collect her ground rents does not appear in any of her records and may very well have been one of the charming but erroneous stories told about her again and again. The idea that all her jewels must have been gifts from Jérôme was quickly discarded once her inventories were thoroughly transcribed; in fact, some of the grandest jewels she bought for herself. As the most famous person associated with the Bonaparte objects, everything in the museum's collection, at one point, was thought to have belonged to Elizabeth. In fact, many of the Bonaparte objects belonged to her sons and grandsons and, by establishing this provenance, new stories about the next generations came to light, and an understanding of the imperial legacy of the American Bonapartes began to emerge. Although past authors have used portraits of Elizabeth as well as some of her objects to illuminate aspects of her history, many of the objects illustrated in this book have never been considered because they relate to the long chronology of Elizabeth's life. In addition, objects from private collections have enriched the story of Elizabeth's descendants, strengthening the narrative of their relationships to their Bonaparte heritage.

Rather than tackling Elizabeth's story chronologically, this book follows the evolution of Elizabeth's identity and addresses specific themes within her story. This allows the trajectory of her story to be told more completely and permits the "human" Elizabeth to emerge. Building upon the work of Helen Jean Burn in *Betsy Bonaparte* and Charlene M. Boyer Lewis in *Elizabeth Patterson Bonaparte: An American Aristocrat in the Early Republic*, this book seeks to further unravel and expand the often-told tale of one of nineteenth-century America's most intriguing women. It also represents an attempt to explore the relationships of Elizabeth's descendants to their Bonaparte heritage. No previous publication about Elizabeth has looked as closely at the history of Elizabeth's son and grandsons and followed her legacy to where it now resides, with her only direct descendants in Denmark.

A timeline of Elizabeth's life that continues through to the marriage of her great-granddaughter, Louise Eugenie Bonaparte Moltke-Huitfeldt, is included in this book because, as I argue, the evolution of the Bonaparte legacy continued long after Elizabeth's death in 1879. The timeline also serves to outline how peripatetic Elizabeth's life was until 1863, when she made her last trip to Europe. In an age when few American women ever traveled to Europe, Elizabeth made nine voyages, a testament to the independent spirit that fueled her life. Although she lived for the last sixteen years of her life in a Baltimore boarding house, she spent much of that time revisiting her past. As Elizabeth reviewed her letters, inventoried her possessions, and filled her journals and books with marginalia, one can see that she reflected on her life with a mixture of awe and disdain. Although embittered by the wrongs she felt her father, brothers, and former husband inflicted upon her, she still reveled in her memories and saved every scrap of paper that documented them.

A true gift to my research came in the form of Martha Custis Williams Carter's diaries, which contain so much of Elizabeth's story. In most cases, the stories Elizabeth told her younger companion are corroborated by other sources. Elizabeth spoke to Martha about her European life, her thoughts about religion, memories of her family, and even about many of the objects she had saved. It is within the pages of Martha's pocket-sized diaries that we come to know a "truer" Elizabeth than can be found in almost any other source. Had Elizabeth's European diaries and others survived, perhaps this would not be the case, but, regrettably, those documents, of which Elizabeth spoke often, have to date not been seen by scholars.

One book that profoundly shaped my thoughts about Elizabeth was Jill Lepore's *Book of Ages: The Life and Opinions of Jane Franklin* (2014). Jane Franklin, Benjamin's sister, was known only because of her famous brother. Historians prior to Lepore solely examined her "Book of Ages," a record of family births, deaths, and other daily details, in the context of her brother's fame. As Lepore discovered, Jane's "Book of Ages" is, when analyzed as a document with its own significance, a window into numerous stories about Jane's life. By lifting the celebrity of her brother away from Jane's history, an entirely new story emerges. Jane was a very different woman from Elizabeth, but *Book of Ages* made me realize how imperative it is to lift the "celebrity" away from a person's story. Within the chapter of this book devoted to Elizabeth's celebrity, my intent was to look at Elizabeth's attitude toward her own fame and the notoriety that came with the Bonaparte legacy she worked so diligently to establish. Simply citing the many quotations about Elizabeth's famously sheer gowns— and the censorious comments of some of her peers—does not present a complete picture of how Elizabeth was perceived.

In researching this book, I centered myself in the documents at the Maryland Historical Society, wedding myself to their content and only looking to additional sources when it was imperative to understand the larger context of the story. Although this produced a relatively limited bibliography with fewer secondary sources, it also allowed the lens to rest on Elizabeth and her descendants with an intensity that brought greater clarity to the history of their legacy. Rather than beginning with the objects in the Bonaparte collection, as many decorative arts catalogues do, I used the documents as a launching pad and then looked at how the information they contained intersected with the surviving material culture. In doing so, the American Bonapartes, beginning with Elizabeth, became more than just celebrities. Theirs became a story that reaches far beyond the romance of "Betsy Bonaparte."

Alexandra Deutsch
Baltimore, Maryland
February 15, 2016

ACKNOWLEDGMENTS

I FIRST "MET" ELIZABETH PATTERSON BONAPARTE IN 1999, while walking through the galleries of the Maryland Historical Society with my mother. Standing in front of Elizabeth's red trunk, I read the label and then reread it, amazed that a woman from Baltimore married a Bonaparte. Turning to my mother in disbelief, I made her read the label and then we walked on, muttering, "How very odd and incredible." I cannot say I thought much about Elizabeth after our first encounter, but when my longtime friend and colleague Mark B. Letzer began talking to me about the Bonaparte silver at the Maryland Historical Society and his discovery that much of the silver thought to belong exclusively to Elizabeth belonged, in fact, to her son and grandsons, I remember thinking back to Elizabeth's red trunk. When I arrived at MdHS in 2008, almost ten years after I had first encountered Elizabeth's story, I returned to that trunk and examined it. For the first time, I realized it had both her names on it, "Elizabeth Patterson" and "Elizabeth Bonaparte." Here was a story to be discovered that needed a proper telling—one woman, two identities. It was so much more than the story of marriage that failed.

Without the generosity, guidance, and patience of many individuals, I could not have told this story. To Barbara Katz I owe the greatest thanks. Mrs. Katz provided the funds to make this book a reality, but she also believed in my ability to tell this story. Her encouragement and enthusiasm for this endeavor fueled my determination and inspiration to tell Elizabeth's story in as much detail as possible.

Many individuals gave their time, expertise, and patience with unstinting generosity and grace. To my editors, Ric Cottom and Donna Shear, designer Jim Brisson, and the unflappable Patricia Anderson, Director of Publications and the Library at the Maryland Historical Society, thank you for recognizing the merits of my interpretation of Elizabeth Patterson Bonaparte's story and for devising a format that let this book be both a catalogue and narrative. Thank you for always sharing my excitement for every new discovery I made, for loving the "chase" as much as I do, and for bucking me up when I began to doubt myself. To my companion in all things EPB, Barbara Meger, you have been a gift to this project and have helped me in every step of this journey. Your keen, scholarly eye is behind this manuscript and your editorial input was invaluable. This book would not be what it is without you. To Jean Russo, who served as my "history police" and pushed me to delve deeper into the complexity of this story, your insights challenged me and your meticulous attention to detail brought a new depth to it. Your remarkable ability to bolster my confidence as well as inspire me to revisit sources again and again changed this book in ways I never imagined.

To Mark Letzer, I do not know where to begin when I think of how you guided me toward Elizabeth. Your study of the Bonaparte silver and realization that Elizabeth constructed an imperial legacy for her son and grandsons was the springboard for my understanding of the Bonaparte collection at MdHS. Your determination to see a Bonaparte exhibition at the MdHS and your continued passion for this history has made so many things possible. To the Richard C. Von Hess Foundation that funded "Woman of Two Worlds: Elizabeth Patterson Bonaparte and Her Quest for an Imperial Legacy," I express my deepest gratitude for your support. Without your generosity, the 2013 Bonaparte exhibition would not have been possible, and without that exhibition this book would never have come to be. To Burton K. Kummerow, former president of MdHS and senior historian in residence, I thank you for believing in my ability to write this book. You continue to be a mentor to me and have taught me that the best history must be a story well told, inhabited by people with flesh, blood, contradictions, and foibles.

I owe a very special thank you to Elizabeth Bonaparte's descendants in Denmark. Your enthusiasm and interest in the project made it possible for me to tell a story previously untold. To Adam Moltke-Huitfeldt, Julie Moltke-Huitfeldt, Elise Moltke-Huitfeldt, Elizabeth Moltke-Huitfeldt and Jacob Rosenkrantz, your willingness to share your family's history with me and your passion for Elizabeth's story and her legacy made this book what it is and allowed me to tell the history of Elizabeth's descendants more completely. My time in Denmark changed this publication in profound ways and I will be forever grateful for that time with you. To Elizabeth Moltke-Huitfeldt, your exquisite photography gilds this book, adding beauty and depth to the tales these objects can tell. The information you continued to share with me about Elizabeth added so much to my understanding of her objects. To Hans Wassard, thank you for providing photographs of objects I had only read about in the Bonaparte papers and allowing me to tell those long forgotten stories. Thank you to Harry Connelly, whose beautiful photographs and wonderful sense of humor made our three-day-long Bonaparte photography session so much fun.

I must thank the knowledgeable and generous costume historians whose contributions to this book cannot be overstated. The unstinting advice and unending store of knowledge you shared with me, as well as important editorial comments, transformed the fashion chapter. Colleen Callahan, Newbold Richardson, Ann Wass, Dr. Karin Bohleke, and Lesley Edwards, I am so very lucky to have you as my mentors in fashion history. To Karin Bohleke, I must extend a very particular thank you for the masterly translations peppered throughout this book. Your understanding of nineteenth-century colloquial French was invaluable and your meticulous attention to every detail of the translations greatly enhanced my understanding of the documents and of Elizabeth's and Bo's psyches. To Charles Germaine, who read Jérôme Bonaparte's letters with me and helped me to see that he possessed a great love for Elizabeth despite the outcome of their marriage, you also helped me understand the French perspective on this history, something I, as an American, could not readily grasp.

To the staff of the H. Furlong Baldwin Library—Damon Talbot, Lara Westwood, Debbie Harner, Cathy McDermot, and Eben Dennis—thank you for pulling countless collections for me again and again and making it possible for me to return over and over to these manuscripts. To Francis O'Neil, MdHS Librarian, I am indebted to your genealogical research and charts. You are and will always be a wizard in my book. To James Singewald, who created, and Joe Tropea, who managed, the vast quantity of images this book required and who willingly helped to untangle the conundrums that arose, thank you. Thank you to Heather Haggstrom, Kate Gallagher, Paul Rubenson, Allison Tollman, and Lauren Ryan, my colleagues past and present in the museum department. You have pulled Bonaparte objects for me, listened to me endlessly talk about this book, and never complained when my writing took me away from some of our other projects.

To my greatest cheerleaders, my husband Kyle Cunningham, my daughter Jane McKee, and my parents, Gail and the late Charles Deutsch, thank you for always believing, even when I did not, that one day I would write a book.

Alexandra Deutsch
Baltimore, Maryland
February 15, 2016

A WOMAN OF TWO WORLDS

Elizabeth Patterson Bonaparte

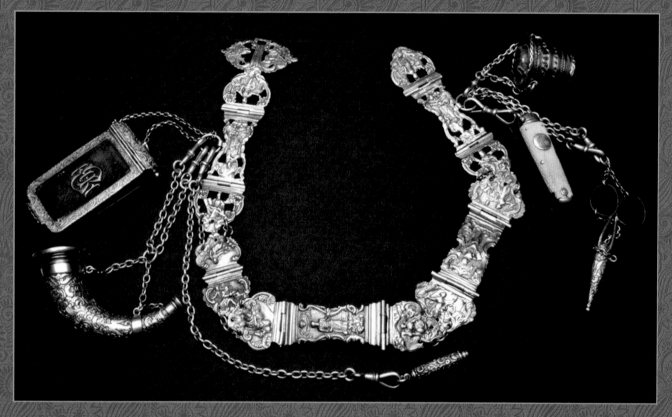

Chatelaine owned by Ellen Channing Day Bonaparte (1852–1924), monogrammed "ECDB"
Circa 1890
Silver with English hallmarks heavily rubbed
Maryland Historical Society, Gift of Mrs. Charles J. Bonaparte, xx.5.425

Traveling Trunk, multiple views
Circa 1805
Chinese
Camphor wood, leather, gilt, and brass
Maryland Historical Society,
Gift of Mrs. Charles J. Bonaparte,
xx.5.552

In 1816, Elizabeth's aunt and financial advisor, Nancy (Anne) Spear, scolded her niece. "You know there is not a being on earth that could make you spend your income. . . . I expect all you do lay out is packed away in little pretty things in your Trunk."[1] Those "pretty things" Elizabeth purchased were almost exclusively for her wardrobe. She invested in clothing and jewelry strategically, knowing her overall appearance outwardly communicated her social status to her peers and reminded them of her imperial connection. Rejecting the typical markers of status usually adopted by the wealthy—a grand home with fleets of servants, vast holdings of material objects, lavish entertainments—she preferred to live with few possessions but believed dress played an important role in creating identity. As she advised her son, Bo, "dress correctly, elegantly, but simply—Finery is the Livery of upstarts & shop men."[2] Elizabeth's numerous trunks contained quantities of clothing, jewelry, and accessories that were, in their time, the height of fashion and European taste. Carefully saved throughout her lifetime and later preserved by her descendants, these things remained sentimental pieces of her life's remarkable history and her royal alliance. Further, they shaped her identity, marking her as a Bonaparte, a woman linked to royalty.

Elizabeth's "Red morocco covered trunk" is emblematic of her nomadic life spent between her two worlds of Europe and Baltimore, as well as her split identity as both Elizabeth Patterson and Madame Bonaparte. One side of the trunk is stenciled, "ELIZABETH PATTERSON" and the other bears two labels that read, "Madame Bonaparte née Patterson." Based on her inventories, Elizabeth appears to have used this particular trunk throughout her adult life, perhaps as early as 1805, when she made her first trip abroad. Preparing for her 1849 trip to Europe, Elizabeth left the red trunk, filled with her silver, at Merchant's Bank in Baltimore. In 1859 she described it in her journal as, "Trunk . . . made of camphor wood and covered with painted red Leather My Name painted in white."* In September 1860, she recorded, "One Red Trunk containing books—a pillow & etc. . . . Deposited at Mr. Bonaparte's Park Street."† That is, before leaving for Paris that fall, she left her red trunk at her son's home. In 1871, she recorded the red trunk "At the Boarding House of the Miss Peters," and noted it contained shawls from her mother, her Brussels Lace marriage veil, and the "black lace dress & ditto Mantilla . . . presented from P. Jerome."‡

---

* Blue Marbled Journal written by EPB, Box 13A, MS 142, EPB Papers.
† Ibid.
‡ Composition Book "for Charles Joseph by his grandmother Madame Bonaparte née Patterson," 1871, Box 13A, MS 142, EPB Papers.

Dorcas Spear Patterson (1761–1814)
with Elizabeth Patterson
Robert Edge Pine (1730–1788)
Circa 1786
Oil on canvas
Maryland Historical Society,
Gift of Mrs. Andrew Robeson, 1959.118.44

Little is known of Elizabeth's mother, Dorcas Spear, except that she was a member of a prominent merchant family and, like her four sisters, was known for her beauty. "She describes her mother as very intelligent & cultivated & very beautiful & often says how elegantly she dressed," wrote Martha Custis Williams Carter in the diary she maintained while living in Mrs. Gwinn's boarding house with Elizabeth.*

_____
* Carter, Diaries, December 1876.

Elizabeth knew how to communicate information about her identity with her clothing and jewelry. For most of her lifetime she firmly allied herself with European taste and sensibility, which she deemed superior to anything found in America. In the last sixteen years of her life, she remained in Baltimore, and her need for admiration and recognition ceased with the decline of her social life. No longer eager to win attention in rarified European circles, she dressed in a manner that stood in sharp contrast to the elegance that was her hallmark as she traveled between Baltimore and Europe eight times. Martha Custis Williams Carter, her friend in Mrs. Gwinn's Baltimore boarding house, described a typical outfit for the elderly Elizabeth, noting, "her nice little foot in a pr [pair] of tight fitting leather slippers, a short black petticoat, a blue checked woolen cape, a bright bandana kerchief pinned across her breast & a little black velvet cap bordered with lace on her head."[3] That was far different from the gown she wore to dine with Madame Récamier in Paris in 1817, "a white imitation cashmere . . . with bands of scarlet cashmere or silk up to the knee & on the waist & sleeves."[4] Nothing about her attire of the 1870s, when Carter talked with her, suggested the elegant woman she had once been, but in her trunks, carefully folded away, were the clothing and other relics of her once fashionable existence.

In fact, Elizabeth was among the first American women to wear the new French fashions of the nineteenth century, setting herself apart from her contemporaries and winning both admiration and scorn for her appearance. As one critic wrote,

> The evening I saw her, she was dressed very plain, at least that part of her body that was covered at all. She exposes so much of her bosom as modesty would permit & I think rather more. Her back was laid bare

nearly half way down to the bottom of her waist. The state of nudity in which she appeared attracted the attention of the Gentlemen, for I saw several of them take a look at her bubbies while they were [in] conversation with her.[5]

Elizabeth skillfully used her clothing to gain attention, and the revealing styles of the early nineteenth century made that an easy task. "I lived on [admiration] while it lasted. . . . I valued my beauty because it gave me immense power." As Elizabeth explained to Carter, she "dressed for admiration."[6] Elizabeth well knew that clothing portrays more than just fashion, it expresses powerful messages about status and identity.

An examination of the costume and costume-related textiles in the Maryland Historical Society's Bonaparte collection reveals connections with Elizabeth's story as told in her letters, account books, inventories, and scrapbooks. Her surviving garments represent "a history of self" that she created for future generations, a material representation of her life, her story, and her legacy. She eventually bequeathed her wardrobe to her grandson, Charles, not as mere clothing but as relics of their shared Bonaparte legacy. In her mind, willing him gowns and laces was no different than willing him a painting of King Jérôme. They both communicated the same important message.

Born in 1785, Elizabeth came into a world in which fashion was undergoing radical changes. By the 1790s when she was a student at Madame Lacombe's Academy in Fells Point, the full skirts and rigid

Gown belonging to Dorcas Spear Patterson with reproduction quilted silk petticoat and fichu.

Gown, last quarter of the 18th century; petticoat created in the 1970s from 18th-century quilted silk; fichu, circa 2013
Silk and silk thread
Maryland Historical Society, Gift of Mrs. Charles J. Bonaparte, xx.5.152
Mannequin made by Studio EIS, Brooklyn, N.Y.

This embroidered silk gown belonged to Dorcas Spear, Elizabeth's mother, and may be the gown listed in Elizabeth's inventories in 1839, 1857, 1862, and 1875. Elizabeth, who remained devoted to her mother's memory throughout her life, traveled at least three times to Europe with this dress—in 1839, 1861, and 1863—but never altered it, suggesting she carried it for sentimental reasons only. Given the cost of a gown like this, it is possible that this was Dorcas's wedding gown. It is highly unlikely that Elizabeth ever wore it, although her figure was very similar to her mother's. Originally, this gown could have been drawn up in the back à la polonaise to create a "bustle" effect.

bodices so fashionable for much of the eighteenth century were giving way to softer, more sensual styles. Muslin gowns made their first appearance in the 1780s, thanks to the influence of classicism and French style on everything from architecture to decorative arts to clothing. Costume historian Ann Buermann Wass points out that women's fashions of the Federal period morphed from a full-skirted silhouette to a tubular shape.[7] The transformation was radical because it allowed the lines of a woman's figure to be seen in a way never before visible in public.

The 1790s and the aftermath of the French Revolution brought French fashions to America, albeit after some delay. One observer remarked, "…the Parisian dress of 1793 [was] in full vogue at Philadelphia in 1795, and that of 1794 did not reach that city until 1796."[8] In Elizabeth's case, her gifts from Jérôme and her later trips to Europe brought her the newest French fashions far more quickly.

As the daughter of a merchant, Elizabeth would have had greater access to imported fabrics and may have been aware of the French fashion plates making their way across the ocean in *Journal des Dames et Modes*, a biweekly illustrated publication.[9] Madame Lacombe, her school mistress whose advertising declared her to be a former French aristocrat who had fled the Revolution, may also have inspired Elizabeth's sense of fashion. At the time, Baltimore was host to an influx of French-speaking émigrés who had fled not only the French Revolution, but also from the bloody uprisings in Haiti. An area near Elizabeth's South Street home, densely populated with these French-speaking residents, came to be called French Town.

Few events in history shaped fashion as profoundly as the French Revolution and the rise of Napoléon—the same man who also redirected the trajectory of Elizabeth's own destiny when he ended her marriage in 1805. By 1803, when Elizabeth married Napoléon's youngest brother, Jérôme, she had already embraced French style. Various descriptions of the bride's attire survive, all of them documenting the sheerness and "smallness" of her clothing. One observer described the wedding gown as "a mere suspicion of a dress—India muslin covered in lace."[10] A green scrap of silk with a lace overlay survives in the Bonaparte collection labeled "a piece of wedding dress," but Elizabeth herself said "She was dressed in white muslin dress with a handsome lace veil given her by her mother."[11] Unfortunately, neither her wedding gown nor the "blue satin [wedding] Coat" sported by Jérôme survive.[12] In 1862, Elizabeth noted the

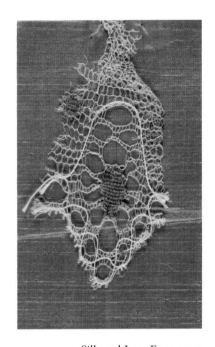

Silk and Lace Fragments
1803
Maryland Historical Society,
Gift of the Enoch Pratt Free Library, 1945.42.1

This fragment of green silk and patch of lace are, according to a note attached to them, part of Elizabeth's wedding gown. It was removed from a trunk with Elizabeth's other clothing and accessories. Other dresses in the collection, as well as a muslin gown at the Metropolitan Museum of Art, have been said to be her wedding gown. Elizabeth never specifically noted "my wedding gown" in her inventories, so its appearance remains conjecture.

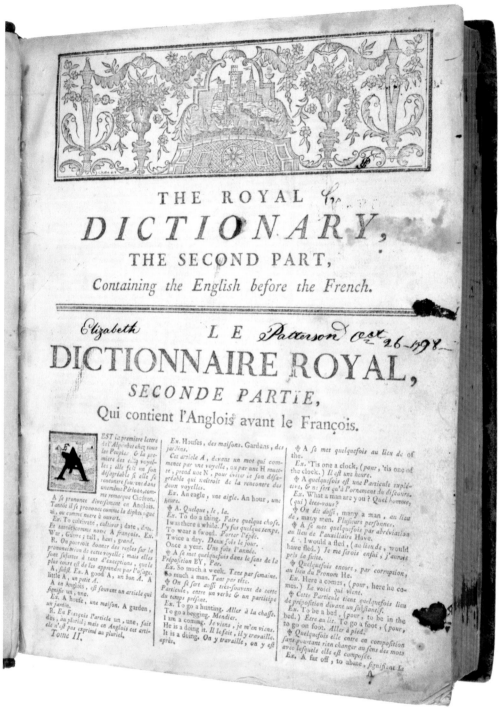

Boyer's Royal Dictionary,
The Second Part
Dated, "Oct. 26, 1798"
Collection of Mr. and Mrs.
Thomas Gorsuch Young

Elizabeth Patterson used this dictionary while at Madame Lacombe's Academy in Fells Point. Originally it was part of a pair, one organized by French to English and the other by English to French. Madame Lacombe, a French-speaking émigrée, promoted herself as an aristocrat who had fled the French Revolution. The school she established at 36 South Street was close to the Patterson home. Elizabeth signed her name four times in this book, twice as "Elizabeth Patterson," once as "Eliza Patterson," and once as "B(?). Patterson." In 1813, when Elizabeth's son, Jerome Napoleon (Bo), was in Baltimore, he wrote to his mother in Washington, D.C., "Don't forget to send me those two Dictionary's of the French Language."* Elizabeth said of Madame Lacombe's, "the teachers . . . were all ladies who had fled France after the revolution & were ladies of the first rank & education—the haute noblesse of France. . . . Madame le Comb had taught [at] a celebrated school at Versailles."†

* Bo to EPB, December 18, 1813," Box 1, MS 144, JNB Papers.
† Martha Custis Williams Carter, Conversations or notations from Madame Bonaparte, [microfilm] Miss Gwinns, 84 Cathedral St., Baltimore: autograph manuscript diary, 1875–1879, H. Furlong Baldwin Library, MICRO 3504, the original from the Department of Literary and Historical Manuscripts, Pierpont Morgan Library, New York, N.Y.

contents of a "Large French round top Box" (in Baltimore), listing: "Wedding Coat of J.B./Wedding Gown. E.P."[13] Only one fragment of her wedding ensemble has been identified, the Brussels lace veil that she wore and recorded in her 1871 inventory.[14] Fragments of this lace veil now edge an enormous net veil made after her death and worn by descendants of her great-granddaughter, Louise Eugenie Bonaparte Moltke-Huitfeldt, as well as other members of the Danish branch of Bonaparte descendants.

Lace and Net Veil
Lace, circa 1803, net,
late nineteenth century
Private collection, photograph by
Elizabeth Moltke-Huitfeldt

The lace edging of this veil, hand-made and similar to other examples of lace found in the Bonaparte Collection, is said to have belonged to Elizabeth. In her surviving inventories, Elizabeth spoke of "a handsome lace veil given her by her mother" that she wore on December 24, 1803 when she married Jérôme Bonaparte. In her 1871 inventory, she noted a "Brussels Lace veil [in] which I was married year 1803." At some point, probably in the late nineteenth century, the remains of what was thought to be Elizabeth's wedding veil were sewn onto a very large piece of handmade netting. The "new" veil has been worn for the weddings of Elizabeth's descendants for several generations.

During their three-year marriage, the ever-extravagant Jérôme bought Elizabeth numerous gifts. "Prince Jérôme sent me $6000 worth of clothes when I was married — I had always a black velvet dress, a black satin, a yellow satin & crimson satin & a blue satin & an elegant black Brussels lace dress to wear over the [illegible] — and a pink satin & a white satin also & the most beautiful India muslin dresses — a number of them embroidered."[15] Jérôme himself loved fashion, and his spending habits appalled his brother, Napoléon.[16] Throughout their brief marriage, Jérôme spent lavishly, particularly during the

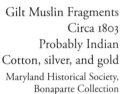

Gilt Muslin Fragments
Circa 1803
Probably Indian
Cotton, silver, and gold
Maryland Historical Society,
Bonaparte Collection

These gold and silver shot muslin fragments may be the remains of the fabric Jérôme bought for Elizabeth during their trip to Lisbon. She recorded that purchase in her journal of 1805.*

_____
* Small green journal,
xx.5.985a-h / Box 13A, MS 142.

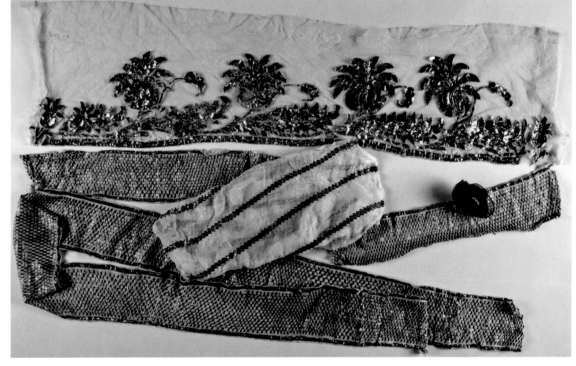

couple's extended wedding trip that took them to Philadelphia, New York City, and even Niagara Falls. Clothing constituted a significant part of their expenditures. During the couple's ill-fated 1805 trip to Europe, they stopped for several days in Lisbon where Jérôme bought Elizabeth "7 yards silver muslin [and] 3 yds gold muslin," $180 worth of topazes, and a garnet necklace engraved "Fidelité" on the clasp.[17] The irony of that inscription was not lost on Elizabeth after Jérôme left her in Lisbon and obeyed Napoléon's imperious order to leave his "so-called wife" behind to make her own way back to Baltimore while he returned to France.

Those gold and silver shot muslins were later made into gowns of the latest fashion, fragments of which survive in the collection today. Ever sentimental, Elizabeth kept the remnants of her spangled muslins in her trunks, recording "Scraps of gold & silver muslin" in the "long trunk with 2 locks" she took to France in 1839.[18] One of her silver-spangled gowns from a slightly later period still survives in the MdHS collection, and after extensive conservation now appears much as it did when Elizabeth wore it. Ellen Channing Day Bonaparte, Elizabeth's grandson's wife, may have repurposed some of Elizabeth's silver scraps to ornament her own gowns. A *Baltimore Sun* article of February 7, 1906 noted, "Mrs. Bonaparte wore a superb gown of black point d'esprit over cloth of silver, with some historic and valuable silver trimmings which belonged to the beautiful Madame Bonaparte."[19] Ellen, much like Elizabeth, knew that clothing proclaimed identity and her association with her husband's famous grandmother was something she not only frequently talked about to the media but displayed in her clothing and jewelry. Her politician husband, self-styled as an American patriot, rarely spoke of his Bonaparte history, but his wife, who donned Elizabeth's relics, let them proclaim it.

Elizabeth, who frequently eviscerated numerous family members in letters, had another deeply sentimental side.[20] This is evident in such things as the gown worn by her mother, Dorcas Spear Patterson. Not only did she save the gown after her mother's death in 1814, she took it with her on three of her eight trips to Europe. To Elizabeth, clothing represented memories, and this fashionable

Muslin Gown with silver embroidery shown with reproduction underdress
Circa 1805
Indian muslin, possibly made in France
Cotton and silver thread
Maryland Historical Society, Gift of Mrs. Charles J. Bonaparte, xx.5.1

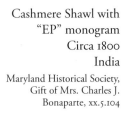

Cashmere Shawl with
"EP" monogram
Circa 1800
India
Maryland Historical Society,
Gift of Mrs. Charles J.
Bonaparte, xx.5.104

In her 1871 inventory,
Elizabeth noted that her
red-covered trunk contained
"four long Cashmir Shawls of
which one white & one yellow
from my Mother."* It is possible
that this one and the surviving
yellow paisley shawl (also
pictured) were given to her by
Dorcas Patterson and are the
ones noted in this inventory.

_____
* Composition Book "for Charles
Joseph by his grandmother Madame
Bonaparte née Patterson,"1871, Box
13A, MS 142, EPB Papers.

Cashmere Shawl
Circa 1800
India

Maryland Historical Society, Gift of Mrs. Charles J. Bonaparte, xx.5.103

This yellow cashmere shawl may have been one of the two given to Elizabeth by her mother. Shawls of this type were called "cashmere," "Kashmir," or "Cashmir" because of the fine goat's wool used to make them and because they were produced in the Indian province of Kashmir. Large quantities of these shawls were exported to Europe and America throughout the nineteenth century.

gown from the 1780s was a reminder of "her kind parent," who stood in sharp contrast to her unloving father. In her old age, Elizabeth described her mother "as very intelligent & cultivated & very beautiful & . . . how elegantly she dressed."[21] She also traveled with her mother's cashmere shawls.

Despite her disdain for her ex-husband, Elizabeth remained sentimental about the gifts he gave her, those material representations of her connection to an imperial legacy. A black lace gown and matching mantilla given to her by "Prince Jérôme" appear in various inventories made throughout her life.[22] Long thought to be simply "scraps" or fragments rather than extant, intact clothing, the lace was revealed after conservation to be "an elegant black Brussels lace

ABOVE: Mantilla given to Elizabeth by Jérôme
Napoléon Bonaparte
1805
French
Silk

Maryland Historical Society,
Gift of Mrs. Charles J. Bonaparte, xx.5.162

After parting from his wife in 1805, Jérôme Bonaparte
enlisted the assistance of the Countess of Elgin (Mary
Nisbet), of Elgin marbles fame, to help him send
several trunks of gifts and money to Elizabeth who, at
that time, was residing in London. In November 1805,
Lady Elgin wrote to Elizabeth, saying, "On leaving
Paris, I was requested by Prince Jérôme Bonaparte to
take charge of some cases of Jewels and Money, that he
had long wished for an opportunity of sending to you
in England."* In February 1806 the trunks finally
arrived in Baltimore, largely undamaged despite fears
that the entire gift had been lost at sea.†

* Countess M. Elgin to EPB, November 5, 1805, Letterbook,
  1805–1809, Box 1, MS 142, EPB Papers.
† James McElhiney to EPB, March 12, 1806, Letterbook 1805–1809,
  Box 1, MS 142, EPB Papers.

LEFT: Lace Over-Dress, given to
Elizabeth by Jérôme Napoléon
Bonaparte, photographed with
reproduction pink underdress
1805
French
Silk

Maryland Historical Society,
Gift of Mrs. Charles J. Bonaparte,
xx.5.209

⚜ 11

Long thought to have been a gift
from Jérôme, this tiara was part of a
large parure Elizabeth inherited from
her sister, Caroline, who died in 1814.
In her 1869 jewelry inventory,
Elizabeth wrote, "Necklace Twenty
Eight Garnetts sett in Pearls – left By
Caroline. – Earrings of same parure
Two Garnets in Each Earring. –
Comb to same parure Twenty one
Garnets pear shaped, sett in Pearls.
Massot copied the comb in his
cabinet Portrait of myself EP."*

---

* Blue and Red Marbled Journal, "Year 1869
Collection," 1869, Box 13A, MS 142, EPB
Papers.

dress to wear over the . . . pink satin & a white satin."[23] Elizabeth referred to this particular gown and mantilla several times in her inventories. An 1805 invoice of clothing sent to Elizabeth by Jérôme included "une robe de dentelle noire superfine sans aucun couture" ("a light/thin/delicate black lace dress without seams") as well as a blue satin gown and a rose or pink satin gown to wear underneath the lace.[24] Rumors circulated that one of the gowns Jérôme bought her cost $1,500, and one can imagine this extraordinary lace gown and mantilla sparking that gossip. Could this gown be the same one mentioned in the *Baltimore Sun* on December 28, 1905, in an article about Ellen Bonaparte? "Mrs. Bonaparte received in an exquisite costume of black lace over rose satin. The skirt was trimmed with flounces of lace that once belonged to Mme. Patterson-Bonaparte. The lace was formed of lace sent to Mr. Charles J. Bonaparte's mother by King Jerome." Although the "robe de dentille," or "Brussels lace" as Elizabeth called it, does not show evidence of flounces, the descriptions of the gown Ellen wore and that treasured by Elizabeth are strikingly similar. In later years, when Elizabeth occasionally received visitors in Mrs. Gwinn's boarding house on Cathedral Street in Baltimore, she sometimes showed them the treasures from her European life. She may have shown them the mantilla and gown while retelling the story of her marriage. Ellen, her grandson's wife, may have continued to show off the gown that always won attention.

Jérôme parted from Elizabeth in Lisbon, leaving her to journey first to Amsterdam and then to England to deliver their son, Jerome Napoleon Bonaparte, or "Bo." During the bleak year after Bo's birth, Jérôme sent his abandoned wife presents. Those that survive are extravagant. The "diadem of Eleven Large Amethysts . . . sett in Gold & Enamel of Pearls of various size" in

the MdHS collection was part of a larger parure or set of jewelry comprising two matching bracelets, earrings, and a comb. Elizabeth noted them in her inventories as having been "sent 1805 by Prince Jérôme."[25] The parure may have been part of the "cases of jewels and Money" that Jérôme entrusted to Lady Elgin to give to Elizabeth for him that year.[26]

On November 21, 1805, Jérôme wrote to Elizabeth, explaining that he had given a box of Parisian clothing to a friend of Robert Patterson, her brother, to be put on board the *Destiny* bound for New York.[27] When Elizabeth returned to Baltimore with Bo in 1806, she brought with her a sophisticated European wardrobe that had grown substantially with Jérôme's gifts. Given the time lag between Europe and America, the clothing Elizabeth brought back to her father's house was probably more up-to-date than that worn by most of her peers. As historian Charlene Boyer Lewis has pointed out, Elizabeth "did not merely dress in American-made clothing that copied European styles, as many of her countrywomen did, but in clothing and jewelry that had actually come from Paris."[28]

The ivory silk taffeta corset in the collection that may date from this early period, perhaps even from her marriage, suggests that Elizabeth was adopting the most fashion-forward trends of the time. The corset is devoid of boning and is the short length that came into fashion in the early nineteenth century. This kind of corset primarily would have provided a more natural shaping to the bust than

Diadem owned by Elizabeth Patterson Bonaparte
Unknown maker, possibly French or Russian
Circa 1805
Amethysts, seed pearls, enamelwork, and gilded copper alloy
Maryland Historical Society, Gift of Mrs. Charles J. Bonaparte, xx.5.297

Elizabeth's 1860 inventory provided a detailed description of this diadem: ". . . one Diadem Eleven Large Amethysts . . . sett in Gold & Enamel of Pearls of various size[s]."* Her inventory also noted that the diadem was part of a much larger parure consisting of "one pair . . . earrings; a Pear Shaped Amethyst for Pendant to one long Pearl compose these Earrings. Nine Amethysts sett per above; & more a Bracelet. Three Amethysts sett per above (one in Comb)."† She concluded that the parure was a gift "sent by Prince Jérôme" in 1805. This was one of the many gifts he sent to her in England after their separation.

---

* "Year 1869 Collection," Box 13A, MS 142, EPB Papers.

† Solid Green Journal, 1862, Box 13A, MS 142, EPB Papers.

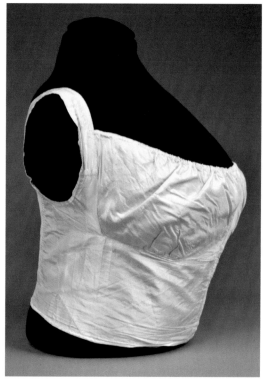

Silk Corset worn by Elizabeth
Patterson Bonaparte (modern
replacement laces)
1800–1810
Possibly French
Maryland Historical Society,
Gift of Mrs. Charles J. Bonaparte,
xx.5.209

the conical shape of the rigid corsets or stays of the earlier period. In an inventory from 1821, Elizabeth noted that she owned both short and long stays (corsets) that she would have worn according to the gown she chose.[29]

Given her daring, French-inspired fashions, and her "story" of an unsuccessful royal alliance, people began to talk. Elizabeth's French alliance, so well represented in her clothing and the presence of her son, also made her an object of political concern for Americans who were faced with the growing tensions among the United States, France, and Great Britain in the period leading up to the War of 1812. She did not shrink from this celebrity, or the controversy that came with it. One commentator described her as an "almost naked woman," and another noted that a crowd of boys once formed outside a party just to glimpse her figure in a see-through gown. An amused onlooker at a party she attended reported that the men in attendance knew not where to look because her breasts were so visible.[30] It is important to recognize that, put into context, Elizabeth's clothing choices were indeed bold and revealing, certainly when compared to the rigid, figure-concealing fashions of the earlier decades and the more conservative American interpretations of French style. Despite one quotation that Elizabeth wore "a gown of dampened muslin that clung to her body,"[31] there is no evidence she was wetting her gowns to make them translucent or wearing nothing under her muslins, but a miniature by Jean-Baptiste Jacques Augustin painted in 1817 depicts Elizabeth with a semi-sheer, revealing bodice, much like those described (and criticized) by her female peers.

Miniature of Elizabeth Patterson Bonaparte and Jérôme Bonaparte in gold and enamel case
Jean-Baptiste Jacques Augustin (1759–1832)
Miniature of Elizabeth Patterson Bonaparte, signed "Augustin à Paris 1817" and Jérôme Bonaparte, signed "Augustin 1801"
Paris
Oil on ivory
Private collection, photograph by Elizabeth Moltke-Huitfeldt

Although these miniatures occupy the same gold case, Elizabeth united her image with that of her former husband. Elizabeth told Martha Custis Williams Carter the history of the miniatures, explaining that a "Mrs. Denon . . . told her of Augustine the great miniature painter in Paris & she went and sat for a miniature of herself to put in a gold book given to Jérôme [her son] by his father 20 years before with his own miniature on one side of the book."* In 1817 when this portrait miniature was painted, Elizabeth had been in Europe two years and had been divorced for four. When Jérôme was painted in 1801, he had yet to travel to America and meet Elizabeth. Bo, Elizabeth's son, did not meet his father until 1821, so it is possible he was given the miniature during that visit.

* Carter, Diaries, undated.

The other subject that set tongues wagging was her figure. Surviving garments attest to Elizabeth's remarkable physique. She told Carter she was five feet one inch tall, but her surviving gowns suggest she may have been taller or worn her gowns with the hem trailing on the ground in the front. Elizabeth told Carter that her small stature had been "a regret" to her throughout her life.[32] Based on extant garments, her frame was petite, and in an age when proper posture and women's clothing required women to stand with their shoulders pulled dramatically back, the distance between her shoulder blades was a fashionably narrow seven inches.

Elizabeth's most striking physical feature aside from her dark hair, pale skin, and languid eyes, was a bust that measured approximately thirty-five inches. The clothing of the early nineteenth century displayed this feature to advantage and elicited comments from men and women alike. Rosalie Calvert of Riversdale heard about Elizabeth's appearance at a ball in Washington. Not a fan of Elizabeth's celebrity or her fashions, Calvert reported that "Madame Bonaparte [wore] dresses so transparent and tight that you can see her skin through them, no chemise at all."[33] Elizabeth did own chemises, or shifts, as she called them in her inventories, and wore them under her gowns, but she may have chosen the thinnest possible fabrics for her undergarments. Surviving evidence attests to the fact that Jérôme also sent her numerous chemises, all purchased in Paris. In 1815, when Elizabeth boarded a ship for England, she had

Elizabeth Patterson Bonaparte
(1785–1879)
François-Joseph Kinson
(1770–1839)
1817
Oil on canvas
Maryland Historical Society,
Gift of Mrs. Charles J. Bonaparte,
xx.5.72

packed, "7 worked Tail Shifts . . . 19 Plain Shifts, 6 cotton Cambrick do. [shifts], 1 do. [shift] Linen."[34] These would have been worn under her gowns, lessening the sheerness of her muslins. In the 1817 portrait of her by François-Joseph Kinson, the outline of her chemise is visible under her translucent gown and the shape of the bodice indicates the presence of a corset. Throughout her later inventories and journals dating from the 1820s to the 1860s, Elizabeth acquired chemises of various types, once paying $4.37½ for "31 yds cotton for shifts" in Rockaway, New York.[35] Her journals also document that she was buying cord to lace her stays, contradicting assertions that she was not wearing undergarments with her gowns. Her address book indicates that her favorite stay maker was in Paris.[36]

Despite the gossip, Elizabeth was not without her admirers. Many friends and family members relied on her to buy clothing and accessories for them in Baltimore (where French goods were available) and later in Europe. Elizabeth moved to Washington, D.C., around 1808, and while there came to know Dolley Madison. She found in the president's wife a kindred spirit, a woman who in many ways resembled her. Both were assertive and willing to defy convention, loved to dress, and relished the power fashion brought to them socially. On November 4, 1813, Madison told Elizabeth, "I will avail myself of your taste, in case you meet with any thing elegant, in the form of a Turban, or even any thing brilliant to make me — such as gause or lace flower'd with Gold or silver," when she visited the milliners in Baltimore.[37] "I shall be in Washington in a few days," Elizabeth replied on the twenty-second. "Should you wish me to execute any commissions in articles of Dress &c, for you (before my departure) which may not be found in George Town at present; I shall esteem myself extremely flattered by such a proof of your confidence in the desire to serve you by which I am ever actuated. There are in the Shops in Baltimore French Gloves, Fashions &c: & the little taste possessed by me shall be exerted, in Selecting, if I obtain your permission, whatever you may require."[38]

The local papers amply attest to the fact that French as well as English goods were available in Baltimore. A Mrs. Gouges advertised in the *Baltimore American & Commercial Daily Advertiser* on October 11, 1813, that she had in her inventory, "2 Cases of very elegant French fashions, lately arrived by the Grampus and Pilot in N. York." On November 6, 1813, Moses Poor at 1834 Market Street also advertised French goods, including gloves, hose, ribbons, and fabrics. Elizabeth may well have patronized these shops and others.

Two years later, after Elizabeth returned to Europe, her sister-in-law, Mary Caton Patterson, wife of Elizabeth's brother Robert, wrote on December 18, 1815, asking, "When you are in Paris you shall know all I want, as I have great confidence in your taste."[39] In 1816, her brother Edward Patterson wrote to request presents for his wife. "I want a couple of merino shawls—one large & thick and raycé I believe the French call it or striped with a good many colors."[40] In only one instance did someone complain about what Elizabeth had chosen for them. When she sent Nancy Spear a gown and shoes that were too small, her aunt remarked that she must have "forgotten my gigantic shape!"[41]

Elizabeth's surviving textiles also document the presence of domestic fabrics and laces in her wardrobe. Within her sizeable collection of lace, numbering over three hundred pieces, numerous examples from Ipswich, Massachusetts, survive. The production of bobbin lace in Ipswich began in the 1750s as a cottage industry and grew until, between 1789 and 1790, more than six hundred women produced almost 42,000 yards of lace in one year. The disruption of trade between the colonies and Great Britain during the American Revolution

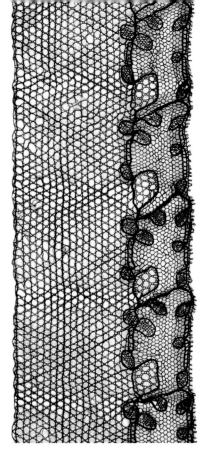

Ipswich Lace Fragment
Mid-1820s
Silk
Maryland Historical Society,
Gift of Mrs. Charles J. Bonaparte,
xx.5.981

Handkerchief
Mid-nineteenth
century
Linen and cotton
Maryland Historical
Society, Gift of Mrs.
Charles J. Bonaparte,
xx.5.9

Fragment of Lace Sleeves
1830–1850
Linen
Maryland Historical Society,
Gift of Mrs. Charles J. Bonaparte,
xx.5.593 a,b

and again during the War of 1812 made this domestically produced lace an affordable, readily available product with which to trim garments. The home-based industry continued to thrive until the 1840s, when machine-made lace took over the market.[42] Elizabeth owned a black net canezou, a vest-like garment, dating to the 1820s and trimmed with narrow black Ipswich lace. She likely acquired these laces in 1823, while visiting with her son Bo who was having difficulties with his studies at Harvard. She kept the Ipswich laces, but referred to them as "beggars lace" in her packing list "to take with me to France" in 1839.[43] They appear again in an August 1860 inventory as "imitation black lace yards of it" and are listed separately from "all my point lace and ditto valenciennes."[44]

Each time Elizabeth traveled abroad, she made detailed inventories of her possessions before her departure, often after her arrival, and upon her return to Baltimore. It is through these records that we come to understand her fashion sense over her lifetime. Though always frugal with her financial investments, she regularly spent money on her wardrobe. Her purchases of shoes between 1826 and 1849 show a pattern of spending that sharply contrasts with the minimal amount of money she spent on housing and household goods. This chart, compiled from Elizabeth's inventories, documents her increased spending in the years after Bo's marriage in 1829.[45] She abhorred her son's union with the American Susan May Williams and, as a sign of her displeasure, terminated Bo's allowance. Free of that financial burden, she spent more on herself, as is clear in the purchases of shoes and fabrics for gowns that Elizabeth made in the 1830s and 1840s.

Elizabeth Patterson Bonaparte's purchases of shoes

Date	Location	Notation	Price
1826			
29 Jun	Paris	2 pr shoes	11 Fr
1827			
3 Feb	Florence	Gloves & L___[?] Shoes	13 Pauls 4 gratz
4 Feb		2 pr Satin Shoes	24 Pauls
16 Apr		Black Satin Shoes	12 Pauls
22 Apr		Black prunel Shoes	10 Pauls
12 May		3 pr of Shoes	30 Pauls
21 May		white Satin Shoes	10 Pauls
19 Sep		2 pr of Cocci's Shoes	16 Pauls
18 Oct		2 pr Shoes Cocci	16 Pauls
21 Dec		Souliers (purchased w/Cherry satin)	
1830			
24 Apr	Florence	Shoes	8 Pauls
May	Geneva	2 pr Shoes	11 Fr 10 sous
5 Jun		Mlle LeMaire Gloves & Shoes	47 Fr 11 sous
29 Jun	Aix	Shoes from Mde Chaberg	5 Fr 10 sous
14 Aug	Geneva	2 pr shoes	11 Fr
20 Sept		5 pr shoes	25 F
1831			
9 Feb	Florence	Satin Shoes	10 Pauls
1 May		4 pr shoes from Cocci	32 Pauls
22 May	Geneva	Shoes walking ones	5 Fr 15 sous
26 May		2 pr shoes at LeMaire's	12 Fr
28 July	Aix	Shoes	5 Fr
28 July		Green slippers	3 Fr
8 Oct	Geneva	Shoes	6 Fr
1832			
25 Jan	Geneva	Shoes	5 Fr 15 sous
13 Feb		LeMaire Shoes & gloves	13 Fr 11 sous
13 Feb		Cleaning shoes	4 Fr 10 sous
Apr		A pair of shoes	6 Fr
20 Jun		Shoes	5 Fr
16 July		Shoes	5 Fr 10 sous
2 Oct		Shoes	6 Fr
22 Oct		2 pr Black P. Shoes	12 Fr
5 Nov		Shoes	6 Fr
1 Dec	Paris	Slippers leather lined with Fur	3 Fr
1 Dec		Shoes	5 Fr 10 sous

Net Mitts worn by Elizabeth Patterson Bonaparte
Mid-19th century
Silk
Private collection, photograph by Elizabeth Moltke-Huitfeldt

Date	Location	Notation	Price
1840			
25 Nov	Baltimore	Shoes from Diengan[?]	$1.50
12 Dec		A pair of indian rubber boots	$2.00
1841			
20 Feb	Baltimore	Shoes	$1.50
26 Mar		Indian Rubber Shoes	$1.00
29 May		Shoes	$1.00
15 Jun		2 pr Shoes	$2.00
9 Sept	New York	Shoes at New York	$1.37
1 Oct		2 pr indian Rubber shoes	$3.50
3 Oct		1 pr Kid walking Shoes	$1.50
6 Oct		Shoes at New York	$1.12
20 Nov	Baltimore	Shoes to Chase	$1.50
27 Nov		Shoes to Chase	$1.50
1842			
4 Mar	Washington	A pr Shoes	$1.25
8 Apr	Baltimore	2 pr Shoes from Chase	$2.50
21 Apr		2 pr Shoes from Chase	$2.50
14 May		Shoes	$1.30
27 May		Making slippers from Chase	$1.12½
1 July		Shoes Chase	$2.25
2 Nov		Shoes	$1.25
15 Nov		2 pr Shoes from Chase	$2.50
1843			
1 Apr	Baltimore	2 pr black red Shoes from Chase	$2.00
4 Apr		3 pr Shoes from Chase	$3.50
23 May		Chase 1 pr Black Buckskin shoes	$1.25
29 Jun		Shoes to Chase Jr.	$1.25
2 Nov		Shoes	$1.12½
1844			
3 Apr	Baltimore	Shoes from Chase ⎫	
12 Apr		Shoes from Chase 1 pr ⎭	$2.37½
1 Jun		6 pr Shoes from Chase	$7.00
5 Jun		Shoes from Rous(?) blue Slippers	$1.00
19 Oct		Shoes from Chase	$1.25
9 Nov		Shoes from Chase	$1.25

Date	Location	Notation	Price
1845			
11 Jan	Baltimore	Shoes from Chase	$1.25
28 Feb		Shoes black kid	$1.25
5 May		2 pr Shoes kid	$2.30
6 Sept	New York	2 pr black kid shoes	$2.25
1846			
23 Apr	Baltimore	3 pr black kid & one pr blue slippers	$4.75
Apr		Shoes Mrs. Hodges	$0.75
6 Oct		2 pr of Shoes	$2.25
31 Oct		1 pr Shoes (& 6 pr Stockings)	$3.00
1847			
Jan	Baltimore	Shoes	$0.50
4 Jan		Shoes	$1.00
22 May		5 pr Shoes	$3.63
8 Oct		Shoes	$1.12
11 Nov		1 pr Shoes	$1.12
1848			
24 Feb	Baltimore	4 pr Shoes at 62½ cents per pair	$2.50
29 Apr		Shoes	$0.50
8 May		Shoes Hemick 1 Pair	$1.50
18 May		Shoes	$0.75
19 May		Pd Hemick for a 2nd pair of Shoes	$1.50
27 May		1 pr Shoes from A Bayle	$1.50
10 July		2 pr Shoes	$2.13
25 Oct		2 pr Shoes Williams	$2.35
1849			
Apr	Baltimore	3 pr Shoes	$2.25
4 May		1 pr Shoes	$1.13
June		Shoes one pair	$1.50
Aug		Slippers by Druang[?]	$1.50
5 Nov	England	Boots	6£2
5 Nov		Satin Shoes	6£6
7 Nov		Velvet Shoes from Marsh	5£6
14 Nov		B Satin Shoes	6£

Elizabeth also purchased large quantities of dress fabric, sometimes taking it to a Baltimore dressmaker and at other times having it made into gowns in Europe. This chart tracks her fabric purchases made between 1826 and 1849.[46]

Purchases of material

Year	Location	# PURCHASES	# YARDS	# METERS	# ELLS	# BRACHS
1826	Florence	12				83
1827	Florence	12				127
1828	Florence	13	25			77
1829	Florence	15				136½
1830	Florence	2				14
	Paris	3			18	
	Geneva	6			32	
1831	Florence	2				16
	Geneva	7			40	
1832	Geneva	8			40¼	
1839	Geneva	4			19½	
1840	Paris	15	10	13	81½	
	Baltimore	3	27			
	Washington	2	20			
	Baltimore	5	68			
1843	Baltimore	2	31			
	New York	2	43			
1844	Baltimore	3	68			
1845	Baltimore	4	65			
	New York	1	9			
1846	Baltimore	1	20			
1847	Baltimore	6	75½			
1848	Baltimore	14	194			
1849	Baltimore	1	12			
	London	7	74½			

Elizabeth devoted considerable energy to refreshing her wardrobe by altering existing garments. Perhaps the best-documented instance of this relates to an embroidered muslin shawl now in the museum's collection. On August 10, 1815, she noted in her "Account of Cloathes" "2 long Worked Muslin Shawls."[47] Commercially embroidered Indian muslin like that used to make these shawls or scarves had been the height of fashion since the latter part of the eighteenth century. She also owned a simple muslin gown with a long train dating to around 1810. Although she did not note when or where she acquired these shawls, she made this particular account of her wardrobe upon

Muslin Gown and
Embroidered Muslin and Silk
Shawl, both worn by Elizabeth
Patterson Bonaparte
Gown, circa 1805 and shawl,
circa 1815
Gown, cotton; shawl, cotton, silk
Maryland Historical Society,
Gift of Mrs. Charles J. Bonaparte,
XX.5.150, XX.5.110
Mannequin made by Studio EIS,
Brooklyn, N.Y.

Alice Patterson Harris (1855–1944)
1876
Collection of Mark B. Letzer

Alice Patterson Harris (Mrs. W. Hall Harris Jr.), Elizabeth's great-niece, served as the first archivist of the Bonaparte papers at the Maryland Historical Society. When Elizabeth's papers came to the Maryland Historical Society library, scholars were initially prohibited from publishing the private correspondence.

Clinedinst   120 & 122 Lexington St.,
BALTIMORE.

Work Bag made by Elizabeth Patterson Bonaparte for her great-niece, Alice Patterson Harris
Fabric, 1850s
Silk and wool
Maryland Historical Society, Gift of Mrs. W. Hall Harris Jr., 1959.92.15

According to the object's history, this work bag was made out of one of Elizabeth's old dresses, probably in the late 1860s. Large fragments of this fabric are in the Bonaparte collection, saved as "scraps" by Elizabeth, providing further documentation that this bag was indeed made by her from old dress fabric.

her arrival in Cheltenham, England. Prior to her arrival in Paris in November 1815, she spent several months in Cheltenham, shopping and seeing the sights. Never one to quickly discard part of her wardrobe, in 1839 Elizabeth recorded "2 brodé Indian muslin long shawls" among the "Contents of long trunk with 2 locks to take with me to France."[48] She mentioned the shawls again upon her arrival in Paris, noting in her "Apparel Inventory . . . 2 long india muslin shawls brodés en blanc." Elizabeth updated one of the shawls in 1840. On "25 avril 1840" she noted that she spent 18 francs for yellow silk "for lining scarf"; three days later she spent 29 francs 10 sous "to Mlle Trouvair Mallet for mending lace and lining scarf."[49] Remarkably, the lined shawl may be the "1 yellow india shawl" she took with her to Paris in 1861. In March 1864, when Elizabeth was seventy-nine, she made her last trip to Paris, listing among her luggage a "flat top box No. 1" that contained "1 india Muslin Shawl lined with yellow silk."[50]

In 1875, four years before her death, she made a list of her personal effects left at "Miss Guinns in my case" and included "2 long white India Muslin Shawls," one of which was probably the shawl lined in yellow silk.[51] This particular example of the shawl documents not only Elizabeth's frugality in preserving her possessions as parts of her personal history, but also her meticulous nature. She invested significant resources in her wardrobe and maintained it with care throughout her lifetime.

Three bodices that may date to the 1820s, all of fine silk, are in the MdHS collection with their skirts and possibly sleeves removed. The frugal Elizabeth probably repurposed the skirts to make other garments. The work bag made for her great-niece, Alice Patterson Harris, is an example of her taking fabric from a dress and transforming it into something else. Her inventory for 1821 included silks, wools, and cottons in colors of lilac, white, rose, yellow, and black.[52] To glimpse Elizabeth's wardrobe of 1830, we can scan her journal to find that on December 22, she was having a white and gold turban made in Florence, and just two weeks later she purchased a pink silk hat. In May, when she was in Geneva, she bought green muslin and two days later took it to the dressmaker to be made into a gown. In the fall of that year, she purchased a black bonnet which she later had trimmed in Paris, a white bonnet, and three belts, one to go with her merino dress, one for her gray dress, and a pink one.[53]

Velvet Turban
Circa 1810
Silk velvet and silk and gilt trim
Maryland Historical Society,
Gift of Mrs. Charles J. Bonaparte,
xx.5.177

LEFT: Turban worn by
Elizabeth Patterson Bonaparte
Circa 1810
Silk velvet with gilt thread
Maryland Historical Society,
Gift of Mrs. Charles J. Bonaparte,
xx.5.182

Violet Silk Bodice
Late 1830s with possible alteration
to waist in the 1840s
Silk and linen lace
Maryland Historical Society,
Gift of Mrs. Charles J. Bonaparte,
xx.5.209

In December 1838, Elizabeth inventoried her lace collection, recording large quantities of Brussels lace, including a veil and handkerchief, and more than twenty yards of various other types of laces, including French point d'Alençon.[54] As mentioned earlier, in 1839 while still in Baltimore and preparing to travel to France, she made a full inventory of all the clothing she was taking with her. One interesting detail of this particular inventory is that she packed garments in need of repair or remaking. For instance, she included a "Puce Silk Pelisse—ripped up," "purple satin brocade in piece for gown," "lilac and blue silk for linings," and "striped muslin in piece,"[55] probably intending to have them repaired or remade abroad. Sometimes the work was accomplished in Europe and sometimes she brought pieces of gowns back to Baltimore to be

Fragments of Bodice
Circa 1820
Silk velvet and cotton
Maryland Historical Society,
Gift of Mrs. Charles J. Bonaparte,
xx.5.210 a–o

assembled by local dress makers. Elizabeth also noted in 1862 that she kept "old gown bodices for patterns."[56] A red silk velvet bodice in the collection that remains in eight pieces may have been taken apart to make a pattern.

Elizabeth recorded, "One Pair of Diamond Earrings—
Sett à Jour—Each Earring composed as follows. One
Solitaire (large diamond) fastens the Ring which enters
the Ear. The Drop or Pendant of Each of the Ear-rings
consists of Three leaves sett in tiny Diamonds—to which
leaves are attached. Eleven large Diamonds (less however
than that one which fastens Each Ear ring—There are
therefore in said Pair of Diamond Ear-rings Twenty Four
Diamonds independently of the small ones which form
the 3 leaves of Each one of the above mentioned pair of
Ear-rings—The whole is intended to represent Bunches
of Grapes. The Drops of above were sett by Bapt in Paris
year 1833—& are now owned by me 1 January 1859, &
owned on 21 July 1870." As was her habit, she reviewed
her inventories, underlining words in red.

In the 1840s, when Elizabeth resided primarily
in Baltimore, her journals reveal the local merchants and milliners she patronized. Mary Ann
Hamilton, who operated her shop on the corner
of Lexington and Sharp Streets, was her milliner.
Elizabeth frequently made purchases at Matchett's
where Charles Mellor sold stockings, undergarments, and imported bobbinet and British lace.
Mrs. Hahn on Lexington Street trimmed Elizabeth's hats and specialized in
bonnets, trimmings, ribbons, and artificial flowers. Elizabeth also engaged the
dressmaking skills of Miss Maria Lee, "mantua maker," on Eden Street, who
made dresses "to order in the neatest manner, and most fashionable style, and
on reasonable terms," and a Mrs. Foy, milliner, who was listed in her address
book as operating on Franklin Street.[57]

As the nineteenth century progressed, fashion evolved from the revealing
high-waisted styles of the Federal period to more structured gowns with volu-
minous skirts and longer, tight-fitting bodices. Based on Elizabeth's inventories,
she kept pace with these changes, enhancing her wardrobe each time she went
abroad and filling the gaps with garments made or acquired in Baltimore. As a
mature woman, she continued to use her fashionable wardrobe to separate
herself from her peers. She no longer distinguished herself with "backless"
muslin gowns but set herself apart by wearing the finest fabrics and the most

Diamond earrings worn by Elizabeth Patterson Bonaparte
Diamonds, 1804, altered in 1823; according to journal set in 1833
French
Diamond and white gold
Private collection, photograph by Elizabeth Moltke-Huitfeldt

Elizabeth specifically noted in her 1875 inventory of her jewelry, "Pair diamond earrings representing bunch of grapes . . . set in Paris 1823. Accounted for in 1875."* According to an inventory made after the death of Elizabeth's great-granddaughter, Louise Eugenie Bonaparte Moltke-Huitfeldt, the original earrings were a gift from Prince Jérôme. The diamonds in these earrings may in fact have come from the diamond earrings Jérôme bought Elizabeth in 1804 for $1,000 in Boston.†

---

* Gray-green Journal, "Memorial of Personal Effects Year 1875," Box 13A, MS 142, EPB Papers.

† Blue Marbled Journal, Box 13A, MS 142, EPB Papers.

current styles Europe had to offer. Ornamented with jewels such as her amethyst diadem from Prince Jérôme described earlier and her long, diamond earrings, Elizabeth stood out as a woman unlike any other.

Her appearance even in middle-age, coupled with her history, made others take note. On February 2, 1837, vying for attention among the young socialites attending Benjamin and Kitty Cohen's fancy dress ball in Baltimore, fifty-two-year-old Elizabeth attracted notice by wearing the costume of Queen Caroline, the wronged wife of George IV.[58] Even when it came to dressing in costume, she exhibited her royal connections and reminded others of her tumultuous story.

In 1860, before she departed for Europe, Elizabeth again made a list of what she was taking abroad. This time her son Bo would accompany her as she tried once more to press suit in the French courts and gain recognition for Bo's right to succession. Among the gowns she chose for the trip were a "cross barred black and green dress," "a cross barred red and brown dress," and a "cross barred white and black dress."[59] Elizabeth was embracing the bolder fabrics and popular plaids that had gained popularity in the years leading up the Civil War. By the time she returned from her trip, she had enhanced her wardrobe with "New unmade black Irish poplin for dress," "New purple silk for dress, brown unmade Barège & blue ditto, all . . . new India muslins."[60] Always one to keep up with the latest fashion, she added a brown cloth Zoauve jacket to her wardrobe, a style inspired by the uniforms of French Algerian infantry units.[61] Elizabeth's last trip to Europe occurred in 1863 and, just as she had on her other trips, she made various purchases to update her wardrobe.

The last surviving inventory of her personal wardrobe dates to 1864 and represents what she brought to Paris and acquired when she was there.[62] In addition to her mother's "old brocade Satin" and the "Black real lace Dress & Mantilla" given to her by Jérôme, Elizabeth took "New black Silk for dress" and "New Purple Silk for Dress" with her, maintaining her tradition of purchasing clothing and textiles in Europe. This last glimpse of her wardrobe represents a combination of relics of her past and more contemporary garments like her "cross barred Silk dress" and a "blue barège dress [with] short sleeves." Her mother's "old brocade Satin" and the muslin shawl lined with yellow silk always traveled with her, as well as several new gowns.

Demi-Parure of Enameled Bracelet, Earrings and Ruby-set Studs owned by Elizabeth Patterson Bonaparte Unknown maker, probably French Gold, enamelwork, and rubies

Maryland Historical Society, Gift of Mrs. Charles J. Bonaparte, xx.5.291 a-e

Paris March 1864

Flat top black Box No. 1

New Muslin

Brown wadded Cloak

Box containing Jewelry & etc.

2 pr. Boots

Black Satin Gown

Purple Satin Gown

old brocade Satin D.P. [Dorcas Patterson]

Black irish Poplin Dress

Black Velvet do.

green Brocade Dress

New black Silk for dress

New Purple Silk for Dress

Black real lace Dress & Mantilla & etc.

Point lace—Valentian[*sic*] Lace

white india cashmere shawl

Ditto yellow—also Tunis shawl

Black blonde Bertha

white Canton crêpe shawl

1 do. smaller white shawl

1 india Muslin Shawl lined with Yellow Silk

2 blue muslin shawls

1 Feather Tippit

1 velvet Sack

1 Do. Cloak

1 Double Calico Robe de chambre

Black lace

12 New unhemmed Pkhs

3 Fans—old blue canton crêpe shawl

Manches Brodés [embroidered sleeves]—Poignets do. [embroidered wristlets]

Real Madras handkerchiefs

Black lace gloves

3 pr woollen knee Caps & pr leggings

2 boxes of hair for front

2 flannel Jackets

8 prs Summer Stockings

old winter Stockings

1 pr Soles for inner of Shoes

long sleeves (under flounces) Cotton Fichus french

Old orange Mousseline laine Shawl

Plaid red & green woollen Scarf

in[dia] double calico Dressing Gown

2 black Silk Jackets—poplin P.Coat

4 new blonde caps for Bonets

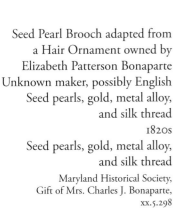

Seed Pearl Brooch adapted from
a Hair Ornament owned by
Elizabeth Patterson Bonaparte
Unknown maker, possibly English
Seed pearls, gold, metal alloy,
and silk thread
1820s
Seed pearls, gold, metal alloy,
and silk thread
Maryland Historical Society,
Gift of Mrs. Charles J. Bonaparte,
xx.5.298

Paris March 1864

Contents of Box with round top

1 velvet Bonnet

Black lace Bonnet

one Straw bonnet

1 cap black lace

one Ditto

white lace trimmed with Blue ribbon

2 Boxes of Hair for Front

yellow india cashmere shawl

1 Red Cashmere indian Shawl

1 Red canton Crêpe Shawl

one lama black lace Shawl

1 chatelaine & Watch of Gold

Pocket handkerchiefs

1 Alpacha Dress : cross barred Silk dress

1 Brown Barège dress—Black & blue
dress :

1 blue Barège dress short sleeves

Parasol with ivory Stick

4 pr black leather gloves : 3 pair of
wristbands;

strings for bonnets. blue; black; &
Purple

new black lace cape in box of col-
lerettes

Agate and Silver Link Bracelet
with Carnelian Charm and
Roman Coin
Circa 1860
Scottish
Maryland Historical Society,
Gift of Mrs. Charles J. Bonaparte,
xx.5.276

For the remaining thirty years of her life, Elizabeth lived quietly in Baltimore boarding houses. Although she did inventory her significant garments—those given to her by Jérôme, those purchased in Paris, and those inherited from her mother and her sister Caroline—a complete inventory of her entire wardrobe from that period does not survive. The precise reason for that remains unknown, but a comment she made to Carter in 1876 provides a clue. "She had dressed only for admiration," the ninety-one-year-old Elizabeth explained, "& now that she can no longer have admiration she does not dress."[63] Despite this, a silver purse of glass beads and a pair of white kidskin shoes with heels dating to the 1870s suggest that Elizabeth may not have abandoned fashion entirely in her last years.

Elizabeth's last two surviving inventories that mention her wardrobe are incomplete and leave out many of the garments, accessories, and fragments of fabric we know survived. In an 1872 inventory she listed "1 Red Moroco Trunk of Shawls & etc. Laces & etc. 4 india shawls therein, 1 white, 1 red, 2 yellow, 1 white Canton Crepe Shawl, 1 ditto red, 1 small, white one — Black Dress, ditto mantilla of real Lace, 2 black real Lace veils, one neckcloth Ditto."[64] Her last inventory of 1875 included a similar list with the addition of her mother's dress, but it does not record any of her contemporary clothing.[65] Toward the end of her life, only clothing with memories merited a mention.

The wardrobe that documented her celebrated past was important enough to Elizabeth that she left it to her grandson, Charles, along with her other material possessions. His wife, Ellen Channing Day Bonaparte, ensured that the surviving garments were preserved at the Maryland Historical Society, giving

Fragments of Silk from Elizabeth
Patterson Bonaparte's dresses
1820s–1860s
Maryland Historical Society,
Gift of Mrs. Charles J. Bonaparte,
xx.5.986-xx.5.998

them to the museum, along with almost six hundred objects and hundreds of documents, in 1921. Ellen also saved the "relics" Elizabeth had given her, noting in an interview, "I have some exceedingly interesting relics of Mme. Bonaparte, but those precious jewels and laces which have been given to me are entirely fabulous." The article went on to note that "Mrs. Bonaparte has some dainty relics of her august relative-in-law in the shape of lovely India gowns" which she claimed to "wear . . . all through the summer and have done for 20 years past."[66] A petticoat dating to the early 1900s and made from an eighteenth-century muslin gown suggests that perhaps Ellen remade some of Elizabeth's India muslins into new garments.

For decades the textiles associated with Elizabeth remained in the trunks where she had stored them. Upon the trunks' arrival at the Maryland Historical Society, the contents were removed, but the order in which Elizabeth originally stored some of her textiles was, in part, preserved. Such was the case with her lace, which until 2012 was rolled into bundles, some of them containing notes in her own hand to indicate their lengths or the pieces' history. Similarly, fragments of garments came to the museum in a trunk labeled "Scraps," a term Elizabeth herself used for them. Only by looking at these artifacts in the context of her inventories and the history of her life can we draw a clearer picture of the role fashion played in shaping her identity.

Fragments of Lace with Parisian
Business Cards
Mid-19th century

Maryland Historical Society,
Gift of Mrs. Charles J. Bonaparte.
Lace, from left to right: xx.5.977, xx.5.635;
business cards, xx.5.975, xx.5.974

When Elizabeth's collection of lace
arrived at the Maryland Historical
Society in a trunk, it was carefully
rolled into bundles, some of which
were wound around business and
calling cards she collected during her
European travels. No piece of lace or
fragment of lace removed from a
garment was too small to keep.

Embroidered Cotton Muslin Petticoat made from
remnants of early-nineteenth century dresses
Embroidered cotton, circa 1805, made into petticoats
in the 1890s
Private collection, photograph by Elizabeth Moltke-Huitfeldt

Even during her lifetime, her celebrity created a mythology that grew
with each publication written about her. This myth-making flattened her story,
freezing her style permanently in the early nineteenth century during the brief
period of her marriage. By looking at the scope of her surviving wardrobe, her
story as a woman who strategically used her appearance to send messages to
observers begins to emerge. She approached her outward style with much the
same planning and care as she took with her investments. As she said about
financial matters, "Never run the slightest risk in the pursuit of great profits,
see clearly the transaction to its termination."[67]

Her "transactions" and "investments" in regard to her fashion were as
shrewd, calculated, and effective as her purchases of ground rents and stocks.

WARNER & HANNA'S

PLAN

of the City and Environs of

Baltimore,

Respectfully dedicated to the Mayor, City Council.

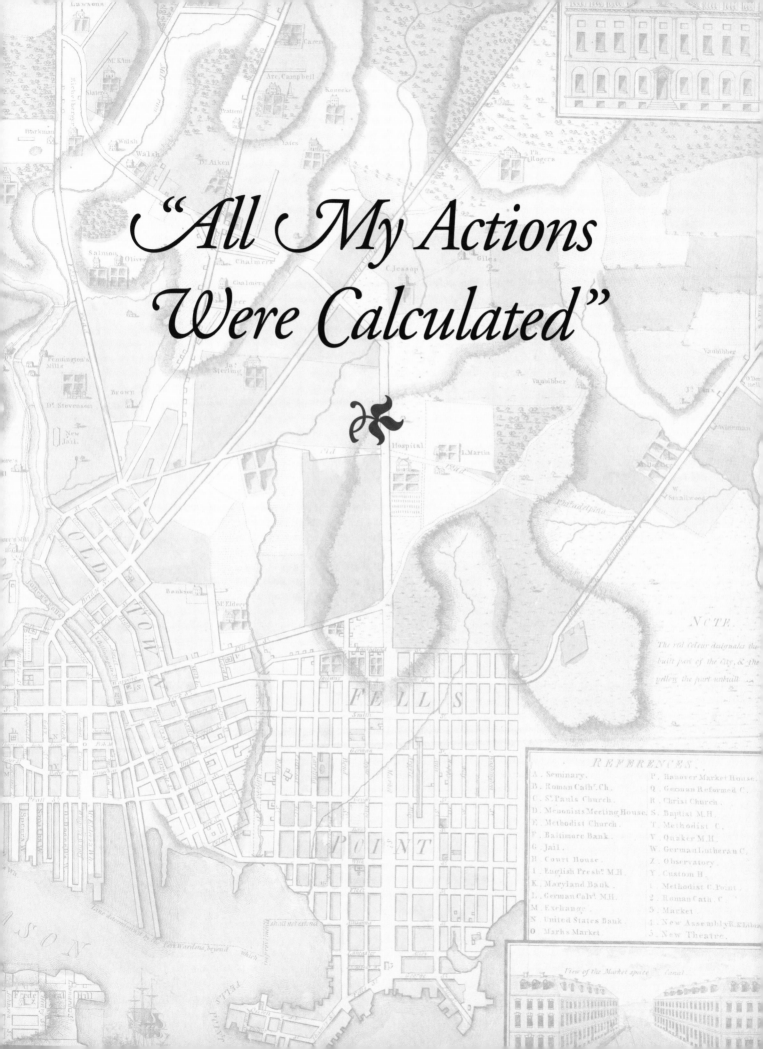

"All My Actions Were Calculated"

I N 1896, SEVENTEEN YEARS AFTER ELIZABETH'S DEATH, the *Sunday Herald* recalled Madame Bonaparte's lesser-known accomplishments as a remarkable business woman. "The admiration which she excited by her beauty and manners was great, but the business ability she displayed caused one critic of her time to claim that he knew 'no woman [was] more capable of creating legitimately with so small a capital, the large fortune she amassed.'"[1] The writer correctly observed that her "lifelong habits of economy" as well as shrewd investments lay behind her financial success. Her business acumen, a talent rarely associated with women during the period, could only be compared to the financial talents of a man. Four decades earlier a friend had called her "a Man of business," a comment that was both a compliment and a slight criticism.[2] Financial success independent of men was not typically a female accomplishment.

Elizabeth's fortune at the time of her death has long been a subject of interest because it was extraordinary for an unmarried woman to amass an estate valued by the probate court in 1879 at $1,017,689.02.[3] Today, that would amount to approximately $35 million. The gradual building of her fortune, as well as the particulars about her investments, provide insight into the economic changes that occurred in nineteenth-century America and, more particularly, nineteenth-century Baltimore. In addition, Elizabeth adeptly moved money from America to Europe, depending on which arena provided a more favorable economic climate.

Unlike her female peers, who benefitted financially through significant inheritances or advantageous marriages, the core of Elizabeth's wealth began with Napoléon's settlement of 60,000 francs per annum. Although her former

FACING PAGE AND OVERLEAF: [Charles Varlé], *Warner & Hanna's Plan of the City and Environs of Baltimore* (1801)
Maps and Atlases, Maryland Historical Society

Two years prior to her marriage to Jérôme, Elizabeth Patterson's native city of Baltimore was in the early stages of rapid expansion that within a few short decades would transform it into the country's third largest city. Elizabeth's early investments in the city's burgeoning infrastructure laid the groundwork for her fortune.

husband Jérôme eagerly sent her gifts of jewelry and clothing after their separation, he sent her money on only three occasions. The 1,300 francs he left with her in Lisbon,[4] the 4,500 guineas he sent her in London after the birth of their son, and the 1,000 Louis d'Or he gave her in 1806 are the only documented instances of his generosity.[5] In an 1807 letter to Anna Kuhn, Elizabeth remarked, "The kindness of my ex Husband the King was ever of the unremitting kind as no money ever accompanied it."[6]

When Elizabeth returned with her infant son, Bo, to Baltimore in 1806, she arrived at her father's house, where her homecoming was anything but warm. Between 1806 and 1809 her financial situation remained uncertain, and her correspondence suggests that her father was only willing to support her if she complied with his wishes. Having lent Elizabeth and Jérôme significant sums during their brief marriage, William Patterson withdrew his financial, as well as his emotional, support from his daughter.[7] Reflecting on this period, Elizabeth wrote, "My position under the paternal roof of the opulent Mr. Patterson after my repudiation by the Emperor and by the husband was painful—it was without pity, sympathy or consolation."[8] It was also, according to Elizabeth, without financial support.

In the margins of her journals and letters, she repeatedly noted that between 1805 and her father's death in 1835 he never gave her any money. "Mr. Patterson's objection to my residence abroad was an excuse for never giving me a cent from 1805 to 1835."[9] Prior to 1805, Patterson had supplied his daughter with funds for her trip abroad, as documented in a letter from him to his banker in Paris asking that a line of credit be established for Elizabeth against over £18,000 owed to him by the French government.[10] Elizabeth later said that her father compelled her to pay some of her debts to him, once demanding half of the money Jérôme sent her in England.[11] To recoup his earlier expenditures, Patterson later sold some of the household goods he had bought for the couple. In a letter written in 1858, Elizabeth also referred to the money her father lent to Jérôme during their marriage that her ex-husband never repaid.[12] After Patterson's death, Elizabeth felt that these debts to her father greatly reduced her inheritance, which may well have been true. Despite her complaints, it does appear that Patterson paid some of her expenses during the period between 1806 and the first payment of her settlement from France. In 1807, he noted that he had paid $44.75 for Dr. Thomas Pinkerton's visit to "Madam Bonaparte," presumably at Patterson's South Street home where she was then residing.[13]

William Patterson (1752–1835)
Thomas Sully (1783–1872)
1821
Oil on canvas
Maryland Historical Society
Bequest of Mrs. George Patterson
1883.1.1

In 1808, Elizabeth began her efforts to gain support for her son and herself. Life in the Patterson house quickly became unpleasant, making her need for financial independence more pressing. Strategically, she wrote to and met with the plenipotentiary to the United States, General Louis-Marie Turreau de Garambouville, who was also a family acquaintance. Turreau eventually referred Elizabeth's situation to Napoléon's advisors, and a long period of waiting for a response ensued.[14] By December 1809, Napoléon had still not communicated his wishes, but Turreau acted independently and used French legation funds to establish a $20,000 line of credit upon which Elizabeth could draw. This would become, in part, the pension that represented Elizabeth's settlement. In need of funds, she immediately drew $6,000 as the first installment.[15]

Eventually, Elizabeth received 60,000 francs a year in monthly installments, estimated to have been approximately $950 a month.[16] That a woman of twenty-three, whose only link to Napoléon Bonaparte was through an annulled marriage to his youngest brother, was able to negotiate so aggressively on her behalf, even refusing to bring her son to Europe, indicates the boldness with which Elizabeth set about shaping her future. Shrewd and calculating, she also knew that having a son gave her more leverage. Years later she reflected that "all my conduct is calculated," and this early example demonstrates the accuracy of that statement.[17] Undaunted by her position as a woman, and an American one at that, who had been acknowledged by Napoléon only as his brother's "so-called wife," Elizabeth resolutely demanded to be recognized as a Bonaparte and continued to advocate on behalf of her son throughout her life. The final settlement she received from the French government provided the foundation of what would one day be her fortune. Unlike most women of her time, the dissolution of a marriage rather than its formation laid the groundwork for her later wealth.

In 1808, upon learning of Elizabeth's correspondence with Napoléon concerning a possible settlement, Jérôme, now King of Westphalia and married to Catherine of Württemberg, offered her 200,000 francs per annum as well as a small kingdom and the titles Prince and Princess of Schmalkalden for their son and herself. Recalling this offer more than sixty years later, Elizabeth remarked that it "was received with the contempt which it merited."[18] She correctly surmised that Jérôme's word was not his bond. As she wrote in one of her books, "Promises one thing; Performance their antipodes I found in the year 1805."[19] Elizabeth was familiar with Jérôme's wild extravagance as well as his inconstancy. Although she had enjoyed his carefree spending during their marriage—when it is estimated he was spending as much as $1,000 a week—she feared a future tethered to his wealth.[20] Wisely, she chose the emperor's offer, famously remarking that she would "rather be sheltered under the wings of an eagle than dangle from the beak of a goose."[21]

Napoléon Bonaparte (1769–1821)
Jean-Baptiste Isabey (1767–1855)
Circa 1806
Watercolor on ivory, gold, and glass
Maryland Historical Society
Gift of Mr. L. Manuel Hendler
1954.158.3

King Jérôme of Westphalia
and Queen Catherine
Sebastian Weygandt (1769–1836)
Circa 1806
Oil on canvas
Private collection

Jérôme Napoléon Bonaparte
married German princess Catherine
of Würtemberg on August 22, 1807,
at the Royal Palace of Fontainebleau
in France.

Despite her self-proclaimed poverty, in 1808 Elizabeth had enough income to invest heavily in the stock of the newly chartered Reisterstown Road, or turnpike, intended to connect Baltimore to the rich farmlands of southern Pennsylvania. Although she later disparaged road stocks as poor investments, she retained this particular stock for the rest of her life. According to her journal, her brothers Edward and Joseph purchased more than $3,000 in stock for her and she bought an additional thirty shares for $675. On New Year's Day 1809 she recorded how well many of her investments had performed:

> Received from the Union Bank a yrs dividend—$92
> Janr. 9 recd from the East India Com a dividend—$200
> Febr. 7 rec'd from Ricester Road Stock—$64.37
> May 24th recd a dividend Ricester Stock—$100.[22]

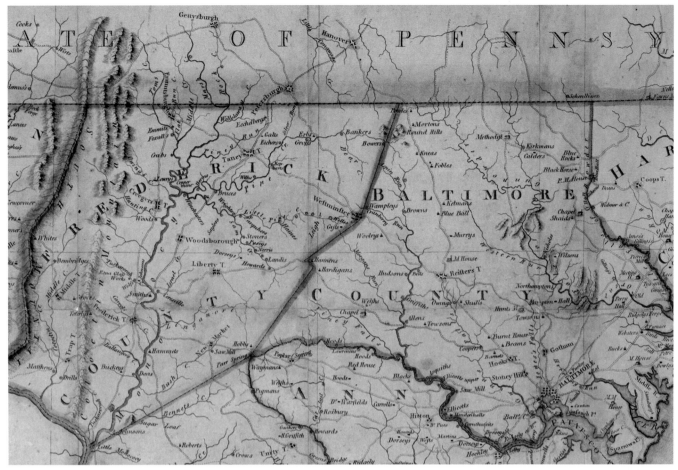

One of Elizabeth's first investments was in the Reisterstown Turnpike Company, which in 1805 began building a toll road from Baltimore northwest through Taneytown and into the rich farmlands of southern Pennsylvania. Detail from Dennis Griffith, *Map of the State of Maryland*, 1794 [1795].

Maps and Atlases, Maryland Historical Society

Elizabeth received dividends from the Union Bank. Cartouche from Thomas H. Poppleton, *Plan of the City of Baltimore*, 1822 [1852].

Maps and Atlases, Maryland Historical Society

Elizabeth's aunt, Nancy (Anne) Spear, as well as her brothers assisted her with financial purchases, but Elizabeth's correspondence shows that she took a strong hand in the decision-making behind her investments. That same year, she noted that "Miss Spear holds 50 shares in the Franklin Bank for me."[23] For a woman who felt financially insecure, Elizabeth was able to invest and spend her money in a way that few Americans could imagine.

By 1811, Elizabeth had sufficient money to buy her own home and spent a sizeable sum to acquire it. Without her payments from France, such a purchase would not have been possible. Robert Patterson, her brother, sent her a receipt on February 25 "for House in King George Street . . . $9.000."[24] Robert continued to manage her affairs during this period, particularly while Elizabeth was in Washington. In November he wrote,

> Since you left Town I have recd for you
> Dividend from Marine Stock $288
> " Franklin Bank Stock $47.60
> " from Mr. Comegys this day—952.38
> [Total] 1287.98.

He also remarked that on October 31 he had paid "Jas Jennings for plastering your house 191.77 and I presume I must pay the other bills as they are presented." By this time, Elizabeth's investments also included "Water Stock" because Robert informed her that "a div[iden]d has been declared."[25] In subsequent lists of Elizabeth's investments she recorded stock in the "B. Water Company," which is probably the same stock Robert mentioned in 1811. This refers to the Baltimore Water Company founded after the city fire of 1804. By 1825, Elizabeth noted that this stock had risen in value to $1,940. She never sold her water stock and continued to add to it for several decades. At the time of her death it was valued at $31,800 in her probate inventory.[26]

Throughout her life, Elizabeth invested in the growing infrastructure of Baltimore, eventually buying shares in the gas company, the B&O Railroad, and numerous roads, including the aforementioned "Reistertown Turnpike Company."[27] Her hometown was growing up around her and she profited handsomely from its expansion. The city she deplored throughout her life, in large part, made her fortune.

Robert Patterson, who managed his sister's finances when she lived in Washington, D.C., arranged the purchase of a house for her in 1811. The house, on King George Street, no longer stands but was located just east of the Jones Falls near today's Little Italy section of Baltimore.
Box 10, MS 142, EPB Papers

Elizabeth invested in manufacturing and transportation infrastructure, including the Baltimore and Ohio Railroad, the country's first railroad. Detail from *E. Sachse & Co.'s Bird's Eye View of the City of Baltimore 1869*. (Baltimore: E. Sachse & Co., 1869.)
Maps and Atlases, Maryland Historical Society

Maximilian Godefroy (1765–1840)
The Union Manufactories of Maryland
on Patapsco Falls, Baltimore County
Circa 1815
Ink on paper
Maryland Historical Society
Mrs. John Jay Schwarz
1934.2.1

How long Elizabeth resided in her new Baltimore house is unclear because by the beginning of 1812 she was renting lodgings in Washington, D.C. Eventually the house became another one of her many rental properties. By 1813, Napoléon's power was showing signs of weakening, and Elizabeth began contemplating her next trip to Europe. To prepare, she built up her resources by selling household goods she would not need abroad. On March 5, 1813, her son Bo wrote, anxiously asking, "Is it true that you are going to sell your Furniture . . . and are going to sell your horses?"[28] An undated entry in one of Elizabeth's journals kept during this period recorded household goods she had sold to members of her family. Her brother Robert bought "a bed, Mat[t]ress, Bolster, Bed Curtains, 2 window curtains & a Bed cover with 2 cornices & 1 saddle horse—[all] $380," while her brother John bought "brass stair rods" for $16, "2 Wilton parlour Carpets" for $162, and a side board for $50. She even sold "5 Salt sellers of cut glass to Mama" for $3.[29] That same year, Elizabeth's modest investments in Baltimore real estate began to yield income. In August 1813 she collected $375 for nine months' rent on a warehouse. This marked only the beginning of her investments in Baltimore properties that would later constitute a large part of her fortune.

In 1812, Elizabeth petitioned the Maryland General Assembly for a divorce from Jérôme, a legal mechanism that freed her, as an American citizen, to accept the annual annuity from Napoléon.
Box 2, MS 142, EPB Papers

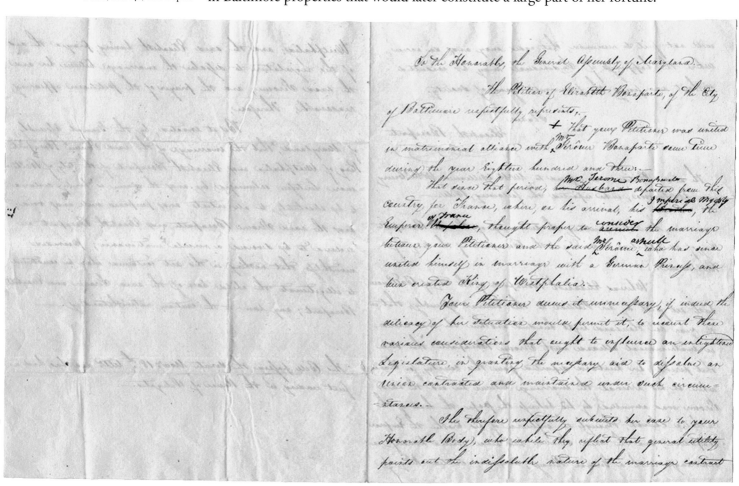

In 1812, the continuing debates in Congress about the rights of Americans married to foreigners placed Elizabeth's finances in yet more jeopardy. Two years earlier, Representative Philip Reed of Maryland proposed a "Titles of Nobility Amendment" which would have prohibited an American citizen from accepting a present, office, or pension from an "emperor, king or foreign state."[30] Had it passed, Elizabeth would have been unable to sign receipts for her pension payments and could only avoid "disenfranchisement of all her rights as an American citizen" by putting all the funds into a trust for her son. That would have left her with a severely restricted income to cover her own personal expenses. In addition, she recognized that if she remained married, her growing financial security would become vulnerable if Jérôme encountered financial difficulties, since, as his wife, her money was legally under his control. In another bold stroke, Elizabeth petitioned the Maryland state legislature to grant her a divorce, which she won in January 1813. This decisive move left her free to operate as a single woman with complete control over her financial destiny.[31]

In 1814, Elizabeth suffered a blow that was both financial and emotional. On May 21, Dorcas Patterson, known to her always as her "kind Parent," died at the age of fifty-two. [32] She had wanted her estate to be divided equally among her children, but William Patterson chose to favor only his surviving sons with their mother's worldly possessions. Elizabeth was left to treasure a few objects that belonged to Dorcas, including two silver pitchers, a shawl, and a silk gown, but no inherited money. [33]

After Napoléon's final exile in 1815, Elizabeth could safely return to Europe, but the end of his power also marked the end of her pension. In 1861, she explained, "my pension had ceased on the departure of [Napoléon] for the Island of Elba." [34] That she would receive no more money from France cast a shadow over her approaching departure. Elation over the prospect of escaping from Baltimore was tempered by her perceived financial insecurity, but she nevertheless proceeded with the trip. Six weeks after Napoléon's defeat at Waterloo, Elizabeth sailed for Liverpool where she arrived on July 26, 1815. On November 18, Nancy Spear advised her, "You may spend 5,000 a year of your own, draw for as much as you please. I am convinced I can get it from your father for you." [35] Barely a month later, on December 15, 1815, Mary Caton Patterson, Robert's wife and Elizabeth's sister-in-law, contradicted that cheerful advice. "Mama," she wrote, "applied the other evening to your Father, and told him how impolitick it was to compel you to return to this country. . . . [H]e replied you might be happy here, and the amount is this, he will not give you the money."[36] In fact, William Patterson had been warning his friends abroad of Elizabeth's arrival, claiming that her mental instability had driven her to make the voyage and that her plans to leave the United States had come as news to her family. Only when Elizabeth contacted James McElhiney of McElhiney & Gerry in London, one of her father's bankers, did she learn that her father had been circulating this rumor in advance of her arrival. This information, coupled with the knowledge that her father was "making another fortune" was all the more galling.[37] Barely masking her sarcasm, she wrote to her father, "The reputation of your fortune would be a great advantage to me abroad, and I am sure you cannot object to my having the honor of it, provided you keep the substance."[38] By then, Elizabeth knew that, when it came to supporting herself, she was entirely on her own.

On February 10, 1816, Mary Caton Patterson asked Elizabeth if her pension had been paid.[39] Elizabeth had grown to envy her brother's wife because in time Mary would benefit from the vast fortune that would be left by her grandfather, Charles Carroll of Carrollton. The isolating effect of great wealth may explain why Mary knew so little about Elizabeth's precarious financial circumstances or that almost two years earlier, in September 1814, she had received her last payment from France.

LEFT: Mary Caton Patterson (1788-1853)
Unknown artist after Sir Thomas Lawrence (1769–1830)
after 1825
Oil on canvas
Maryland Historical Society
BCLM-1991.66.1

Though they were at one time close, Elizabeth and Mary Caton Patterson, who stood to inherit enormous wealth from her grandfather, Charles Carroll of Carrolton, became rivals, at least in Elizabeth's mind.

RIGHT: Charles Carroll of Carrollton (1737–1832)
Michael Laty (1826–1848) after Robert Field (1769–1819)
Circa 1847
Oil on canvas
Maryland Historical Society
Gift of Mrs. Richard Caton through her daughter Mrs. Emily McTavish
1846.2.1

Unlike her father and former husband, the emperor had remained true to his promises, which in large measure contributed to her lifelong respect and admiration for the fallen leader. Nevertheless, the termination of her pension meant that in the future Elizabeth would have to rely solely on income from her investments and whatever interest the annuity yielded. Past scholarship has shown that the 60,000 francs from Napoléon amounted to slightly more than $50,000, but Elizabeth calculated that she received the equivalent of $65,174 from the French government. This figure excludes the money Prince Jérôme gave her in 1805 and the $20,000 line of credit established by Turreau that was part of her settlement. She received regular payments from 1810 to 1814:

List of Monies received from French Govt, circa 1814,

Rec^d from French Government from 21 Nov 1809	20,000 Dollars
Rec^d from Ditto from 1st October 1810	952..37 ½
Rec^d from Ditto 1st Nov 1810	952..37 ½
Rec^d from Ditto 1st Decr 1810	952..37 ½
Rec^d from Ditto for Year 1811	11,428..50
Rec^d from Ditto for Year 1812	11,428..50
Rec^d from Ditto for Year 1813	11,428..50
Rec^d from Ditto for nine months of year 1814	8571..37 ½
amount Recd as above from France	$65,714..

after paying 20,000 Dollars as above Stated; they agreed to pay me 60000 francs per annum; & by *their* calculation, the amount of Sixty thousand francs was 11,428 dollars & fifty cents

from P Jerome [portion cut out of paper] left to me at Lisbon 1300 Dollars

[portion cut out of paper] remitted me thro England one thousand guineas of which guineas Mr W Patterson kept half

Bring down the sum rec'd from French Government of $65.714

add there to [cut out of paper] [Jérôme] left me at Lisbon by PJ   1300

add his guineas at for gone   4500

Amount total received $71,514

This document also reveals that William Patterson took 500 guineas from the money Jérôme sent his daughter in an attempt to recoup some of the money he had spent on Elizabeth and his son-in-law during their marriage.[40]

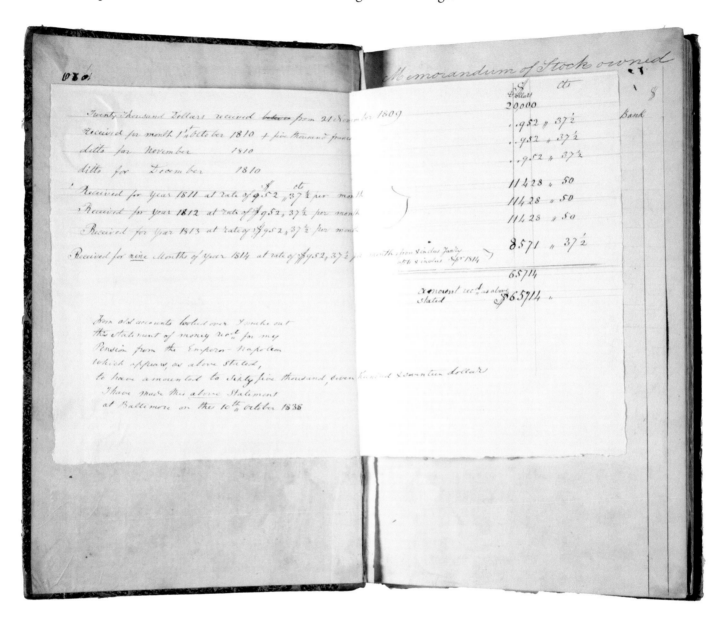

Elizabeth was fundamentally conservative when it came to investing. The economic downturn and subsequent subsequent inflation brought on by the War of 1812 brought financial instability to the United States. Although her portfolio of investments comprised real estate and stock holdings during this early period, Elizabeth's concern for her finances heightened in the winter and spring of 1813, but by May she was relieved to receive £500 from her investments.[41] Her father then demanded twenty percent of that money for his

Elizabeth copied her 1814 "monies received from the French" government list twenty-four years later, "at Baltimore on 10 October 1838," and pasted it in the front of this account book. The tattered original is among her papers.
Box 14, MS 142, EPB Papers

assistance in securing this payment. For Patterson, business was business, and he expected compensation—even when aiding his daughter.

Although Elizabeth's pension was certainly a majestic sum by most nineteenth-century standards, far more than most people would ever see, fully invested at 6 percent it would "only" yield between $3,000 and $4,000 a year. According to her friends, such a small income would make life in a major European city difficult for a woman of her social level.[42] Spear, who mistakenly thought she could get money for Elizabeth from Patterson, advised: "If you do not spend 2000[d] [pounds] a year whilst in England you will be considered mean & miserable & it will injure you a great deal more than the saving of it will do you good. You have 2000[d] in the Bank I am astonish[d] you dont draw." Her aunt went on to list how profitable Elizabeth's investments had been, except for her stock in the "fire company" and "the falls turnpike," and assured her that "dividends are daily coming in."[43]

Elizabeth followed her own counsel—she was determined to invest the principal of her money, and to live solely on interest and as little of that as possible. "Do spend your money," Spear repeatedly urged in 1815, knowing full well that her niece would probably only spend money on her appearance, her expenses for Bo, and basic accommodations.[44] On April 16, 1815, Patterson, who had no intention of giving Elizabeth any material help, advised, "If you are Determined to Remain in Europe, and find that your present Income is not Sufficient you must break in upon your Capital a Thousand or Two a year."[45] Although Spear regarded spending only one or two thousand dollars a year as "miserable," Patterson saw it as perfectly acceptable for his daughter. Socializing with royalty and high society in Europe was a costly proposition, but adopting an iron will with regard to preserving the core of her wealth in prudent investments was perhaps the most significant step Elizabeth took to attain her fortune.

Before she sailed for Europe in 1815, she prepared her finances as well as settled her son in school in Mount St. Mary's College in Emmitsburg, Maryland. Her concern regarding her ability to support her son seems to have been excessive, for there is little indication that the child's expenses were a drain on her finances. In 1814 she paid "$126.50 [for] Bo's Schooling" as well as $70 to Mr. DuBois, Bo's tutor, and $5.50 for "pocket money" for the boy. The following year, she paid $68.32 for "six months of Bo's schooling," but her father also contributed. Spear reported to Elizabeth that Patterson paid

$100 for his grandson's tuition and equipped him for the school year in grand style. Patterson made sure Bo departed "ladened" with clothing and other supplies and did not ask Elizabeth for reimbursement.[46] Patterson doted on and spoiled his grandson, fostering an extravagance in the boy that would later appall Elizabeth and lead Edward Patterson to remark upon his nephew's "inordinate desire for money."[47]

Despite Elizabeth's careful financial preparations for her trip abroad, only a year into her stay she began to sense that a return to Baltimore was inevitable because her funds were insufficient. In 1816 she wrote to Spear expressing concern about her income. "I think you are unnecessarily anxious on the score of your income," her aunt responded. "You cannot expect to add to your capital during a sojourn to Europe; . . . Bo's prospect of a provision, from his grandfather's estate is great; so you need not be solicitous on his account."[48] Given her own experience with her father's generosity, Elizabeth found little comfort in

Jerome Napoleon Bonaparte, "Bo"
(1805–1870)
Attributed to Anna Pecchioli
Circa 1817
Watercolor on ivory
Maryland Historical Society
Gift of Mrs. Charles J. Bonaparte
xx.5.62

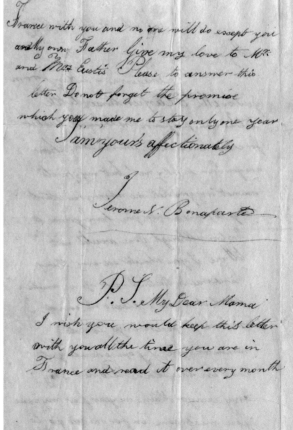

Letters such as this one that Bo wrote to Elizabeth in 1815 reveal the lonely child she often left behind.
Box 1, MS 144, EPB Papers

her aunt's reassurance. In 1816, Spear wrote to Elizabeth, "It was much against my Judgment making you a remittance of 20 percent but you wrote so many importunate letters about starving & want of credit. & the Lord knows what that I was obliged to act against my judgment. But the remittance only cost you 2,400^d [dollars] & the price of the Bill of Exchange was 2,666 [dollars] your Father does not ask for the other part of the Purchase money." This suggests that Patterson may have obtained the money for Elizabeth but in this case did not charge his daughter a commission. In addition, Spear notes that Patterson paid $200 for Bo's tuition. In another letter written that year, Spear encouraged Elizabeth to "spend part of your principal—you cannot live forever." She also added that the only unflattering thing she ever heard about Elizabeth was that she didn't spend "money enough."[49] Elizabeth confessed to John Spear Smith, her cousin, on August 22, 1816, that she anticipated that "pecuniary difficulties" as well as the "impossibility of sending for my dear child" would force her to return to the United States.[50]

By 1817, the economic downturn in the United States had become evident and Elizabeth was keenly aware that her finances were dwindling. Edward Patterson began his letter to her on January 3, 1817 by "Supposing your funds in Europe must be nearly exhausted by this time,"[51] but on January 11 he wrote another letter saying, "you have now in the bank 1000 Dollars & more coming every day."[52] Nevertheless, when her uncle, Samuel Smith, lost his fortune in the panic of that year, the financially conservative Elizabeth took it as a warning. On September 12, 1817, she set sail for the United States. This was but the first occasion that financial concerns compelled her to leave Europe; in the decades to follow money, more than family, drew her back to Baltimore. Her correspondence is frequently peppered with worries about money, more so than with anxiety about her son.

Elizabeth returned to the United States in 1817, but few records of her financial transactions between 1817 and 1819 survive. In 1818, her recorded expenditures related to repairs on her property on King George Street which had been rented to a Dr. Steward, tuition for Bo, and payment of her taxes to Baltimore County. In 1819, she purchased Baltimore City bonds in the amount of $1,000 at six percent interest and stock in the Bank of the United States, but clearly noted, "it stands in my name altho' it belongs to my Son." This is the first recorded instance of her making an investment specifically to benefit Bo. In looking at her stock and property holdings in the 1820s, there is little evidence that Elizabeth sold stocks she held prior to the financial crisis. After 1819, her next records of her investments date to 1824 and 1825 and her "Reicester Town Road" stock, her "Water Stock" [Baltimore Water Company], and her investment in the Bank of Maryland continue to appear in her records.[53]

In 1819, Elizabeth decided it was time for another trip to Europe. Her losses in the financial market, if indeed she suffered any from 1817 to 1818, did not hamper her ability to plan another extended journey. Moreover, she thought that Bo, at fourteen, should complete his education in Europe. "Embarked the third of May 1819 for Amsterdam," she wrote in her journal, adding that she brought with her "a Bill on the House of Willink from the Gilmors for three thousand current Florins" and another from "the Wirgmans for twelve hundred & fifty guilders Holland currency." These bills of exchange, amounting to $1700, functioned like checks to be "cashed" upon her arrival in Amsterdam, which she did on June 12.[54] In advance of her departure, she had looked to prominent Baltimore merchants and investors Peter and Charles Wirgman, who both had relationships with the House of Willink, for this assistance, providing them with the funds in advance of her trip and then using their "bills" to draw the money.[55] "I found the Willinks, of Amsterdam, very agreeable and useful acquaintances during my short residence in their country," she wrote to Gilmor, who had also assisted her. "I thank you infinitely for the letters you wrote to them."[56]

When Bo and his mother arrived in Geneva in 1819, Elizabeth quickly discovered that her son did not emulate her own prudence and economy. The young man's extravagance, reminiscent of his father's, concerned her almost as much as his longing for his home in Baltimore.[57] Elizabeth also knew that if she denied her son anything, he would turn to his indulgent grandfather. In 1820, Elizabeth wrote to her father saying, "I know Bo has written to you for money to buy a horse which I beg you *not* to send him. He pretends it will be more economical for him to keep a horse than for me to pay nine francs per week for riding lessons."[58] In an attempt to instill some frugality in the boy, she bought him a dog instead of a horse to prove her point.[59]

During this period, two developments dramatically affected Elizabeth's finances. The first occurred in Geneva, where she began a friendship with John Jacob Astor. America's first millionaire, she observed with some irony, "seems afflicted with possession of a fortune which he had greater pleasure in amassing than he can ever find in spending," a thought she would later have about

When Jérôme's family made overtures to have Bo visit them in Rome so they could meet him, Elizabeth worried about the expense and turned to her friend John Jacob Astor for advice. In a letter to her father she relayed Astor's opinion that the Bonapartes' hints at aiding Bo financially were hollow.

Elizabeth Patterson Bonaparte to William Patterson, June 23, 1820, Bonaparte Vertical File, Maryland Historical Society

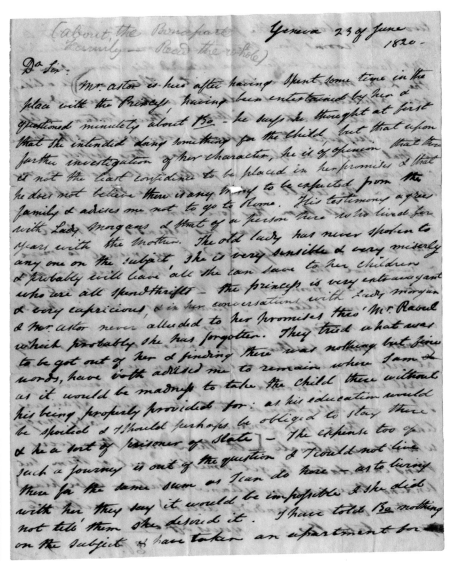

John Jacob Astor (1763–1848)
John Wesley Jarvis (1780/81–1839)
Circa 1825
Oil on canvas
National Portrait Gallery

herself.[60] Astor soon became her financial and personal advisor. The second arose from the Bonaparte family's desire to know Bo. When Elizabeth had to decide whether to send Bo to meet his father's family, particularly Pauline Borghese, Napoléon's sister living in Rome, she relied on Astor for advice because he had met several members of the Bonapartes during his time in Rome. Although Elizabeth felt Bo should know his Bonaparte relatives, the financial side of this decision outweighed the emotional. Before she committed to the expense of traveling to Rome she wanted some assurance that the journey would benefit her son. Perhaps the family would fund the rest of his education. Astor was not sanguine. She related his assessment in a letter to her father on June 23, 1820. "He [Astor] says he thought at first that she [Pauline Borghese] intended doing something for the child but that upon further investigation of her character he is of the opinion that there is not the least confidence to be placed in her promises & that he does not believe there is anything to be expected of the family."[61]

Pauline, Princess Borghese
(1780–1825)
François-Joseph Kinson (1771–1839)
1808
Oil on canvas
National Gallery of Ireland

The Panic of 1819 was still undermining the American economy, making Elizabeth especially cautious with her finances. When Joseph Bonaparte, Prince Jérôme's brother, offered her the use of his isolated chalet outside Geneva, she declined because she could not afford to keep a carriage to transport her back and forth to the city. She initially considered a trip to Rome, which might well be pointless, to be an imprudent expenditure, but in 1821 she and Bo finally made the journey to meet the Bonapartes.[62] The trip, though successful in establishing Bo's relations with his father's family, did not significantly relieve Elizabeth of expenses related to his education. Astor's appraisal of the situation had been largely accurate: Borghese may have showered Bo with gifts, but her promise of $8,000 when Bo married was never fulfilled.[63]

In February 1823, Bo enrolled in Harvard, where his spending shocked and dismayed his mother. During his first year and a half back in the United

States, he spent $2,150, an amount that approximated what Elizabeth spent in a year.[64] Whenever she questioned him, and she did so repeatedly, Bo petulantly declared that he would rather leave school than face "uninterrupted complaints about his expenses."[65] Elizabeth responded by putting her son on a budget, hoping he would adopt the "economy" she had so long practiced. Until Bo's marriage to the wealthy Susan May Williams in 1829—a marriage Elizabeth disdained—she continued to support him while constantly expressing the hope that he would adopt some degree of financial responsibility. After

Dinner Forks
Unmarked
Circa 1820
Silver, engraved "EP"
Maryland Historical Society
Gift of Mrs. Charles J. Bonaparte
xx.5.24, xx.5.25

This pair of forks is recorded in several of Elizabeth's inventories and remained with her until her death. She purchased them in Geneva in the 1820s.

Elizabeth lived frugally whenever she went to Europe, keeping detailed accounts of even the most minor expenses.
Red Journal, Box 13A, MS 142, EPB Papers

violently opposing the marriage because Williams was an American, she accepted the reality that the union was "the only sure way of relieving myself of the expense he occasions me and I can ill-y afford." Although Elizabeth claimed she could "illy afford" Bo's support, by 1829 her holdings had grown sufficiently so that her income made her son's expenditures "affordable." Upon his marriage, she terminated his allowance and determined to spend more freely on herself.[66]

During this period and despite her commitment to ease her financial discipline, Elizabeth maintained her socially active—but frugal—life in Europe. Her accounts from 1826 to 1832 include the cost of renting her rooms, taking carriages, hiring servants, and franking letters. In the matter of her wardrobe, she relaxed her spending habits the most, but she never allowed herself to be extravagant. After Bo's marriage in 1829, Elizabeth's expenses do not appear to have changed radically despite her decision to spend more freely on herself. She continued to spend little on food, relying instead on the hospitality of her friends. She also kept careful records of what she tipped various servants, including the Russian and Swedish ministers' servants in Geneva and the servants of the Sardinian and Swedish ministers, and Prince Borghese in Florence. Her "pantry" appears to have contained only basic necessities such as tea and sugar, bread, and butter.[67] While at the baths in Italy, she watched her expenses for dining, or "nourriture," but that kind of extravagance occurred rarely. More often, she relied on social invitations for her meals and largely eliminated this expense from her day-to-day life. The fact that she owned the barest minimum of tableware, notably two forks purchased in Geneva, for most of her life attests to the fact that she maintained the habit of dining out rather than entertaining.

While in Europe, Elizabeth never ceased watching her investments and building her fortune. Throughout the 1820s and 1830s, she relied on her aunt Nancy Spear and her friend, John White, for financial advice. Despite their contentious relationship, she and her father exchanged letters about financial matters, and she undoubtedly benefited from his astute guidance. Having become seasoned by the sharp financial swings in the American economy, she grew even more conservative. "I have no confidence in banks, insurance companies, road stocks, or, in short, any stock in Baltimore," she confided to her father. Her friends thought her "almost a miser."[68] Despite this, she continued to buy property in Baltimore and invest in stocks. Her philosophy was simple. "Never run the slightest risk in the pursuit of great profits—see clearly the transaction to its termination."[69]

By the early 1830s, Elizabeth's investments were providing her with significant profits. In 1831, when she was in Paris, William Patterson brought her up-to-date on affairs back in Baltimore. "You have now floating capital here of perhaps fifty or sixty thousand Dollars for which employment is obliged to be changed & shifted frequently from one kind of security of another: this is precarious, dangerous & troublesome." He warned her that Spear and John White, who were handling her "monied affairs," were "both delicate," and she had caused "Mr. White "a great deal of trouble" for which he had not charged a commission. Patterson recommended sending him a watch as a thank-you gift.[70]

She continued to invest most of the interest she earned, holding back only enough for her modest personal needs and a wardrobe suitable for her social life. On April 14, 1833, John White wrote via the American consul at Le Havre, "I have now the pleasure, in obedience of your request, of handing you enclosed a Bill for one thousand dollars, which I caused to be purchased at New York, being the cheapest market . . . & drawn by R E Patterson at sixty days rights, in favor of John S Delaplaine & Co upon M Rouqumont de Lowenberg, Paris for five thousand, three hundred and fifty francs. . . . I feel confidant that its disbursement under your good judgment will amply repay you in gratification of the cost in money."[71] That same year, Spear wrote regarding her desire to buy a property. "I should like to get it where property will probably rise in value, the insurance & taxes I will pay my self & see that it is well taken care of."[72] Like Elizabeth, her aunt followed politics and its effect on the economy with a shrewd eye and knew that sound investments were often a matter of timing.

The following year, 1834, Elizabeth left a Europe once again plagued by a cholera epidemic and disrupted by revolution. These were ample reasons to leave, but her departure was in large part motivated by the need to attend to her finances. Her father had alerted her to the increased economic instability in the United States. "We are in great confusion & distress in this country on account of President Jackson's arbitrary conduct in respect to the Bank of the United States, there is no saying how it may end or that it may not ultimately produce a revolution." Patterson was speaking of the bank crisis, which caused even the soundest investments to founder. He went on to assure her that upon her arrival home he would look after her comfort, even providing her with $1,000 annually, the settlement from her mother's estate he had previously denied her. In 1867, Elizabeth annotated his letter, crediting her father with his

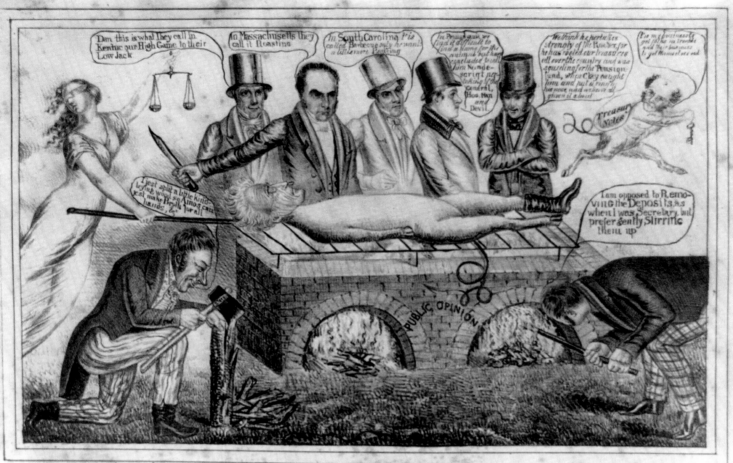

THE POLITICAL BARBECUE

"The Political Barbeque," 1834. The figure of Justice in this cartoon roasts President Andrew Jackson over the fires of Public Opinion following the decision to move federal deposits from the Bank of the United States as part of his strategy to destroy it.
Library of Congress

"sagacious" advice, but noting, "The promise to endeavor to make my situation as comfortable as he would was kept in the same good faith as that made at the time of my marriage. To pay me one thousand dollars annually; that of complying with the wish expressed on her death bed to him of his Wife that her property should be given to her daughters & to Henry & Octavius."[73]

When Patterson died in 1835, Elizabeth received the greatest financial shock of her life. Her inheritance, promised to be the equal of that left to her brothers, was in fact a pittance. Fortunately, Elizabeth had managed her finances well and never appeared to depend on an inheritance. For the rest of her life, she referred to what little she did receive with growing wrath. According to her notes, corroborated by Patterson's will, she received interest in six properties in the city, including the "home in which she was born." On an undated fragment of an account book, she recorded the profit she made on her portion, listing "rent on one house in South Street $400 per anum/rent of 3 in Market Street [$]1150/one . . . rented to Priestley [$]326/one next to Priestly occupied by Daly—[$]300/amount of rents on the inheritance annually [$]2,175."[74]

Edward Patterson (1789–1865)
William Edward West (1788–1857)
Circa 1830
Oil on canvas
Maryland Historical Society
Gift of Mrs. Andrew Robeson
(Laura Patterson Swan)
1959.118.48

Reflecting upon her father's will, she wrote, "The clause in his will which relates to myself plainly betrays the embarrassment of a loaded conscience & of a bad cause. He violated every principle of honour & of equity to make a ruin of my ambition, of my hopes & of my happiness."[75] Patterson justified his lack of generosity in the will, writing that his daughter had "caused more anxiety & trouble, than all my other children put together & her folly & misconduct has occationed me a train of expense that first and last has cost me much money."[76]

Feeling slighted by her father and encouraged by Bo, Elizabeth and her son filed suit against the estate. Always eager to increase his wealth, Bo wanted his mother to have an equal claim to his grandfather's estate because her portion would eventually be his. In addition to the perceived financial loss Elizabeth suffered as a result of the will, the lawsuit brought with it deep emotional betrayal. It was bad enough that her father had castigated her behavior throughout her life, but now her brothers turned on her. If that were not hard enough to bear, Spear, so long her confidant and friend, sold them Elizabeth's letters to strengthen

In 1835, upon her father's death, Elizabeth inherited the South Street house. This idealized view of the city shows the street as it looked during her lifetime. (Detail, *E. Sachse & Co.'s Bird's Eye View of the City of Baltimore*, 1869.)

their case against their sister. Elizabeth lost not only her aunt's emotional support but an astute financial manager as well. In 1835, she wrote a poem to immortalize Spear's betrayal, noting that it was the first poem she ever composed. In verse after verse she poured out her feelings:

> Honest Nancy, to fraud & Perjury.
> Sons will then threat an action
> 'gainst private scandal of a Sister
> For years hoard'd by family faction . . .[77]

The rift with her aunt never mended. On the wrapper of a package of Spear's letters, Elizabeth wrote, "Thou also! et toi Brutus," a lasting reference to her betrayal.[78] Unwilling to forgive those who had wronged her, Patterson's will marked the end of her close ties with her brothers. Only George Patterson, who shared some of his inheritance with her, was spared her wrath. Elizabeth told Martha Custis Williams Carter, her friend in Mrs. Gwinn's boarding house in the 1870s, "He [George] was the one . . . instrumental in getting the others to consent to letting her have the property left to her by her mother."[79] Around 1861, Elizabeth wrote in her journal, "He [Patterson] & his Sons Bob the Brutal, & John the Drunken, never failing on all occasions to insult the affliction & distress of a daughter & a Sister, who had Every right to expect from Every member of the P[atterso]n family protection aid & hospitality. The family, inflicted by nature, not by choice on me, have Ever been my Evil doers, maligners & Selfish persecutors."[80]

Unlike many people who associated security and sense of place with family, Elizabeth saw Baltimore and her family members who lived there as a blight on her existence. This translated to an aversion to permanently tethering herself to the city with a residence. Life in boarding houses not only provided the freedom to quickly leave for Europe, it was a significant component of her

Nancy Spear, Elizabeth's aunt, turned on her niece when Bo and Elizabeth sued her brothers to gain an equal portion of William Patterson's estate. Feeling deeply wounded at being betrayed, Elizabeth penned this poem—it ran to three pages—to vent her anger with her onetime confidante and financial advisor.
Box 10, MS 142, EPB Papers

frugality. In forgoing a house and servants, Elizabeth removed a financial burden. She owned real estate solely for the purpose of rental income. In 1824, prior to her return to Baltimore, her father had suggested she move into her rental house rather than return to his South Street home. He advised, "you cannot be ignorant of the situation the Family were placed in when you were here before & everything was confusion & out of order about my House. we are now tranquil & wish to remain so, & if you were to take up your permanent residence at my House it is to be feared that the same confusion & dissatisfaction would take place as formerly." Patterson continued, "I think it will be best for you to remain with me until you can make arrangements & open House for yourself, your House over the Bridge is now in good order for your reception & no doubt you can get possession of it ere long from Mr. Sterett[?] the present Tenant, your means are ample to keep House, far beyond any of the Family."[81] The statement that Elizabeth's means exceeded those of her family must have angered her, given her anxieties about supporting herself.

The boarding houses she occupied, all in the elegant Mount Vernon district of Baltimore, provided her with comfortable temporary quarters, eliminated most of the costs of a household, and afforded her the freedom to travel. Her decision may seem perplexing, particularly as her wealth grew, but given her frugality and aversion to anything that would prevent her from going to Europe, it makes sense. Besides, she was accustomed to living this way during her travels.

By 1838, Elizabeth's annual income had risen to $10,717.76, a remarkable achievement given yet another financial panic that struck the country in 1837.[82] Her investments were growing slowly and her real estate holdings had more than doubled. Her portfolio had expanded in both stock holdings and real estate. In addition, she had lent considerable sums to three individuals at six percent interest.[83] In 1839, just before she and Bo departed for Europe, Elizabeth wrote to Alexander Yearly, "I hand to you . . . my Power of attorney to collect & receive the rents on my Houses, & to do every thing for the advantageous management of my Real Estate."[84] Several of her properties were in need of repair. Yearly often wrote to ask for permission to execute necessary work. If Elizabeth's correspondence with her property managers during her later years is any indication, she wanted to spend as little as possible to make her houses and shops rentable. Upon her return to New York in July of 1840, she wrote to Yearly inquiring about several of her renters. "I am ignorant whether Mr.

R._____ has vacated one of the granite front houses, and whether Mr. F_____ has succeeded him in the occupancy of the said house. . . . Please have the goodness to inform me of all these circumstances, and at the same time state for me the dates of the days on which, subsequent to my departure from Baltimore, the new tenants had entered my houses."[85]

Despite the steady growth in her investment income, Elizabeth still worried about money. Upon her return from Paris, she established herself in a Baltimore boarding house but took frequent trips to Rockaway, New York, to visit the Astors. By 1845, she listed her annual income at $14,963.80. On a scrap of paper among her journals, she noted that in 1845 she had $100,000 invested in Europe. Just one year later, she calculated her income had risen again, to $16,498.50, later adding $253 to make the total a more accurate $16,751.50.[86] Between 1845 and 1848, she only once spent more than $1,200 a year and for several years kept her annual expenses around $900, a remarkably low figure considering her income. Every penny remained accounted for, even when she could not remember quite how she had spent it. In 1848, she noted that she spent $4.49 "I know not how."[87]

By early 1849, Elizabeth was again contemplating a return to Europe. She wanted to see her old friend, Lady Sydney Morgan, the Irish novelist. In a letter to Morgan dated March 14, 1849, Elizabeth wrote, "I shall emancipate myself, *par la grâce of Dieu* [by the grace of God], about the middle of July." She confessed her correspondence with her friends in Europe had languished during her "vegetation in this Baltimore." "What could I write about, except the fluctuations in the security and consequent prices of American stocks. There is nothing here worth attention or interest save the money market.[88] Clearly, despite Elizabeth's increased wealth, she remained concerned about her ability to afford a trip to Europe. Her friend Harriet Stewart wrote to her from London, attempting to allay her fears about the cost. "As for your means, I will give you a rough idea—it is very rough & crude, but it will show you that your means are ample for position and comfort—it is only whims that you need deny yourself." She outlined:

A House will cost 300 pounds

Taxes   50

Furniture, say 10 p.cent on 1500 lbs.   150

Carriage & horses 300

800 pounds

She went on to add that Elizabeth might with her income "live in luxury at Brighton—in comfort competence & position in London." She also agreed that Elizabeth should spare herself the expense of traveling with servants, something Elizabeth rarely did.[89]

On October 17, 1849, Elizabeth boarded the *Canada* and set sail for Liverpool.[90] She arrived only eleven days later and wasted no time in traveling to London. The first stop recorded in her journal was a visit to George Peabody, the multimillionaire banker who had offered to assist her with her finances while she was abroad. Peabody, founder of George Peabody & Company banking house in London, advised her about investments, paid her bills, and offered advice both financial and personal.[91] Peabody had taken up residence in London in 1837, knew the city well, and was one of the best people Elizabeth could have approached for financial guidance. He offered favorable terms on her money as well. Elizabeth noted "G Peabody has promised to allow me 3 per cent interest for Money in his hands & to charge me 3 per cent if I should borrow from him. He charges nothing for the Bills I gave him from Wm Brown at Liverpool." In early November she brought her "Bills from Brown to George Peabody on 3 November 1849 who holds them at my disposition."[92] During this European visit, Elizabeth also conducted considerable business with her Paris bankers, asking them to sell her French investments and remit the money to London. According to her journal, "on 27 November 1849 G Peabody gave me credit for said remittance [from France] of francs 1250 40 centimes—say 49 pounds—2 sterling—Peabody gives me credit 1 april 1850 for 417 francs 30 centimes . . . say 16 pounds." Peabody oversaw the transfer of these funds from France to England and helped her convert them to pounds.[93]

She also turned to longtime friend and New York banker James Gallatin to manage her finances in the United States and relied on a property manager to collect her rents.[94] While abroad Elizabeth continued her usual manner of investing, acquiring ground rents in Baltimore, state bonds, and utility stocks. In 1854, two years after she returned to Baltimore, a newspaper article entitled, "The Baltimore Bonapartes," described Elizabeth in the city, saying, "She may be frequently seen on the wharves, at the post office, visiting brokers, bankers and other gentlemen of business, collecting rents, buying stocks and participating in other speculative matters."[95] It is perhaps in this article that the idea of Elizabeth collecting her own rents had its origins, but her personal correspondence and journals suggest she relied on property managers for that job. Despite this, Elizabeth was known to be a woman

George Peabody (1795–1869)
Photograph by Mathew B. Brady
(1822–1896), engraved by
John Chester Buttre (1821–1893)
1850–1890
Library of Congress

who handled her own finances, negotiated her own terms, and controlled her own investments. Few contemporary women acted with such independence.

A letter to her grandson, Jerome Jr., in 1858 shows that her frugality continued unabated long after her wealth rendered it completely unnecessary. Although she had wanted Jerome to purchase "a French Bonheur* & a sandal wood box," for her in Paris, she told him "[they] would cost too much money; therefore, I prefer to do without either. My poverty & my personal insignificance ne sont pas traînés à la remarque par l'Empereur des Français.† Not being a *Bassesse imperiale‡* I can be forced to pay my debts; therefore I must practice Economy." She went on to warn Jerome against investing in "Road Stocks & of any investments in Joint Stock Companies. I followed the advice of other people when I foolishly bought R.R.Rd. Bonds—had I obeyed my instinctive repugnance to this kind of Stock I should now be far better satisfied." In later life, financial misjudgments comingled in Elizabeth's mind with what she deemed her own personal misjudgments. "I made a terrible miscalculation when I invested in Malaparte [Prince Jérôme]; & I hate Joint Stock Companies, Taxes & himself de toute la force de mon âme."** Elizabeth also added with considerable resentment that the South Street house left to her by William Patterson had required considerable repairs, remarking, "It was a poisoned gift & has, from first to last, been a source of annoyance."[96] She spoke truthfully; of all her properties the South Street house required the greatest expenditures.

Elizabeth and Bo traveled to Europe again in late fall, 1860, this time in a final attempt to secure the legacy left by Bo's uncle, Cardinal Fesch. She took with her the financial records she needed to follow her investments and while abroad continued to invest in additional holdings. In January 1861, James Gallatin, president of the National Bank of New York, bought additional New York City bonds for Elizabeth and on April 1, 1861, Elizabeth recorded that, according to Gallatin, she held $71,200 in "New York City sixes."[97] Although Elizabeth's finances just before the war continued in their

"The Late Jerome Bonaparte, Husband of 'Miss Patterson' of Baltimore," *Harper's Weekly: A Journal of Civilization,* July 28, 1860
Box 15, MS 142, EPB Papers

This image is from an article about Jérôme Bonaparte's death that Elizabeth annotated with derogatory comments about her former husband and added to one of her scrapbooks.

---

*a bonheur du jour is a lady's writing desk

†"would not attract the notice of the French emperor." She is implying that money is the real emperor of the French and she does not have enough to attract attention.

‡ imperial lowlife or his Royal Lowness

**"with all the strength of my soul," or, as we would say, "with every fiber of my being"

usual good order, a downturn in 1857 and the economic decline prior to the Civil War were having their effect. Explaining her reduced rents, her current property manager, William Mentzel, wrote, "You can scarcely imagine the depression of the money market and business here owing to the disunion excitement." The $800 or $900 she had been receiving each month from her properties was now shrinking by hundreds of dollars each month. Following the riot of April 19, 1861, when a mob attacked Federal troops passing through Baltimore, the situation grew sharply worse. On May 14, Mentzel reported,

> "We are so fully engaged in War here now that all business is well nigh suspended indeed since April 19th the general fear has been that our City would be burned up. On that date owing to the passage of Massachusetts troops through the city, we had a civil war in our streets in which some 15 or 20 were killed and a number wounded. This resistance on the part of our citizens brought the indignation of the Government and the entire North upon us threatening immediate destruction. The Rail Road Bridges were burnt up to the state line by authorities, our Port was blockaded, and business at an end."

That month Elizabeth received only $244.96, less than a third of the amount she had received the year before. Mentzel added that two of her rental houses "came near being in ruins" when "the arch and alley between Reuter and Coates (upon which a heavy dividing wall rests)" collapsed and significantly damaged the stock in a tenant's hardware store. He assured her that he had seen to the repairs "as economically as I could costing about $100." The roof on the South Street house was in such poor condition that part of it was almost "past repair." In addition, war depressed the rental market. Men left daily to enlist in the armies, and Mentzel could not get tenants to pay their rent. The situation got no better as the months passed. On December 8, 1863 he wrote, "Herewith you will find your account for November. It is rather small, owing mainly to the draft of 3200 men in the last two weeks which has for the time almost stopped business. I have the promise however after the 10th of several amounts which I have tried to get before rendering my account, but failed."[98] There is no surviving evidence that Elizabeth increased her real estate holdings during the war. In 1862, Elizabeth recorded that she owned "47 perpetual ground rents"; just after the war in 1866, she owned the same number of ground rents but had enhanced her stock portfolio.[99]

In 1863, Elizabeth returned to an old account book with some blank pages remaining and entered her financial records. "I am very much richer than when this book was begun year 1805," she observed with pride and some irony.[100] This comment also suggests that although the war brought poverty and devastation for many, for her it had presented financial opportunity. As the war dragged on, rents remained low, with owners sometimes reducing them further in order to retain tenants, but investments in the bonds of northern states grew profitable, particularly her New York City "sixes." Elizabeth acknowledged that a Virginia bond bought prior to the war was not a good investment, but it was her only investment in bonds or stocks of a Confederate state. Despite its low yield, the Virginia bond remained in her estate until her death in 1879.[101] In 1864 she invested $20,000 in a subscription to the "Soldier's Bounty Fund" and by the end of the war, her overall wealth had increased, not diminished.[102] Her decision to shift her focus away from real estate in wartime had been wise.

After 1865, Elizabeth's investments solidified and her relationship with her grandsons, particularly after Bo's death in 1870, became more generous and

Massachusetts Militia Passing through Baltimore
Virtue and Company
1861
Maryland Historical Society
Hambleton Print Collection
H-254

On April 19, 1861, a pro-Southern mob attacked Massachusetts volunteers traveling through Baltimore, marking the first bloodshed of the Civil War. Although the war's effect on Baltimore's economy was profound, Elizabeth managed to prosper during the conflict.

dependent. Age and impending mortality softened her. Writing in 1869 to her youngest grandson Charles Joseph she explained, "I had promised . . . to give you next January one thousand dollars. Life at my age is of short & uncertain date, therefore I bought for you Cert. No. 99 for Two Thousand Dollars Balt. City Hall Sixes, in preference to what had been promised. . . . May you live long to enjoy it!"[103] Like her father, she had tried to use her money to manipulate first her son's and then her grandsons' decisions, to no avail.[104] Now, at eighty-four, she only wanted her son and grandsons to enjoy the money she gave them. That same year, she confided to Charles Joseph,

> "I have recd the certificate No 390. date "Annapolis 13 September 1869" redeemable at pleasure of State of Maryland after year 1883. Since purchase of said Cert No 390 for $15,000, I now own forty five thousand Dollars of above Maryland Defense 6 perc[en]t Loan. The $1700 Gold, which I had kept at McKims, was sold by them on 20 of this month, & only brought me premium net of $629—I am ever unlucky; the chances of life have ever been against me; & I owe nothing except to prudence, toil & Economy!"[105]

Her mantra of "prudence, toil & Economy" never changed. Wealth never eased her concerns about money or led her to extravagance. Six years prior to her death, she could be detached from the ups and downs of investing, but her attention to financial matters never diminished. She meticulously recorded her stock and bond holdings and ground rents in 1871 in a small composition book that she labeled, "For Charles Bonaparte."[106]

In her last years she entrusted most of her finances to Charles's management. In 1873, having just recovered from a major illness, she wrote to him, saying, "The late Monetary Panic was met by me with the same stoical composure that did my expected death last winter. Fatality has ever pursued me thro' life, has been my chronic dire Malady; which now that I shall soon shift off the Mortal coil, I have no time left to fight with."[107]

At the time of her death in 1879, Elizabeth's estate consisted largely of municipal and state bonds. She was heavily invested in bonds from New York City, Philadelphia, and her hometown. She had gradually acquired more than fifty-one ground rents throughout Baltimore, as well as other rental properties, including a wharf, a factory, and numerous shop fronts and residences. Proudly she wrote in her journal, "All my *Ground Rents were* bought out of my *own* Purse. EP."[108]

During the last decades of her life, Elizabeth maintained again and again in her journals that her financial success was of her own making. Late in life she claimed all the credit for that, forgetting the roles Spear, Astor, Peabody, her father, and many others played in helping her create and maintain her wealth. Elizabeth saw herself as the sole agent of her destiny. "Like a Silkworm I spun my own suit & my own Lodging—& had no aid nor partner in my labors." She looked back on her decision to remain independent with a mixture of pride and melancholy. In the same journal, she confessed: "To run through one's own Solitary cycle & work out one's own weary problem alone—I have found it a sad thing to do."[109] She was a single woman who had made her own way on her own terms, an achievement of which few of her peers could boast. Although she had always followed the advice of others, often turning to the most influential men of the period, the final decisions had been hers, and she "thanked God for the capacity he had given her to make money."[110]

The story of Elizabeth's wealth, overshadowed for decades by the romance of her marriage, is that of a single woman in the nineteenth century protecting herself by building a fortune through prudent investments, frugality, and a willingness to seek sound advice. Her ties to Europe, her connections to powerful advisors, and her understanding of world events helped her manage money between two continents, but investing in the burgeoning city of Baltimore, the place she most hated, turned out to be the greater influence on her life. More than family obligations, her American holdings drew her home again and again and, ironically, made her the wealthy woman she became.

Undated (1870s) list of Elizabeth's investments late in her life, when she had made her considerable fortune.
Box 13A, MS 142, EPB Papers

Two Pairs of Ice Cream Coolers
Stone, Coquerel et Le Gros
Circa 1815
Paris
Porcelain and gilt
Maryland Historical Society, Gift of Mrs. Andrew Robeson Jr. (Laura Patterson Swan). 1935.15.8 a–c and 1935.15.9 a–c

In 1815, when Elizabeth departed for Europe, she inventoried her French porcelain along with her possessions. "Four ice cream vases" are noted in a list that contained a total of 102 pieces. Although it had long been thought that all the porcelain associated with Elizabeth was purchased for her own use, current research suggests that some of the tableware was purchased for her brother, Edward Patterson (1789–1865). In 1815, Elizabeth's account book notes on April 15, "recv'd from Edward for china six hundred and thirty dollars and 85 cents." The correlation between Edward Patterson's marriage to Sidney Smith (1794–1879) in 1815 and the purchase of these and other Parisian housewares indicates that Elizabeth helped the newlyweds furnish their new home. Later, she may have sold Edward the tableware, such as the ice cream coolers, that she no longer wanted.

"O, for celebrity . . ."

*"I am constantly asked for . . . photographs of myself. . . . I have
become too old & too ugly to leave to posterity . . . I am much
annoyed by people asking after my portrait & what I think of the
Emperor of France—& of his dispositions toward our Country."*[1]

FOR MORE THAN SIX DECADES Elizabeth Patterson Bonaparte's story
captivated the public, yet in all that time her celebrity barely diminished.[2] She could not escape that which she valued most, her association
with the Bonapartes, nor did she desire to. Newspaper articles about her
appeared with regularity. Sometimes press attention waned, but then the tides
of her life drew interest back to the American woman who might have been a
queen. Frequent trips to Europe, her lawsuits in the French courts, even her
grandsons' success kept her in the public eye. In her old age, people were still
watching Madame Bonaparte, the faded beauty who walked the streets of
Baltimore, inspecting her properties and visiting her brokers. When she was
eighty-five, a reporter from the *Baltimore Sun* wrote, "On the street then, she
carried yet the traces of that beauty and vivacity which were the charms of
her youth, and her keen eye flashed with a luster remarkable for her age and in
her figure she showed no bending, and her step was firm and even elastic."[3]
Even in old age, Elizabeth caught one's eye.

People she did not know wanted her image, her money, her story. Fed up
with a particularly tenacious reporter who ventured to her boarding house, she
answered the door and snapped, "Madame Bonaparte is not home."[4] Other
visitors appeared on her doorstep in the hope of seeing the "celebrated" Madame
Bonaparte. The lucky ones might be invited to her rooms and shown the

A daguerreotype of the triple portrait painted by Gilbert Stuart in 1804. As she grew older and photography became popular, Elizabeth declined to use the medium, preferring to have images made of her earlier portraits.

csph 293 02, 01,
Maryland Historical Society

relics of her European life. Others less fortunate were turned away with, "Today is not a show day!" The last known image of Elizabeth dates to 1840. It is the silhouette of a middle-aged woman with a softened jaw line and a modest bonnet. Although others thought she remained beautiful, she lamented her lost looks and did not want the loss memorialized in photographs or portraits. Given the popularity of photography after the invention of the daguerreotype in 1839, the fact that photographs of Elizabeth do not exist is telling. Even people of modest means could document their appearance in a *carte de visite,* but Elizabeth avoided the photographer's lens, preferring instead to have her portraits photographed. If people wanted her image, they would get only a vision of her former self. Elizabeth explained this to Martha Custis Williams Carter at Miss Gwinn's boarding house when she asked her for her autograph. In her diary, Carter recorded their conversation.

> I asked Madame if she would not give me her autograph seeing that she wrote with comparatively little trouble and very distinctly. . . . no she said nothing would induce me to give my autograph to any one— then just a little sentiment—no not a word she replied—you know I once wrote very well and I do not intend to have these signs of decrepitude descend to posterity any more than I wd ever allow myself to be photographed or a likeness of any kind to be taken after I grew old.[5]

In 1873, W. T. R. Saffell seized upon the public interest in Elizabeth's private life and published *The Bonaparte-Patterson Marriage*, based on a large group of letters that he purchased "from Houtine & Murdock, dealers in paper-makers' material, on Centre Market Space, Baltimore," who bought them as "waste paper" from a warehouse William Patterson owned on Gay Street. Saffell told readers he copied the letters and then returned them to Elizabeth's grandson.[6] Although Elizabeth had spent most of her life deeply concerned with how she was perceived by the public, in later years she claimed to care little about it. In the preface, Saffell wrote that he had contacted "Mde. Bonaparte" about the book and been told, "the publication of the volume was a matter of perfect indifference to her."[7] An unbound copy of the manuscript resides among Elizabeth's papers at the Maryland Historical Society, evidence that Saffell indeed shared his work with her. She may well have read it, but she did not annotate it or underline key passages, as was her habit with everything else she read. She may have been indifferent to Saffell's portrayal, but she kept her copy for posterity, suggesting that she did not dismiss the volume entirely.

Despite what she told others, her private writings betray her true feelings again and again. She could not, no matter how she tried, "shake off the Curse of Memory!!"[8] It was decades before she could claim "perfect indifference," but

Oval Waiter
Marked by George W. Riggs, Baltimore
Circa 1795
Silver, engraved with the Patterson arms and motto "I die for those I love/Patterson" and "Elizabeth Patterson" on verso
Collection of Mr. and Mrs. Charles Newhall

in fact she held many grudges. As she observed about Scotland's motto, *"Nemo me impune laccesit"* ("No one can harm me unpunished"), "[it] might suit E P." She could not forget the battles she had lost and the disappointments she had suffered. "There are wrongs which we never pardon, & injuries which we never forget." She exhorted herself, "oublié le Passé!" (Forget the past!), but added, "no *Pas* EP 1857" (no, not), and never succeeded in doing so.[9] It is perhaps accurate to suggest that Elizabeth at once loved and loathed her legacy and the fame that came with it, just as many modern celebrities do. Most troubling was that the public's perception of her life did not match reality. To the newspapers, she was beautiful and wealthy, her story romantic and dramatic. Yet, in her own mind, life was "a grinding martyrdom," filled with concerns about money, her son's future, and her fading looks. This is the fate of most people in the public eye, but Elizabeth could not reconcile the disparity, noting "the disproportion of my fame & mode of life."[10] Despite her inner despair, she documented her life in objects and on paper to preserve her fame for posterity.

Foremost among the memories Elizabeth could not forget or forgive were her ill-fated marriage to Jérôme Bonaparte and her lifelong struggles with her father. As early as 1845 she confessed, "I am fatigued, disheartened with the hard battle of existence, what with the B[onaparte]s & P[atterson]s, I am tired, worn out mentally & physically." She may have been "worn out mentally," but over and over she released her venom in writing. For the most part, she placed her thoughts in private places, inscribing them in the margins of her books and among records of her investments. Sometimes her fury spilled into her correspondence. She reflected on this written vitriol, saying, "The tongue & the pen are great outlets for wrath and resentment."[11] Well-read as she was, Elizabeth expressed her anger with a power that makes a reader wince, and she offered no apologies. "My words are severe," she wrote on one occasion, "and designed to be severe."[12]

The collection of Elizabeth's papers at the Maryland Historical Society contains more than one hundred newspaper clippings, most of them annotated in her own careful hand. From announcements of her marriage to articles published in France, Italy, Great Britain, and most of the major newspapers in the United States, she kept an archive of her fame. As a young girl, she had wanted a bigger stage than Baltimore afforded and she had found it, but what lay beyond its curtains had not been what she envisioned. "I certainly did expect both honor & profit from the marriage & [have] been cruelly disappointed, having obtained neither,"[13] she wrote, an acknowledgment that love alone had not motivated the marriage. She had hoped it would bring her a title and a fortune. Instead, she had had to establish her identity and wealth on her own.

Elizabeth admitted her "love of Eminence & of Society . . . ambition in me [was] a revolt against destiny."[14] Ambition, a trait considered more admirable in men, led her to marry Jérôme and later allowed her to succeed in the highest ranks of European society. It also made her a fortune. In his memoirs, Jérôme recalled Elizabeth's "womanly ambition," and in her copy she wrote "True" next to the words. In fact, her ambition was not womanly; her drive to succeed in nineteenth-century culture was, if anything, masculine. She never denied her desire for greatness or ceased to record her achievements. "I suppose no one ever lived who was more ambitious than I was unless it might have been Napoleon & Alexander the Great."[15] When it came to ambition, she could only find her equals among men.

In the late 1820s, Elizabeth began writing her memoirs. Perhaps encouraged by the *femmes d'esprit* and the female authors she encountered in Europe, she set pen to paper and recorded the events of her life. In 1870, Elizabeth confessed to her grandson Charles, "In reading my European Diary, it appears like a fairy dream that I should have lived in the highest circles of Rank & of fashion & of intellectual cultivation. I had no money to invite the attentions, no relations to buoy me up; yes, it appears fabulous to myself the position I occupied & the appreciation beyond my deservings." Despite her resentments, Elizabeth's accomplishments both awed and humbled her.[16] Her social circle included some of European society's most influential women writers, including Madame de Staël and her close friend, the Irish author Lady Sydney Morgan.[17] Her memoir may have begun with the "European journal" she started in 1826. In a letter that probably dates to 1826 or 1827, her aunt Nancy Spear playfully lamented that she had not heard from her as often as in the past: "Your letters have come very scarce, do your literary pursuits so fully occupy you?"[18] In her 1839 inventory, Elizabeth noted, "12 volumes of my Journal kept in Europe from 1826, to & inclus., part of 1834, 5 cahiers, Covered with red paper of a sketch of my memoires." Decades later, on January 9, 1873, she wrote in her account book, "There are in the Black wooden Box at Baltimore Safe Deposit: 13 volumes of Diary, 4 volumes of Dialogues of the Dead, 5 volumes of Skeleton of my Memoirs covered with red paper; one volume leather covered, of my life, copied from above five cahiers."[19] By the 1870s, when Elizabeth was in her early nineties, had she ceased writing about her life? An account book from 1875, written in a strong hand, attests to the fact that she was still taking pen to paper, but in her last years her surviving writing was confined to records of her accounts and letters to her grandsons. Did she simply feel that in her tenth decade she had written enough?

Her journals must have been distinct volumes from her account books because neither the "13 volumes" nor the "5 red cahiers" are to be found among her papers, but more than twenty account books survive. Only one volume answering to the description of a red notebook remains. Of all her account books, it is closest to a journal or memoir. Held in one direction it is a typical record of her investments and her inventories. Turned 180 degrees, the book is filled with phrases, sentences, and short paragraphs, all of which express deeper thoughts about her life. It is, in fact, "a skeleton" of a memoir as she herself called the volumes. This particular red journal provides some of the most powerful evidence of Elizabeth's internal struggles. Given the comments about the 1861 lawsuit in the French courts, it appears to date to that period. If in fact this red journal is one of the "5 cahiers," it is the only surviving glimpse of what might have been in Elizabeth's memoirs. The author of her obituary claims Elizabeth was offered $10,000 for those memoirs and refused to accept the sum.[20] In the end, the woman who wrote so prolifically, and assiduously documented her life, did not want to be an autobiographer.

Upon her death, Elizabeth entrusted her writing to her grandson Charles, stipulating that he should receive "all my Diaries, my dialogue of the Dead, the letters received by me from various correspondents, and all manuscripts whatsoever belonging to me."[21] Martha Custis Williams Carter noted, "Madame B spoke of her 'Memoirs' & of her 'Dialogues with the Dead' which she intends to have published after her death."[22]

Like the diaries, the "Dialogues of the Dead," a play about her estranged husband, Jérôme, and William Patterson, her father, meeting in Hell, has not survived. Donor records in the library of the Maryland Historical Society suggest that the memoirs never came to the museum, even though the letters and account books did. The precise circumstance behind their disappearance remains unknown. Charles, who had vehemently opposed the publication of Saffell's book, may have destroyed them once they reached his possession, but

Charles Joseph Bonaparte (1851–1921). PVF, Maryland Historical Society

At the end of this letter from James McElhiney, Elizabeth wrote a note about her father's mistresses. Box 2, MS 142, EPB Papers

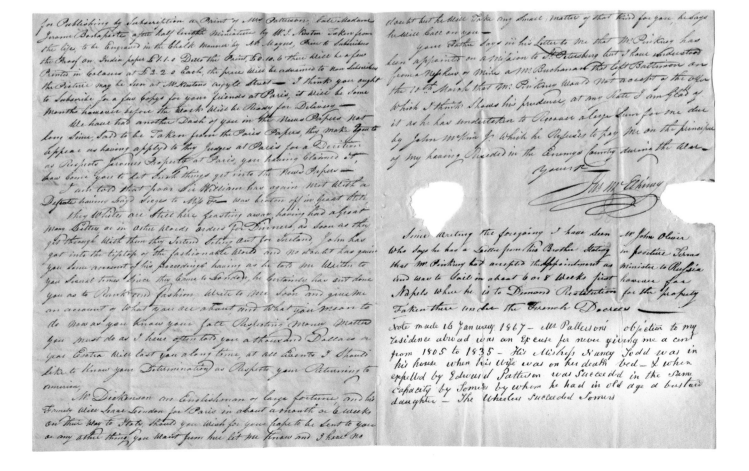

that seems unlikely because on one occasion he read "hilarious passages" of his grandmother's memoirs aloud to friends at his country residence, Bella Vista.[23] It is also possible that Charles felt that amusing aspects of Elizabeth's writing could be shared, but her more pointed commentaries should not be preserved for posterity. In Victorian society, a woman could be amusing, but she could not be frank.

Regardless of how the journals, memoirs, and other writings came to be lost, surviving evidence attests to the diligence with which Elizabeth worked to memorialize her life. Letters, account books, and other documents are often underlined in red pen and annotated to put events and individuals in context. She revisited her former life by rereading her own words, much as she unpacked her trunks to look at the relics of it. She annotated her own correspondence so that future generations could better understand her history and recorded her objects and textiles with their histories in much the same way. Sometimes pointed accusations appear in the margins of her letters, such as the note about her father's mistresses—Nancy Todd and a woman known as "Somers"—made on an 1816 letter from James McElhiney.[24] If she wanted future generations to know some hidden truths about her esteemed father, her marginalia serves that end. She also intended "Dialogues of the Dead" to contribute to a better understanding of the Patterson patriarch. "Whatever may be the character of the confessions adopted for the late WP in Dialogues of the Dead—they are the truth, not indeed the whole startling astounding truths . . . nothing however but the sad truth."[25]

Elizabeth believed her son and grandsons could benefit from the lessons she had learned and experiences she had had in Europe. If she kept careful records of her history and her possessions, they were sure to know the precise nature of the legacy they had inherited. In the 1860s, she created scrapbooks, carefully pasting newspaper articles into their pages and making notes in the margins. Her oft-noted sense of humor appears in the commentary she placed on cartoons of Louis Napoleon Bonaparte, Jérôme's son, and his failure to rule the French people.[26] Sometimes, she labeled her newspaper clippings, "For my Grandson;" some were saved for Jerome and others were intended for Charles. In the scrapbooks, articles about her grandson Jerome's military successes in the Crimea lie side by side with articles about herself and the lawsuit she pressed in 1861 to gain acknowledgment of Bo's right to succession. She lost the case but obsessively documented it in her scrapbooks, letters, and red journal.

Elizabeth was clearly torn by her memories. On one hand she wanted to escape them, on the other she memorialized her past with a paper archive and a collection of objects relating to her marriage and her ties to the Bonapartes. Jérôme may have abandoned her in Lisbon, pregnant and friendless, but she did not toss his portrait on the rubbish heap or throw his wedding suit in the fire.[27] She lived with his face gazing upon her until she died and kept his wedding clothes carefully tucked away in a trunk, preserved like flowers pressed in a book. "The sentiment of hatred to old Jérôme is in my heart & circulates with Every drop of blood in my body—I look upon him as belong[ing] to the lowest type of humanity,"[28] she wrote, but she still treasured the things he gave her. In her mind, hatred for Jérôme the man comingled with reverence for the power he represented.

Every time she left for Europe, Elizabeth had to find a safe place for her possessions, particularly her paintings. Sometimes she left the portrait of Jérôme at the Maryland Historical Society for safekeeping, a benefit to members of the society.[29] On April 1, 1875, she noted that the painting of Jérôme was in the Mercantile Library in Baltimore.[30] According to her account book, it had been there since 1871, but it was in her room at the boarding house when she died.[31]

In her will, she left the painting of "King Jerome, his grandfather," to Charles, along with her triple portrait also by Gilbert Stuart, the "cabinet portrait . . . painted at Geneva by Massot, and . . . the portrait made of me by Kinson." She also left Charles all her "furniture, silver-plate, books, clothes and

Jérôme Napoléon Bonaparte
(1784–1860)
Gilbert Stuart (1755–1828)
1804
Oil on canvas
Private collection, image courtesy of Sotheby's

This unfinished portrait of Jérôme was done when he and Elizabeth sat for Gilbert Stuart in his Washington, D.C., studio. Jérôme intended to give the portrait to his mother. Elizabeth, with the help of her friend Robert Gilmor Jr., reclaimed this portrait. It was hanging in her room at Mrs. Gwinn's boarding house when she died in 1879.

A view of the Athenaeum. Elizabeth often stored her treasures at the Maryland Historical Society for safekeeping when she traveled. The society had rooms in the Athenaeum building in Baltimore.
Maryland Historical Society

house linen."[32] Her youngest grandson, her favorite, inherited the material world she had created. His imperial legacy came to him first in name, but then in wood, silver, cloth, and on paper. As historian Jill Lepore observes, "The things people kept are all that remains of them," and Elizabeth kept almost everything.[33] In death, she made Charles the keeper of her possessions and, therefore, her memories.

Despite their painful associations with her ex-husband, Elizabeth's material world was populated with reminders of the celebrity her marriage had created and which, though relatively few in number, reinforced who she was and what she once had been. She owned more than twenty portrait miniatures of the Bonapartes, all gifts from the family to her and to Bo. In her own words, she was, "Not an aristocrat by birth, but one by associations, by instinct & by ambition."[34] She kept the miniatures of the Bonapartes because she *was* an important part of their family, and they were her legacy.

Maria Anna Elisa Bonaparte
Baciocchi Levoy (1777–1820)
Unattributed European, possibly
Jean-Baptiste Isabey (1767–1855)
Circa 1800
Watercolor on ivory, gold, and glass
Collection of the Maryland Historical Society
Gift of Mrs. Charles J. Bonaparte
xx.5.54

Elizabeth owned more than twenty portrait miniatures of Bonaparte family members, including this one of Napoléon's younger sister.

Charles Maurice de Talleyrand-Périgord
(1754–1838)
Pierre Paul Prud'hon (1758–1823)
1817
Oil on canvas
Metropolitan Museum of Art, New York

Elizabeth saw herself as a new kind of aristocrat whose title came not through bloodlines but by other means. In her mind, her ambition and talent, her personal links to the aristocracy, and her comfort in that echelon made her as much an aristocrat as anyone born to the role.[35] Others thought so, too. The author of her obituary quoted Lady Morgan, who said of Elizabeth, "With her airy manner, beauty and wit, she would have made an excellent princess, American as she was . . . ," and Talleyrand added, "If she were a queen with what grace would she reign."[36] Her appearance and possessions, from her clothing to her silver, were mostly French and all of a quality suitable for royalty.

A study of Elizabeth's inventories and her objects at the Maryland Historical Society substantiates this theory. Few pieces of Elizabeth's silver were American. In 1875 she owned "six Tea Spoons French Silver, one old Silver ditto, make unknown" as well as "the articles made by LeBrun," the silversmith who had served Louis XVI. Among the LeBrun pieces, all of which were made for her in Paris, were "1 Tea pot, 1 Sugar Dish, 1 Cream Pot, and 1 Slop Bowl." The service survives in the museum's collection. "May no Silly Descendant or Relative of Mine," she warned, "ever change the form of any Plate or Jewelry possessed by myself!" To change the form of her French silver was to destroy what it symbolized, to undo the legacy it had established. To alter or sell the

Tea Service
François Durand and
Marc-Augustin Lebrun
Circa 1830
Paris
Silver, each piece engraved
"Elizabeth Patterson"
Maryland Historical Society
Gift of Mrs. Charles J. Bonaparte
xx.5.a-d

"O, for celebrity . . ." ⚜ 83

two American silver pitchers her mother had given her would dishonor the memory of the parent she loved best. Elizabeth's friend, Martha Custis Williams Carter, wrote, "She speaks with the greatest reverence of her dear mother." She also remarked throughout her diary how often Elizabeth talked about her mother, Dorcas, describing her as "beautiful, talented" and possessed of "ambition," a trait she particularly admired.[37] Elizabeth's possessions transcended their material qualities; they were symbols of her memories.

Elizabeth also dictated how her armoire should be used after her death. In 1873 she asked her nurse, Mrs. Rosa McLaughlin, to write a note "on the large

Armoire
Unknown maker
by 1804
Mahogany and poplar
Maryland Historical Society
Gift of Mrs. Charles J. Bonaparte
xx.5.94

Elizabeth recorded that it was a gift from Jérôme in 1804. It was in her room when she died in 1879.

Mahogany Wardrobe with large Brass hinges; given me 1804 by Prince Jérôme" directing that "after my death all my books should be placed in it; & this wardrobe called Library of my Grand Mother." The armoire is now at the Maryland Historical Society, and the note to her grandson is in her account book. "Dear Charles," it reads, "I bequeath this wardrobe to you, Never permit it to be sold, my child. . . . Carefully keep it at your own rural home; It was presented to myself by King Jérôme."[38] Elizabeth left her library and armoire to Charles, but whether he created the "Library of my Grand Mother" on its shelves remains unknown.[39] Today that library rests on the shelves of the Maryland Historical Society library and contains volumes Elizabeth owned, as well as books owned by her son, grandsons, and even her father. Ironically, one book in the Bonaparte book collection is a French dictionary originally owned by William Patterson, a man who scorned all things European.

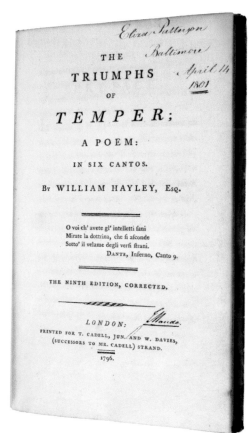

Title pages from William Hayley's *Triumphs of Temper*, 1796, and Mary Wollstonecraft Godwin's *Maria or, the Wrongs of Woman*, 1799, both of which Elizabeth read closely.
MS 3134, books 12 and 11, Maryland Historical Society

The books donated as part of the Bonaparte gift contain more examples of Elizabeth's desire to document her personal story. Always an avid reader, those she passed on to Charles date from her early teens almost to the end of her life. In 1858 she wrote to her grandson Jerome, "I read five hours a day to keep my mind from rusting." Reading helped her remember. Although her library ranged from French literature to histories of aristocrats to popular contemporary publications, she had a particular fondness for women's memoirs. Toward the end of her life, she preferred memoirs of European society or books about history. Most are annotated with commentary in the margins that constitutes a running dialogue with the book's content as it related to her own experiences. Her marginalia transformed the biographies of others into autobiographies of herself. One of the earliest books in the collection is William Hayley's *The Triumphs of Temper; A Poem in Six Cantos*, published in London. Hayley's work enjoyed eighteen editions and ranked among the most popular poems of the period. When Elizabeth received the book from "J. Maude" on April 14, 1801, she was sixteen and had just completed her schooling at Madame Lacombe's Academy. Hayley intended his poem to be a study of the "effects of spleen" on the female character and a lesson to young ladies that the "gentle qualities of the heart" and general "good humor" were the appropriate traits of a virtuous young

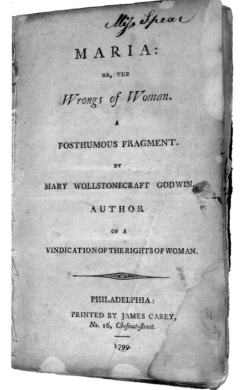

Mary Wollstonecraft (1759–1797)
John Opie (1761–1807)
Circa 1797
Oil on canvas
National Portrait Gallery, London

woman. Perhaps "J. Maude" gave it to Elizabeth as a guidebook for future behavior or a warning against repeating previous indiscretions. Regardless of the giver's intent, Elizabeth does not appear to have read the volume with great attention. The tight binding and almost pristine condition are markedly unlike her other books, almost all of which are heavily worn and bear numerous underlined words, annotations, and general marks. She did, however, mark one line, "No proud parental folly spoils the child," undoubtedly a reference, and perhaps one of her earliest, to her father's lack of attention.

Elizabeth's copy of Mary Wollstonecraft Godwin's *Maria or, the Wrongs of Woman: A Posthumous Fragment* boasts numerous underlines and cross-marks.[40] In contrast to Hayley's poem that encouraged young women to behave with a pleasant disposition devoid of anger, Wollstonecraft boldly wrote about the plight of women in a society dominated by men. Elizabeth underlined passage after passage. She marked the protagonist's lament, "Why was I not born a man, or why was I born at all?" and the observation, "Such are the partial laws enacted by men; for, only to lay a stress on the dependent state of woman in the grand question of the comforts arising from the possession of property." Both sentiments resonated with this independent, self-determined young woman who from a very early age recognized the inequities of the society in which she lived. Living in the Patterson house, where her father dominated his wife and children and favored his sons over his daughters, she knew all too well the plight of women who could not control their own property and, therefore, their own lives. Wollstonecraft spoke to Elizabeth in language she understood well. She did not have to suffer the disappointment of her marriage and experience her future struggles to learn that independent women faced an inhospitable world. Only by possessing her own property and amassing her own fortune could she avoid "the dependent state," and avoid it she did.

From the profuse annotations in her personal copy, it is clear that *Mémoires de Frédérique Sophie Wilhelmine . . . Soeur de Frédéric-Le-Grand: Ecrits de sa Main* by Wilhelmine, granddaughter of Frederick William I of Prussia, ranked among Elizabeth's favorites.[41] She purchased the two-volume memoir in Paris in 1840 and re-read it numerous times—her last comments are dated 1872. Wilhelmine's life paralleled Elizabeth's in several ways. Her unhappy childhood in a household of fourteen children, her tyrannical father, and her profoundly disappointing marriage to the unfaithful Duke of Anhalt-Dessau, all reminded Elizabeth of the trials she had suffered and prompted her to remark upon the similarities. Beside the underlined phrase "n'ayant jamais manqué à la respect et le tendresse qu'une fille devoit avoir pour son père" (never having lacked the respect and tenderness that a girl ought to have for her father), Elizabeth retorted, "Yes, for a bon père [good father], EP, 1857." Respect and affection were due to a good father, but, as Elizabeth wrote beside the phrase again in 1872, "Neither love nor respect are due to bad Parents."[42] Her comments referred to William Patterson, whom she often called "her Blast of the Desart [desert]."[43]

Despite Wilhelmine's personal struggles, she became a champion of the arts and an accomplished composer and lute player. She did not succumb to the forces exerted upon her by her husband and father and was therefore a woman after Elizabeth's own heart. Inspired, she wrote, "Toujours avancer, ne pas reculer" (always advance, never retreat) in the margin. Using the language of war, Elizabeth saw her life and her struggles with the Bonapartes as a battle to be fought without retreat. No matter what obstacles she had encountered, Elizabeth had moved forward with her own life. "Like an indian Rubber Ball the more I am knocked about, the higher I bound," she proclaimed, echoing Wilhelmine's memoir.[44]

Elizabeth found such memoirs of women who defied society's conventions with their independence and intellect deeply appealing. Just as she returned to the story of Wilhelmine throughout her life, she repeatedly re-read the *Mémoires of Madame de Staal*, the life story of Marguerite de Launay, Baronne de Staal (1684–1750). On the title page, she noted that she bought the book in Paris in 1817: "August 1857 forty years since I first read & owned these Memoires EP." She pronounced them "admirable" because they told of de Staal's triumph over being orphaned while still very young, her imprisonment in the Bastille, and difficulties in love. Despite it all, de Staal became a writer, something Elizabeth aspired to be. In de Staal, Elizabeth found another kindred spirit, one whose experiences mirrored her own. Always an admirer of ambition, Elizabeth underlined, *"L'ambition étoit le grand ressort des mouvemens*

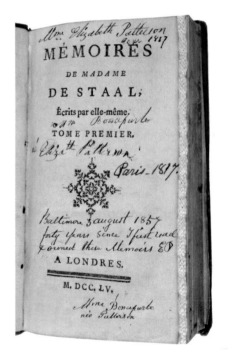

Title page from *Mémoires of Madame de Staal* [1755]
MS 3134, book 31,
Maryland Historical Society

In her copy of Madame de Staal's memoir, Elizabeth underlined, among others, the passage: *"L'ambition étoit le grand ressort des mouvemens de son âme, & peut-être en avoit-elle altéré les vertus,"* which translates to, "Ambition was the mainspring of the movement of her soul and perhaps corrupted its virtues." In the margin she wrote, "It ever was of mine."
MS 3134, book 31, Maryland Historical Society

Madame de Staal (1684–1750), from the 1787 reprint of *Mémoires de Madame de Staal* (London, 1755).
MS 3134, book 237, Maryland Historical Society

de son âme, & peut-être en avoit-elle altéré les vertus" which translates to, "Ambition was the mainspring of the movement of her soul and perhaps corrupted its virtues."[45] Beside those words, she wrote, "It was ever mine EP," meaning that ambition was the force that shaped who she was and what she became. Elizabeth never viewed ambition as a corrupting force, always believing it was the ultimate virtue. Her additional underlines in this part of the book attest to her fervent belief that the highest European circles were her proper place. As she wrote to her father, "nature never intended me for obscurity," and this belief became a driving force behind her ambition.[46]

Madame de Staal's descriptions of people often reminded Elizabeth of individuals she had known. For instance, de Staal's jealous and domineering benefactress, the Duchesse of Maine, reminded Elizabeth of Pauline Borghese, Jérôme's sister, whose capricious and demanding ways she and Bo knew first hand. If her grandsons ever read the books, they would find them to be guidebooks of a sort, filled with men and women who had populated their grandmother's own history.

Elizabeth's library contained any number of passages that reminded her, painfully, of Jérôme and her ill-fated marriage. On a page of the *Lady Morgan's memoirs* containing one of Elizabeth's own letters, she confessed, "I cannot keep dipping my pen in my thoughts."[47] Neither could she turn away. Lady Morgan's *Memoirs* presented Elizabeth's own history in letters she had written to Morgan and the commentary said to have been written by Morgan herself.[48] The women enjoyed a long friendship that stretched from 1815 until Morgan's death in 1859, and Elizabeth's letters show her deep affection for Morgan and her respect for her friend's literary success. In one of the earliest, written in 1816, Elizabeth proclaimed, "I hope you have not forgotten me, as I admire and love you more than anyone else." Such a passionate declaration of affection was unusual for one who never in her surviving letters wrote the equivalent to her son or grandsons.

For her part, Morgan wrote in her *Memoirs* that, "Madame Bonaparte's friendship for Lady Morgan was more for her own sake. She found in her friend some substance of character, and one who could sympathize with the romantic discomforts of her position." To that, Elizabeth added, "real as well as romantic discomforts."[49] Outside observers might see Elizabeth's discomforts as romantic, but she viewed the end of her marriage and her relationship with her father as authentic tribulations and disappointments.

On the covers of all three volumes, Elizabeth wrote a "finding aid" where future readers would find pages relevant to her story as well as the story of "Old Jérôme." The second volume of the *Memoirs* presented Elizabeth's marriage to Jérôme both in letters and a history, and provided Elizabeth with an opportunity to comment on the accuracy of Morgan's portrayal. Elizabeth "had been subject to the bitterest insult and outrage that could be offered to a woman," Morgan wrote. "Her marriage was broken; her child made illegitimate; her prospects in life killed; and she herself stripped of her husband's protection when little more than a girl, flung upon the world to sink or swim as she could."[50] Beside that passage, Elizabeth scribbled intertwining lines of red and black ink and wrote, "True" twice. She also underlined the words in both red and black, adding particular emphasis so that anyone reading it after her death would know that Morgan's portrayal was accurate and her description of Jérôme was a "True Portrait." "Jérôme Bonaparte had been, from

Lady Sydney Morgan
(1781–1851)
René Théodore Berthon
(1776–1859)
Circa 1818
Oil on canvas
National Gallery of Ireland

Pages from Lady Sydney Morgan's memoirs, on which Elizabeth wrote comments.

MS 3134, book 229,
Maryland Historical Society

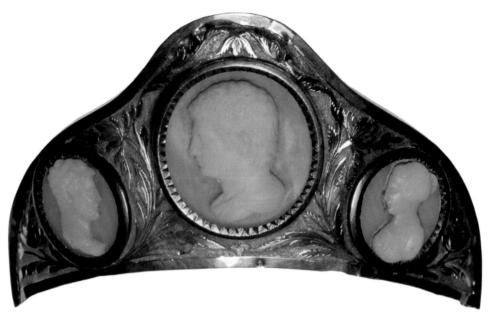

Comb with Cameos
Unknown maker, possibly
French
Circa 1825
Gold on ivory
Maryland Historical Society
Gift of Mrs. Charles J. Bonaparte,
xx.5.292,

Fragment of the cloth
draped over Napoléon's coffin.
Maryland Historical Society
Gift of Mrs. Charles J. Bonaparte
xx.5.380

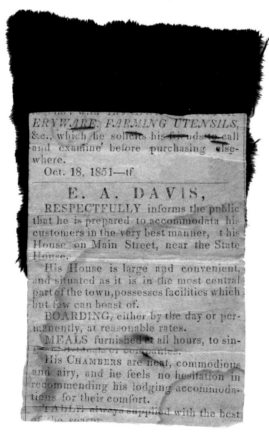

the beginning, the plague of his family," Morgan wrote, "thoughtless, idle, vain, extravagant and inconsiderate." To this, Elizabeth added, "This Portrait a faithful resemblance of the King" and, "True." Then, anger rising, she added: "He was all this & worse—worse!"[51] Morgan's *Memoirs* gave Elizabeth a springboard to call Jérôme a "liar" and more. After her death, those who read her copy as well as the other books in "Grand Mother's Library" would know the truth—she had written it in black and red in the margins of her books.

Looking back on the dissolution of her marriage, Elizabeth reflected, "I was sacrificed upon the altar of mistaken political expedience by the Emperor Napoleon," yet she never disparaged the man who ultimately changed her life. Jérôme was the focus of her wrath, not his brother. Elizabeth valued ambition and power above almost all else and felt a lasting admiration for Napoléon.[52] For most of her life, she lived with images of the emperor, including a miniature and a lapis box with a cameo of his profile. When younger, she even wore a gold comb, set with a cameo of Napoléon's profile as well as Jérôme's. Among her possessions was a piece of black cloth that was taken from the cloth draped over Napoléon's coffin, and she scolded herself for parting with a "Flacon with Emperor's head on it," writing in a later note, "since given foolishly away."[53] Images of Napoléon, the man who ended her chance to become royalty, ornamented her material world and later assumed prominent places in the homes of her son and grandsons. On the lone occasion when she parted with his image, she regretted it.

French plate with portrait
of Napoléon
Stone, Coquerel et Le Gros
Circa 1815
Paris
Porcelain and gilt
Maryland Historical Society
Gift of Mrs. Andrew Robeson Jr.
(Laura Patterson Swan)
1955.15.25d

Elizabeth purchased large
quantities of French
porcelain for her brother
Edward, including this
plate which is part of a set,
each depicting a Bonaparte
family member.

Napoléon even appeared on the household possessions of her family and can been seen on a plate bought by Elizabeth for her brother, Edward. No Patterson was above capitalizing on the brief alliance with "the Emperor."[54] Elizabeth's jewelry includes pieces that memorialized her European alliance and, interestingly, documented her life following her marriage. After real estate and stock holdings, jewelry was the most valuable part of her estate, amounting to more than $3,000. She inventoried the individual pieces with the same frequency and rigor she devoted to her investments. She also commented on many items, an unusual practice. Inventories are generally compiled for estates in probate and almost always consist of summary lists of the decedent's personal property. In a sense they are "biographical" in that they are created by someone other than the person who owned the objects. Elizabeth, though, wrote her own inventories and made them into lessons for those who would eventually own her possessions. Like the volumes in her "library," they were guidebooks for her heirs, an autobiography written in material goods.

Elizabeth inventoried her jewelry throughout her life, but her last inventory, made in 1875, is the most detailed. She gave this list the fitting title, "Mme Bonaparte's née Patterson's Memorial of Personal Effects"—fitting because, like her account books and scrapbooks, she made her jewelry and other household objects annotated pieces of her own history. She wanted Charles, to whom she would leave the account books and most of the jewelry, to comprehend fully the origin of his inheritance and the "meaning" of his grandmother's material world.

Despite a long- and widely held assumption that all of Elizabeth's jewelry dates to her marriage, her inventories tell a different story. Only a small number of pieces were gifts from Jérôme. They are always noted as such and, in her mind, their value was greater because of the Bonaparte association. In one instance, the value increased significantly because the jewelry had come from Jérôme via his brother, the emperor himself. "One Breastpin from a Lyre, contains Thirty-one diamonds. . . . Had been a Present to Prince Jérôme from his Brother the First Consul of France, Napoleon; who had worn it three days himself, rendering such a Present of great value. The Prince gave it to me year 1804."[55] This pin's symbolic value could not be forgotten. Other pieces came in the sad months after their separation in 1805, when Jérôme misleadingly sent her reassurances of his love and gifts that included "a case for perfume; gold striped with Rubies Emeralds & Diamonds with a little Padlock to it" and a "cornelian & gold Box, or vinaigrette," both "sent by him from the Brazils to me." He also sent her a "diadem of 11 large amethysts set in green, blue enamel and pearls," (see page 13) one of his most extravagant presents, but it still did not rival the pin that had once been Napoléon's. Such efforts to solicit her "forgiveness" did little to temper the hatred she later felt for her ex-husband. In a fit of anger, she wrote of a "Locket . . . and chain . . . given me by Prince Jérôme & contained his hair which I threw to the winds." It is the only known instance of Elizabeth throwing out a memento. Some of the jewelry held especially unhappy memories, such as "My Wedding Ring!!! Plain gold a fraud a delusion & a snare it proved to me EP."A simple gold band held the most complicated story of all.

Lyre Pin
Unknown maker,
probably French
Circa 1805
Gold, diamonds,
blue enamel,
and pearl
Private collection,
photograph courtesy
of Hans Wassard

Elizabeth also filled her mahogany jewel box with gifts from friends. A "finger ring given me by Pauline, Princess of Borghese . . . antique, The Engraving is a cock & a cornucopia" sparked her to comment on its symbolism, derived from the motto, "Vigilance is the father of abundance." It was, she observed, "a most fitting Emblem for me EP Who owe my fortune to care, labor & vigilance." This may also have been a stab at Borghese, Jérôme's sister, who had promised her nephew Bo a great legacy but gave him little more than extravagant gifts before her death. Bo benefited from the hard-won fortune of Elizabeth's making, not the one falsely promised by Borghese, another disappointing Bonaparte. Countess Schouvaloff, who was both a confident and a frequent correspondent during the 1830s, gave Elizabeth "a Breast pin . . . small Turquoises sett in Black enamel" and a "Finger Ring, two hands Embracing." To better identify the countess, Elizabeth added that she was "born Princes[s] Zoltikoff." Sometimes, the person who gave the jewelry was not identified, as

"My Wedding Ring!!! Plain gold a fraud a delusion & a snare it proved to me E.P."
Box 13A, MS 142, EPB Papers

Pauline, Princess Borghese
(1780–1825)
Marie-Guillemine Benoist
(1780–1825)
1808
Oil on canvas
National Chateau Fountainbleu, Paris

was the case with "a green Enamel & gold box or Vinaigrette given me at Paris Year 1816." One can surmise that an admirer, perhaps a suitor, gave her the elegant memento, but she discreetly omitted that detail from the record.

Despite her frugality, Elizabeth bought jewelry throughout her life, for her own use and for others out of appreciation for their kindnesses. In 1833, encouraged by her father to do so, she thanked her friend and financial advisor, John White, for his help with her properties and other investments by presenting him with a watch, and on July 1, 1849, she gave James Gallatin, who was also advising her on financial matters, a "turquoise ring surrounded by diamonds."[56] In 1850 she gave her close friend Harriet Stewart "a pair of garnet earrings" that she had intended for herself.

Elizabeth also inherited jewelry and listed those pieces with particular attention to the person they memorialized. She had "the breast pin of amethyst [and] pearls" that had belonged to her "blessed mother," Dorcas Patterson, as well as an "old fashioned blue enamel watch chain" her mother had worn. In 1840 she made note of an enamel watch she had bought in Paris to go with it, attesting to the fact that she wore it.[57] From her sister Caroline, who died in 1814, the same year as her mother, Elizabeth had several pieces, including the "inherited parure" of garnets that in-

Elizabeth Patterson Bonaparte
(1785–1879)
Firmin Massot (1776–1849)
1823
Oil on canvas
Maryland Historical Society
Gift of Mrs. Charles J. Bonaparte
xx.5.69

cluded a "garnet & pearl head ornament on comb with 20 garnets set in pearls." [see page 12] From her vast collection of jewelry, Elizabeth chose to wear the garnet and pearl comb for her 1823 portrait by Firmin Massot, a detail she noted in the inventory. In immortalizing a part of Caroline's parure in that painting, Elizabeth was also memorializing the sister she had loved best and whose shawl she took with her to Europe six times. A "gold ring" that had been her mother's was a double memorial because it also held the hair and monogram of Augusta Sophia, Dorcas's last daughter, who "died very young," in 1793. With no little irony she noted the "bracelet of 7 American five dollar coins" that she had made from "the sole money given to me from 1805 to 1835 by the late Millionaire Father WP [William Patterson]."[58] Some jewelry only awakened grudges, but she kept her father's coins, which she had gone to the expense of having made into a bracelet, just as she kept her wedding ring. Symbolic of her "duplicate miseries," the Pattersons and the Bonapartes, these were important parts of her story. Elizabeth might offer harsh commentary in her inventories, but she also preserved the sentiments she felt for those she had lost. To those who came after her, the jewelry would continue to speak of her life—the good, the bad, the sentimental, and the painful.

Stick Pin mounted with Bo's tooth
Circa 1810
Gold
Maryland Historical Society
Gift of Mrs. Charles J. Bonaparte
xx.5.335

Creating jewelry with children's teeth was not uncommon during the first quarter of the nineteenth century, and Elizabeth had her son's tooth mounted on this pin. Note the engraving of the *fleur de lis*, a symbol of the French monarchs, but not one favored by the Bonapartes.

Elizabeth gave some of the jewelry to her grandsons before she died. Jérôme received "an oval clasp locket containing hair of PJ [Prince Jérôme] and given by PJ." She gave Charles a locket in which she replaced a lock of Prince Jérôme's hair with one of her own; she had, after all, thrown her former husband's hair "to the wind." The gifts to her grandsons were small when compared with her more extravagant pieces, such as her topaz necklace of thirty-two stones and earrings of "3 topazes each." That particular parure, another inheritance from her sister Caroline, remained in her collection until her death. The gifts to her grandsons were more significant, not for their size or value but because they related to their grandfather, Jérôme. They were parts of their legacy wrought in gold.

Elizabeth placed great personal value on her jewelry, far surpassing her concern for most of her other possessions and evidenced as early as 1829. Upon learning of Bo's marriage to Susan May Williams, Elizabeth wrote to her father that she would instruct her aunt, Nancy Spear, to send her various household goods by "the first vessel sailing to Leghorn [Livorno, Tuscany]." She went on to say, "The Box of Jewels of which Jerome has the Key . . . could be sent by some one coming here" and that "an inventory of its contents" should be included.[59] She did not want to risk Bo giving her jewels to his new wife.

Elizabeth spent her last years among Spartan furnishings in Mrs. Gwinn's boarding house on Cathedral Street in Baltimore, but she had her vast collection of jewelry with her. To this day a story survives among her descendants that, perhaps not fully trusting the other lodgers, she carried the jewelry around in a bag and hung it on the back of her chair during meals. Prior to her death, she must have communicated her wishes for her jewelry to her grandson, Charles. "Mme. Bonaparte . . . left all her jewels and especially valuable possessions to the women of her blood," Charles's wife, Ellen Channing Day Bonaparte told an interviewer in 1907. "In a clause of her will she stipulated that none of these things should get to 'strange women,' that is women who had married into the family."[60] "Strange women" were not Bonapartes and therefore should not receive her legacy. Elizabeth's will did not in fact make that stipulation, because she left Charles all her remaining jewelry. Ellen Channing Day Bonaparte, who in turn inherited the jewelry from her husband, gave it to the Maryland Historical Society in 1921, but some pieces that passed to Elizabeth's grandson, Jerome, in turn went to his children, particularly Elizabeth's great-granddaughter Louise Eugenie Bonaparte Moltke-Huitfeldt.[61]

Baltimore 1st august 1838. List made by me EP, or Inventory of the Jewels belonging to me. verified August 22 1869 a French watch, dark Blue Enamel: Twelve large diamonds (monté à Jour) & Twelve Pearls Surround it: a Dart, composed of small diamonds points to the hours, which said hours are designated by aforesaid Twelve diamonds: Said watch is attached to Seven Eight smaller diamonds than those round the watch & then the whole is attached to a ring containing or Sett with five diamonds: Maker's name "L. Roy. au Palais Royal N° 88." number of watch is 4212." a present year 1805 from King Jérôme, &.c. &.c. intact 22 August 1869 June 1875 a Diamond Brooch or Breast Pin, Form a Lyre; contains thirty one Diamonds, monté à Jour; Three of said diamonds are on dark Blue Enamel: There are five gold cords in said Lyre: There is a short gold chain & a gold pin headed by a large Pearl attached

Despite her collection of jewelry and clothing, Elizabeth herself lived with few furnishings, particularly during her last years in Baltimore. Martha Custis Williams Carter, who visited her at Mrs. Gwinn's boarding house in Baltimore in the 1870s, described the contents of Elizabeth's room. "An inch stump of a candle. . . . Three large black arm chairs, two wardrobes, a bed & a cabinet & a table compose the . . . furniture." For a woman who had lived such a privileged life and amassed a considerable fortune, such an interior, devoid of luxuries, is incongruous. There was no carpet, no wallpaper, and no gas in the room because Elizabeth believed it to be unhealthy. In 1863, Elizabeth inventoried her own room, corroborating the evidence that Carter offered in her diary. She listed:

> one Mahogany Ward Robe, one walnut wardrobe, 1 ditto Bureau with Looking Glass & marble Top, 1 Ditto walnut wash Stand marble top, 1 walnut Bedstead, Spring Matress & 1 hair Matress, 1 small walnut Table, 3 French arm Chairs, 1 woollen Blanket & 1 ditto cotton, 2 dressing gowns round the Blankets & Soap in, Mahogany Dressing box, in which are the Keys of Trunks & of the Boxes in the Merchants Bank, one Mahogany writing Desk, 2 Flat irons, 1 Demi John.[62]

Watch given to Elizabeth
by Jérôme Bonaparte
Unknown maker, probably French
Circa 1805
White gold, enamel, and diamonds
Private collection, photograph by
Elizabeth Moltke-Huitfeldt

"French watch, dark blue enamel,"
a present from Jérôme, and a
description of same in her 1875
record of personal effects.

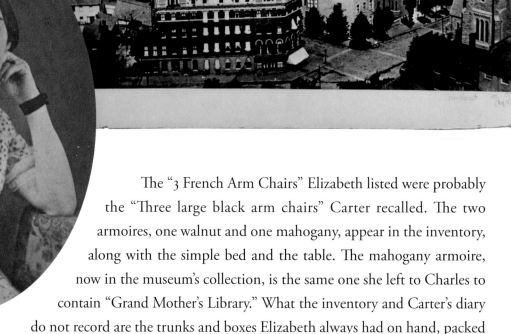

Martha Custis Williams Carter (1827–1899) lived in the boarding house and frequently visited Elizabeth's room.

Image courtesy of Tudor Place Historic House and Garden

The "3 French Arm Chairs" Elizabeth listed were probably the "Three large black arm chairs" Carter recalled. The two armoires, one walnut and one mahogany, appear in the inventory, along with the simple bed and the table. The mahogany armoire, now in the museum's collection, is the same one she left to Charles to contain "Grand Mother's Library." What the inventory and Carter's diary do not record are the trunks and boxes Elizabeth always had on hand, packed with the mementos of her long life.

Her probate inventory taken in 1879 provides yet more evidence of the austerity in which Elizabeth lived. In addition to the furnishings noted by Martha Carter and listed in Elizabeth's inventory from 1863, the probate record shows that Elizabeth's room contained "1 Large easy chair, 1 Bookcase, 1 Stand, 1 Towel rack, 1 Clock, 2 Plaster casts, Busts, 1 Cushion, 1 Commode" and her small collection of silver. Possessions, including furniture, paintings, and jewelry, accounted for less than one percent of her total wealth; her stocks and other investments represent the rest of her $1.1 million estate.[63]

Between 1875 and 1878, Carter visited "Madame B" in her room almost every day and asked if she could record their conversations. "Madame B. does not at all seem to object to my taking notes of what she says & on one occasion

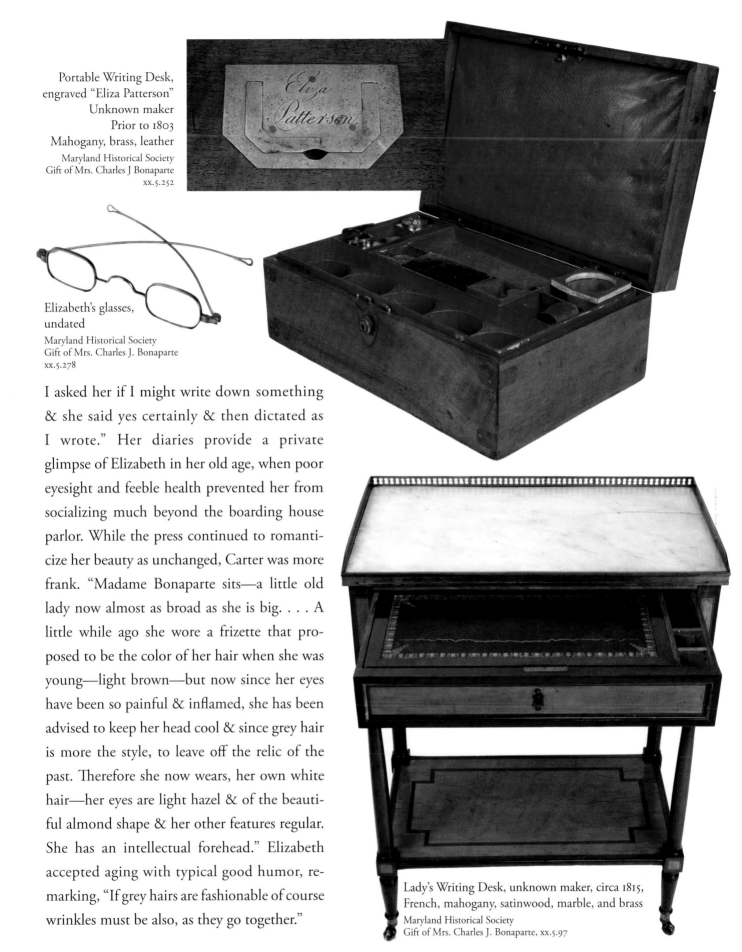

Portable Writing Desk,
engraved "Eliza Patterson"
Unknown maker
Prior to 1803
Mahogany, brass, leather
Maryland Historical Society
Gift of Mrs. Charles J Bonaparte
xx.5.252

Elizabeth's glasses,
undated
Maryland Historical Society
Gift of Mrs. Charles J. Bonaparte
xx.5.278

I asked her if I might write down something
& she said yes certainly & then dictated as
I wrote." Her diaries provide a private
glimpse of Elizabeth in her old age, when poor
eyesight and feeble health prevented her from
socializing much beyond the boarding house
parlor. While the press continued to romanti-
cize her beauty as unchanged, Carter was more
frank. "Madame Bonaparte sits—a little old
lady now almost as broad as she is big. . . . A
little while ago she wore a frizette that proposed to be the color of her hair when she was
young—light brown—but now since her eyes
have been so painful & inflamed, she has been
advised to keep her head cool & since grey hair
is more the style, to leave off the relic of the
past. Therefore she now wears, her own white
hair—her eyes are light hazel & of the beautiful almond shape & her other features regular.
She has an intellectual forehead." Elizabeth
accepted aging with typical good humor, remarking, "If grey hairs are fashionable of course
wrinkles must be also, as they go together."

Lady's Writing Desk, unknown maker, circa 1815,
French, mahogany, satinwood, marble, and brass
Maryland Historical Society
Gift of Mrs. Charles J. Bonaparte, xx.5.97

Throughout the diary, Carter remarked upon Elizabeth's mental vitality and her ability to recall the stories of her youth. "Her conversational powers are wonderful—one never sits with her even for a few moments without hearing something very interesting & told in a very interesting way."[64] Always sensitive about her age, but witty, Elizabeth recalled for Carter the story of a gentleman who "came up to her at a party & said, 'Madame B may I be permitted to ask what is your age?' She replied, 'No, you may not be permitted to ask, for I should never think of asking such a question of you!'" She added, "To grow old is an infirmity which no one likes to have brought to mind & to do so, reminds one of what is disagreeable." Just as she advised Bo never to ask a woman her age, she thought others should observe the same courtesy.

Her friendship with Carter gave Elizabeth an outlet for her stories. "It seems to me that there is a scrupulous attention to accuracy in narrating things," Carter wrote about reading newspapers to Madame B., especially the stock reports, as well as memoirs of European aristocrats and society figures. For months, she read the memoir of Madame Le Brun (Louise Elisabeth Vigée Le Brun [1755–1842]) to her. Although Elizabeth did not know Le Brun, they had traveled in similar European social circles and she knew many people in the memoir who sparked memories of her time in Europe.

> This morning Madame B said as I read of the Luxembourg Palace—Ah! once when I was in Paris . . . I was going to take the Marchioness de Vilette to drive & on my way passing the Palais de Luxembourg I got out of my carriage & walked through the Luxembourg gardens. I had an elegant wardrobe then, for Prince Jerome had given me a trousseau costing six thousand dollars. I had on a beautiful blue pelerine dress & hat—the costume was elegant but perfectly unsuitable to the street but I did not know that. Some young gentlemen followed me & conversed together gazing at me most impertinently. I turned around & said in French—gentleman I have valets at home and I am not in need of servants to attend me.

Le Brun's discussions of various Russian and Polish aristocrats Elizabeth socialized with in Geneva and Florence in the 1820s provoked great nostalgia. "Ah M Demidoff!" Elizabeth exclaimed to Carter on December 18, 1876, after she had read a passage about Prince Nicholas Demidov, the wealthiest aristocrat in Europe, who had been a close friend of hers until his death in 1828.[65]

By recounting these stories to Carter, Elizabeth could remember the best of her past, when her beauty and wit won her a place in European society. When Carter read to her Le Brun's description of the Palazzo Pitti (Pitti Palace) in Florence, Elizabeth remembered, "There is where the Grand duke held his Court & there I went every week for five years." In contrast to these memories, she "bemoan[ed] her solitary uncared for life." In old age, she felt alone and deprived of affection, saying "her relatives have left her to Providence." The woman who once counted aristocrats, artists, and authors among her friends now waited for infrequent visits from her grandson, Charles, and entertained herself in the boarding house parlor. To Carter, Elizabeth admitted that "she had plenty of admiration, but her life was one of extreme loneliness & desolation." "She bemoans the fact that she never knew domesticity & that she never knew love," Carter observed.[66] Although many thought she had taken lovers after her divorce, some friends accused her of "prudery."[67] "She dwells particularly on the chastity of her life—on her never having had lovers—on the preservation of her character." To marry or even associate herself intimately with another man meant to risk the Bonaparte connection for her son and grandsons and that was a risk, in her mind, too great to take. In addition, she told Carter, "she never had a way of thinking men were in love with her—although of course many men made love to her, she never believed them." She distrusted all men, probably based on her experience with her father and her former husband, and did not believe any man was sincere. "They did it because she was the fashion & to do so gave them éclat," Elizabeth remarked cynically.[68] Even when she encountered Prince Alexandre Mikhailovitch Gorchakov, the chargé d'affaires at the Russian Legation in Florence, and began a close friendship with him, it ended abruptly seven years later.[69] When he wrote to her in 1861, she drafted a reply that recalled their friendship but also complained about the injustices of her life and referred to an inaccuracy found in "Mr. Thiers Histoire du Consulat," which claimed she received a pension from Napoléon "for life."[70] The unsent copy of the letter, a mixture of fond reminiscences about their time together and long-held grudges against the Bonapartes, remains among her papers.

During her many conversations with Carter, she often spoke of her ambition and recalled with wonderment how she had made the decisions she did. "She says she is constantly wondering why she did not accept the Emperors

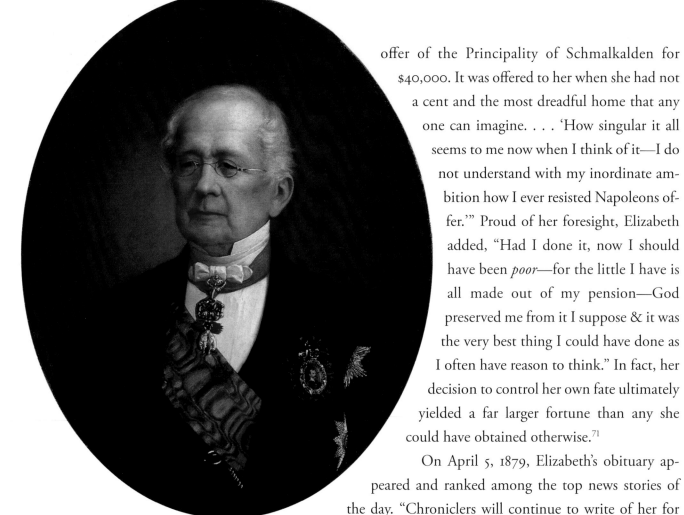

offer of the Principality of Schmalkalden for $40,000. It was offered to her when she had not a cent and the most dreadful home that any one can imagine. . . . 'How singular it all seems to me now when I think of it—I do not understand with my inordinate ambition how I ever resisted Napoleons offer.'" Proud of her foresight, Elizabeth added, "Had I done it, now I should have been *poor*—for the little I have is all made out of my pension—God preserved me from it I suppose & it was the very best thing I could have done as I often have reason to think." In fact, her decision to control her own fate ultimately yielded a far larger fortune than any she could have obtained otherwise.[71]

On April 5, 1879, Elizabeth's obituary appeared and ranked among the top news stories of the day. "Chroniclers will continue to write of her for these many days to come," the *Baltimore American* concluded. "Her career will be told over and over again, and the curious will wait with anxiety to see whether the personal reminiscences which she is said to have committed to paper will ever be permitted to see the light."[72] Although her memoirs never were published, the prediction that her "career" would win attention long after her death turned out to be true. In 1879, just months after her death, Eugene L. Didier published *The Life and Letters of Madame Bonaparte*, a book inspired by Elizabeth's remarkable celebrity as "one of the famous women in the country."

Despite the disappointments at the end of her life, in 1872 Elizabeth told her grandson Charles, "I never wished to be fixed like a Plant on its peculiar spot, there to draw nutrition, propogate & rot. I desired an elevated position in the World & world wide celebrity; no efforts on my part however disappointed have ever been spared to accomplish my ambitious aspirations."[73] For more than one hundred years, books, movies, plays, and exhibitions have attempted to retell her story, a testament to the world's enduring fascination with her life.

Alexandre Mikhailovich Gorchakov
(1798–1883)
Nikolai Timopheevich Bogatsky
(1798–1883)
1873
Oil on canvas
State Hermitage Museum,
St. Petersburg, Russia

"Mésalliances are Fatal in Most Families"

"Mésalliances are fatal in most families."
—ELIZABETH PATTERSON BONAPARTE, 1871

No MENTION CAN BE MADE of Elizabeth's descendants without a reference to the union that began it all, her marriage to Jérôme in 1803. The *mésalliance* with Prince Jérôme remained a defining event in their lives as well as hers, and if they had any desire to separate their identities from her past, the newspapers made certain they could not.[1] Even the obituary of Susan May Williams Bonaparte included the story of Madame Patterson, the mother-in-law who thought her unworthy of her son. In the newspapers, the Bonaparte legacy that began in 1803 endured for more than one hundred years. Elizabeth's actions, the meticulously saved letters and documents, and the objects she amassed attesting to the Bonaparte heritage became lasting reminders to the next generations, who related to their imperial history in ways far more varied than previous scholarship has explored.

Elizabeth's desire to perpetuate the legacy greatly affected her relationships with her son and grandsons, and, not surprisingly, it is in the story of the next generations that one discovers an added layer of ironies and disappointments. Only by looking at how Elizabeth's son, grandsons, and great-grandchildren related to their Bonaparte history can we reach a clear understanding of their material world. It is not a legacy summed up simply by a Bonaparte coat of arms on a piece of silver, or an image of Napoléon on a porcelain plate, but reaches much deeper, and stretches from Baltimore to France, and ultimately to Denmark.

Elizabeth's obsession with documenting her own history as a guide for her son and grandsons continued for more than seven decades. During her lifetime, she preserved every mention of herself in European and American newspapers, annotating and underlining the numerous versions of her story as they appeared. Her son and grandsons, who later read these scrapbooks, learned what she thought of the press and how it portrayed her, as she repeatedly reminded them that *their* Bonaparte story was the most important one to tell.

FACING PAGE:
Medallion originally on an oval mahogany mirror
Maryland Historical Society
Gift of Mrs. Charles J. Bonaparte
xx.5.99b

Elizabeth's son and grandsons perpetuated their Bonaparte heritage in symbols such as this coat of arms.

Camberwell Grove,
birthplace of Jerome
Napoleon Bonaparte.
Photograph by
Elizabeth Moltke-Huitfeldt

The birth of Jerome Napoleon Bonaparte, "Bo," in Camberwell Grove, London, England, on July 7, 1805, marked the beginning of Elizabeth's lifelong quest to establish herself and her son as acknowledged members of the imperial family. In her mind, the birth of a son meant she had produced a future king of France, an idea that profoundly shaped her decisions. Had she given birth to a daughter, her life would have taken a far different course. A daughter could never attain the power of a son. Her ambition to achieve royal status for Bo was shaken only decades later, after many failed attempts to attain it. As she remarked in the margin of one of her books, "[Ambition] is not a character flaw."[2] Elizabeth calculated every step in her son's upbringing to strengthen his Bonaparte ties. In some cases, her judgment did not yield the outcomes she desired; in others, her decisions are remarkable for their sagacity.

At Bo's birth, Elizabeth followed a protocol typical of royal births by calling for witnesses, five in number, who attested to the event lest members of the Bonaparte family call it into question. Given that her husband was not present for the birth, the signatures of these individuals provided "insurance" against any claim of illegitimacy. They included her close friend from Baltimore, Eliza Anderson; Baltimore native Mrs. Hannah Stene; Charles Aveline, "accoucheur" at Camberwell; "nurse" Elizabeth Orton; and "servant" Charlotte Crouch. Benjamin Lane, a London notary public of the king, authenticated the document; the Austrian ambassador, Louis Comte de Starhemberg, and Baron de Jacobi-Kloest, the ambassador of the Prussian king, attested to the certification.[3] Elizabeth had produced an heir to the French throne and, as a result, his upbringing from the moment he entered the world had to be a calculated endeavor. Every decision made for Bo had to be weighed in view of a single fact: he might one day rule France.

Notarized statements and signatures of the witnesses present at Bo's birth. MS 142, EPB Papers

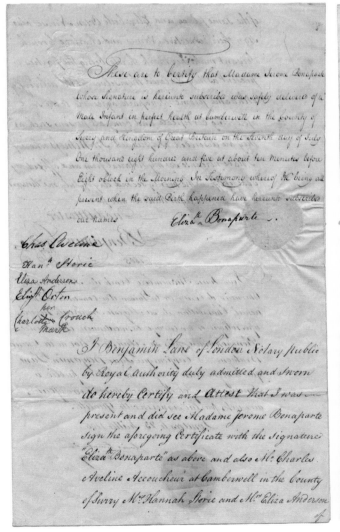

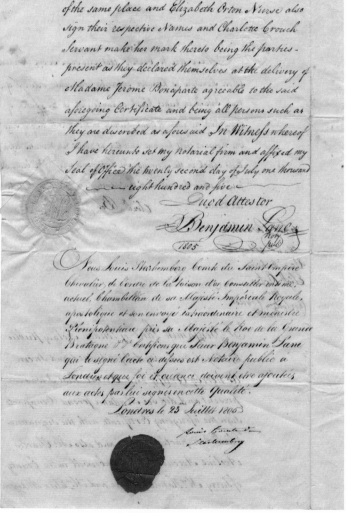

Although Elizabeth herself had never placed much importance on religion, she recognized the political significance of raising her son in the ways of his French family and realized he must be brought up as a Catholic. When, in May 1809, Archbishop John Carroll wrote Elizabeth asking to delay Bo's christening for a few days, he referred to the child as "the perhaps future Prince." This characterization of the child's importance relative to France must have been shaped by Elizabeth's own thoughts about her son's prospects.[4] On May 8, Carroll, who had married Elizabeth and Jérôme six years earlier, baptized Bo in Baltimore. Elizabeth then appointed Carroll godfather and Mary Ann Caton Patterson, her Catholic sister-in-law, godmother.[5] In 1806 the absent father, Jérôme, who, on Napoléon's order, was sailing aboard the *Veteran* to Brazil, advised Elizabeth, "*Ne te rends pas malheureuse, occupe-toi de élever mon fils, surtout ne m'en fais-pas un Americain; mais un françois, que les premiers môts qu'il prononcera soient ceux de son père; et de son souverain; qu'il sache de Bonne heure que le Grand Napoléon, est-son oncle et qu'il est destiné a faire un prince et un homme d'Etat.*" (Do not make yourself unhappy, busy yourself with raising my son, especially do not make for me an American of him, but a Frenchman so that the first words that he will pronounce will be those of his father, and of his sovereign. Let him know early that the Great Napoléon is his uncle and that he is destined to be a prince and a statesman."[6]) Elizabeth shared her estranged husband's hope that Bo would be a Frenchman, a prince, and a "statesman." He would be a European aristocrat who, only by circumstance, lived in America as a boy. His education must prepare him for the role he would eventually attain—ruler of France, in the line of succession originating from Napoléon. This vision for her son, first articulated by Jérôme, became the guiding force in Elizabeth's life. To date, scholars have attributed this vision entirely to Elizabeth's ambition, but, as his letter reveals, Jérôme, too, foresaw a royal future for his son during the boy's first years.

Archbishop John Carroll
(c. 1735–c. 1815)
Joshua Johnson
(c. 1763–c. 1824)
Before 1812
Oil on canvas
Image courtesy of the
Archdiocese of Baltimore

Acknowledging the importance of Bo's Catholic heritage, Elizabeth named Archbishop John Carroll and her sister-in-law Mary Ann Caton Patterson as her son's godparents.

Just as Elizabeth's mastery of the French language influenced the trajectory of her life, Bo must learn to speak like the Bonapartes. Even his father asked Elizabeth to "speak to the boy in French."[7] In December 1809, General Louis-Marie Turreau de Garambouville, the French minister plenipotentiary to the United States, who had arranged her pension from Napoléon, aided Elizabeth in securing a French tutor for Bo. Louis Tousard, a veteran of the French army and the American Revolution, undertook the boy's earliest education and acted as a caretaker. Thus, Bo's exposure to a French education began by the time he was four. He might not be a French prince yet, but he would learn to speak like one and to know his royal lineage. By 1814, when Bo was nine, his letters to his mother began to include French words and phrases, and he routinely closed with *"Votre plus affectueux fils Jerôme Bonàpàrte"* (Your very loving son), using the formal "vous," rather than the more intimate "tu" when

Mary Ann Caton Patterson (1788–1853)
SMPR, Maryland Historical Society

General Louis-Marie Turreau de Garambouville (1756–1816), French minister plenipotentiary to the United States, helped Elizabeth find a tutor for Bo.

Georges Six, *Dictionnaire Biographique des Généraux & Amiraux Français de la Révolution et de l'Empire, 1792–1814* [Paris: Gaston Savroy, 2003]

addressing her. Elizabeth, in turn, sent French "exercises" that Bo complained were too difficult. On April 4, 1814, he wrote in frustration, "I received your last letters which had French at the end of it but I would wish to have it in a small paper with a few easy lines in French to translate into English." He asked that she send her French dictionaries to help him with his studies, the same ones she had used as a girl at Madame Lacombe's in Baltimore (see page 7). "Do not forget to send me those two Dictionarys of the French language," Bo reminded her on December 26, 1813.[8] Just as Elizabeth always strove to prove her accomplishments to her father, Bo eagerly demonstrated his knowledge of French to his mother and grandfather, even writing a letter to Patterson entirely in French. Years later Elizabeth advised him, "It would be unnecessary to say that the French language should be as familiar to you as English."[9] In fact, Bo achieved fluency by the time he was a teenager and throughout his life conducted more than half of his correspondence in French. Elizabeth lamented his lack of aptitude for languages, but his letters to his Bonaparte family as well as his negotiations in the French courts attest to his proficiency.

Bo mastered the language of the Bonapartes at an early age, but he also developed strong ties to America through his Patterson family, in large part because of Elizabeth's absences. Beginning in 1809, Elizabeth lived primarily in Washington, D.C., and saw her son only occasionally. His grandparents, William and Dorcas Patterson, and Elizabeth's brother Robert and his wife, Mary Ann Caton Patterson, were the closest family he knew. On March 5, 1813, Bo apologized to Elizabeth for not writing, explaining, "The reason that I have not written to you lately is because I expected you up." Thinking he would see his mother in Baltimore, he did not want her to miss his letters when they arrived in Washington.[10] In fact, Elizabeth had not visited her son as he had hoped, and he heard about her mostly from others who had seen her at parties and events in Washington. In letters, his passionate, albeit boyish, expressions of his love for his mother suggest that he missed her terribly throughout his early childhood.

Although there is no known testament to Bo's grief after his grandmother Dorcas's death on May 21, 1814, at age fifty-two, he must have felt that loss of his other "mother" deeply. In letters written prior to her death, Bo always noted the state of his grandmother's health, either better or worse, and two months prior to her death remarked, "Mother [Dorcas] has not been out since your department [departure]."[11] A letter from Mary Ann to Elizabeth dated July 15, 1815 touches upon the motherly role she played for her nephew, particularly after Dorcas's death. Bo had an insect bite on his face that required lancing. Mary Ann reassured Elizabeth that should Bo tell her about the bite in his letter, "it is not material, and in fact nothing."[12] Distanced from the day-to-day care of her child, Elizabeth was a much longed for and somewhat shadowy figure during his formative years. Others stood in for her, first her mother and then her sister-in-law, and even the boy's tutor, a fact that later may have influenced Bo's turning away from Elizabeth's European ambitions for him and his decision to live his life in America.

For most of his childhood, Bo's primary links to his mother and father were letters from Elizabeth, occasional letters from his father, and newspaper articles that mentioned "Prince Jérôme," who, by 1807 had become King of Westphalia, in Germany. Bo accepted his father's absence from an early age and followed his career closely. In the sixteen months after he left Elizabeth, Jérôme wrote to her with some frequency, and his surviving letters frequently mention their son. On July 17, 1806, he wrote, "Kiss Napoleon for me," meaning his son. In another letter from that year, he spoke of envisioning Bo "sur mon genou" or "on his knee." Although his letters to Elizabeth grew slightly less affectionate after his marriage to the German princess Catherine of Württemburg on August 22, 1807, his thoughts about their son did not. On May 16, 1808, Jérôme wrote to Elizabeth from Cassel, Germany, confessing, "The events which have succeeded each other since our separation have not been able to efface you from my recollection." He added, "I have not ceased to occupy myself with the care of your happiness & with that of our child." Jérôme may, upon Napoléon's command, have married another, but he wanted his first family to enjoy every advantage he could offer. The repeated reassurances he gave Elizabeth of his affection and his ambitions for their son suggest that Elizabeth was not the sole driving force behind imperial ambitions for Bo. In the same letter, Jérôme made a single request: he wanted his son to be with him. He acknowledged the pain it would cause her to send Bo to Europe but warned, "you will not be so blind to your true interests, & to his, as not to consent to his departure." By sending Bo to live with his father, the boy would "enjoy all the advantages to which his Birth & his name give him a right."[13] By allowing him to remain in America, she would deprive him of what he deserved.

Jérôme Bonaparte (1774–1860)
Unattributed European artist
Circa 1800
Watercolor on ivory
Maryland Historical Society
Gift of Mrs. Charles J. Bonaparte
xx.5.58

Despite Jérôme's efforts to persuade his first wife and her father, William Patterson, of the wisdom of sending the boy to Germany, Elizabeth staunchly refused. Jérôme's letter did, however, echo a concern she often expressed. As a Bonaparte, Bo must be raised to attain a rank suited to his birth, yet the title Elizabeth wanted for her son was not to be had. On November 22, 1808, Jérôme wrote to her in obvious exasperation: "Is it to have Jerome recognized as a French Prince? That cannot be done—The Constitution of France opposes itself to it." Jérôme touched upon the one thing Elizabeth wanted for Bo and could never achieve, to be a "French Prince," the very thing he had once led her to believe would be possible. According to Jérôme, "A brilliant destiny is reserved for him," but it would not come with a royal title.[14] In his November 22 missive to Elizabeth, Jérôme included a letter to Bo that does not survive and a miniature of himself. Not only did he want Bo to know him as his father, he wanted to give the boy a miniature to remind him.

"Adieu Westphalia Ich eit nach Corsica"

Adieu Westphalia Ich eit nach Corsica
Caricature of King Jérôme's abdication, circa 1814
Deutsches Historisches

Cossack troops drove Jérôme out of Cassel on September 30, 1813, after Napoléon's failed invasion of Russia. A European coalition including Austria, Prussia, and several German states pushed the emperor out of France and into exile in Elba.

How much about his father Elizabeth shared with her young son is unknown, but by the time Bo was nine he could read his father's letters and the newspapers. In January 1814, he wrote to his mother, "My Dear father has lost his kingdom," and a month later worried, "I hope your spirits are not depressed on account of the late calamities which have befallen the French."[15] Bo may or may not have known that his father was called "König Lustik," the "laughing king," by his subjects and mocked for his extravagance and incompetence during his reign, but he did know that Cossack troops drove Jérôme out of Cassel.[16] He also knew that his uncle, the emperor, had come to the end of his power in France.

Even as a boy, Bo knew that the fate of the Bonapartes affected his mother and, in turn, his prospects. They were, after all, his French family, and their fate remained inextricably linked to his own. Despite the fact that Bo had never seen his father in anything other than a miniature or perhaps as an engraving in a newspaper, he "knew" him and loved him as only a child could. Conversely, Elizabeth made certain Jérôme knew what his son looked like, sending him a miniature of the boy in 1808.[17] Jérôme may have been struck by the boy's undeniable resemblance to his powerful uncle, Emperor Napoléon, a similarity so striking that later it would prove a political hindrance for Bo.

In 1812, after some years of silence, Jérôme wrote to his son directly, claiming that his other letters must have been lost. He was affectionate and expressed concern to the child he had never seen: "I hope that you will not forget me because I could not do without your affection." Jérôme then exhorted Bo to be a "good and loving son" to Elizabeth, who "will always set you the best example."[18]

Bo's feelings for his father remained strong, as did his longing for his mother, who was often absent. Between 1812 and 1815, when Elizabeth departed for Europe, she spent most of her time in Washington, enjoying the society of the

Madison White House. Bo, who was living with his Patterson family during this period, closed one of his letters with, "Your mos[t] affectionate son Jerome Napoleon Patterson Bonaparte," the only known instance of his affixing the Patterson name to his own.[19] Whether this was a boyish mistake or a deliberate rebuke for her absence is unknown, but no other letters survive with this "mistake."

Bo often regretted that he had not heard from Elizabeth and wondered when she would visit him, suggesting that he did not see her often. She did not spend Christmas 1813 with her son, but sent presents for which he thanked her on December 26: "I am very well satisfied with that Christmas gift that I have got." He closed with, "For you know that I love you better than all the world together." She must have written to Bo about her time with the president because the boy wrote back and asked, "How are Mr. and Mrs. Madison?"[20]

Several letters document the boy's longing for his mother. "Be sure you attend to your precious hea[l]th as what would become of me without you I would be a forlorn creature," he wrote when he was ten, clearly fearing a life

"Mésalliances are Fatal in Most Families" ❦ 113

without her. In 1814, Elizabeth's friend, Elbridge Gerry, visited the boy in Baltimore and reported, "he is impatient to see his dear mamma, his first inquiry having been, when was she to leave Washington?"[21] Often Bo did not know where his mother was or what her plans for him might be. Elizabeth's decision to leave her son in Baltimore rather than take him with her in 1815, the year she returned to Europe, changed his life in ways his mother did not foresee. Bo, who had not seen his mother for months, thought he would see her before her departure, only to learn that she had already left. In a pitiful letter, he wrote,

> I am pretty well but my spirits are not very good. Tell me when you stand to go to France. I know you have gone to Boston although you would not tell me. . . . Please to send me one of your rings for to remember you if you should get lost in the sea. Do not stay any longer than one year for my sake you must come for me to go to France with you and no one will do except you and My own Father. . . . Please to answer this letter. Do not forget the promise, which you made me to stay only one year.

His postscript was, "I wish you would keep this letter with you all the time you are in France and read it every month. My dear Mama I love you very much."[22]

After Elizabeth had sailed, Mary Ann, her sister-in-law informed her of Bo's sadness and desire to have accompanied her:

> your child . . . supports your departure with the manly firmness, and good sense so peculiar to him. His spirits were some what depressed at knowing you had actually gone; for hearing your intention so often doubted, he could not at first realize it, [which] added to the disappointment of not joining you in New York, made him a little sad.[23]

Mary Ann noted that Bo "thought it for your advantage to go," a remarkably mature reaction for a boy of only ten to have about a mother who had left him for an unknown period.

In 1816, Elizabeth described her life abroad in a letter to John Spear Smith, an uncle living in Baltimore. "I have been immersed in Balls, soirée Dinners which have not left me a single moment to dispose of. Every day adds to my disinclination to return where no pleasures no hopes await me." She broke her promise to Bo to stay only one year and remained abroad until 1817. Given the pleasures Europe offered, Elizabeth eventually returned to Baltimore more out of concern for her finances than for her son. She justified her time abroad by claiming that the social connections she formed in Europe would form the foundation for Bo's future, that by establishing herself in European society, she could guide him to his imperial destiny with greater ease. Bo would have been an impediment to her in Europe. "To carry children or Dogs with one on a visit of ceremony is provincial & vulgar," she explained, callously. "Even in half ceremonial visits, it is necessary to leave one's Dog & nurse in the ante Room." She concluded: "it is a thousand times better not to have them [children] at all."[24] Elizabeth's attitude toward Bo explains the emotional distance soon to grow between mother and son. Her expectations, made clear to him from an early age, ultimately generated resentment even as they successfully instilled in Bo the pride she wanted him to take in his Bonaparte heritage.

From 1815 to 1817, as Elizabeth charmed her way through European social circles, her son's emotional and cultural roots grew deeper into American soil. Having chosen to be absent during his childhood, Elizabeth could only influence her son in his formative years through her letters. The domineering but doting influence of Bo's grandfather, William Patterson, ultimately shaped his attachment to America more than his mother's often demanding mandates. In 1826, reflecting upon Bo's upbringing in Maryland, Patterson told Elizabeth, "He . . . seems greatly attached to it [America]," something understandable to his grandfather considering Bo's "republican education," but incomprehensible to her.[25]

Despite his French tutoring, Bo's education had been fundamentally American. In 1814, Elizabeth sent him to Mount St. Mary's College in Emmitsburg, Maryland, a school recommended by Bishop Carroll that boasted high academic standards and strict discipline. She was determined that Bo should complete his education in Europe, but he must remain in Maryland until she had formed beneficial connections with influential people abroad. Even her brother, Edward Patterson, agreed, given "the almost utter impossibility of giving an education in this country together with the great necessity of his case to have him brought up at some distinguished seminary in Europe."[26] The "great necessity" of Bo's "case" was, of course, his French legacy that demanded carefully "calculated" plans. After meeting John Jacob Astor in Geneva in 1817, Elizabeth learned that the American millionaire believed the best education could be obtained in Switzerland, where he had placed his own teenage daughter. By 1819, when Bo was graduated from Emmitsburg, she heeded Astor's advice and decided Geneva was where Bo should prepare for his royal destiny.

Detail of Elizabeth's engraving plate for her calling card (shown in reverse)
William J. Stone (1798–1865)
Maryland Historical Society
NN.1411

Elizabeth legally changed her name back to Patterson after the divorce, but continued to be called Madame Bonaparte throughout her lifetime.

Elizabeth returned to Baltimore in 1817 and remained there until 1819. Little correspondence survives to shed light on her relationship with her son during this period, but a return to Europe remained paramount in her thoughts. In 1819 she and Bo sailed to Amsterdam on the first leg of what proved to be an arduous trip. Just as she had been refused entry to Amsterdam in 1803, she was now informed by the French consul that they would not grant Bo a passport to enter France, claiming that the boy's strong resemblance to Napoléon might stir political unrest among the remaining Bonapartists.[27] Despite the fact that Bo traveled with a passport as "Edward Patterson," the name of his uncle, and Elizabeth traveled as "Mrs. Patterson," mother and son had to change their plans and pass through Germany to reach Switzerland, rather than traveling through France as she had intended. To be an American Bonaparte often made life in Europe difficult. This was, perhaps, the first time Bo became aware of the complexity of his situation as the son of the former king, Jérôme. In the post-Napoleonic France ruled by Louis XVIII, the boy's appearance, regardless of the name he used, attested to his lineage. This would be but the first of several occasions during his life when Bo's identity became politically problematic to the French government.

Born to an American mother in Britain and fathered by a French Bonaparte, Bo's citizenship presented problems throughout his adolescence, resulting in not only frustration but also a divided identity. Was he French, American, or both? In fact, in 1819, prior to leaving Baltimore, Bo signed an oath of American citizenship.[28] Similar conflicts of identity arose for Elizabeth throughout her life. Although legally she reverted to the Patterson name and subsequently used it when traveling, she continued to be called Bonaparte by almost all who knew her, and continued writing that name long after her divorce in 1813. Throughout his life, Bo carried papers to document his Bonaparte identity, including Elizabeth's marriage record, his birth certificate, and proof of his baptism.[29] In America, he could be a Bonaparte, but in Europe his identity, as well as his lineage and family connections, always raised questions. Documents alone could prove who he was.

Jerome Napoleon (Bo) Bonaparte
(1805–1870)
Unknown artist
Circa 1819
Watercolor on ivory
Private collection, photograph by
Elizabeth Moltke-Huitfeldt

Not until Bo left America did his deep attachment to Baltimore reveal itself in his correspondence. While aboard ship, he wrote to his grandfather, lamenting his departure from Maryland. "Then again when I think to myself of the many Dear relations and friends I have left behind I wish myself at home, and am sorry that I ever left Baltimore. I would have come to take leave of you, But the thought of leaving one to whom I was so entirely devoted, and whom I loved so much . . . prevented me from doing so."[30] Perhaps a face-to-face parting had not been possible, or he loved his grandfather too much to say good-bye in person. After the long and troublesome journey to Geneva, complicated entirely by his name, Bo longed for the home he knew and the place where his identity as a Bonaparte was not questioned.

Elizabeth quickly settled herself and Bo in a boarding house and, eventually, an apartment in Geneva. She enrolled Bo in the best school and began executing her plan to educate her son for a life abroad as a prince. Should fate turn against her aspirations, Bo's education would prepare him to succeed through his own accomplishments. Writing to her father, Elizabeth explained,

"My wish is, then to educate him with the idea that he has his fortune to acquire by his own exertions, but at the same time to profit by all the good intentions of his relations in a way that will not interfere with his attainment of personal distinctions, which, after all, is better than money."[31] Bo should benefit as much as possible from his relationship with the Bonapartes, but he should also be prepared to make his own way in life.

Here lay an inherent contradiction in Elizabeth's vision for her son. She wanted to give him an aristocratic future, but, if he did not attain such rank, he must seek "personal distinction" through hard work, a very American sentiment. Self-sufficiency and ambition, though, were antithetical to aristocratic ideals. Elizabeth addressed this contradiction pragmatically. "The uncertainty of events in this century confirms in me the opinion that the only certain fortune parents can give their posterity is some lucrative and respectable profession, such as the law, which renders them at the same time proper for foreign embassies or the situation of a statesman at home." Bo might live abroad as a diplomat or even be an American politician should the French throne prove unattainable. Toward that end, fencing, drawing, dancing, equitation, politeness, and "usage du monde" (ways of the world) complemented his studies in Greek, Latin, mathematics, French, English, the sciences, history, mythology, geography, and jurisprudence. On Saturdays he attended balls where, according to Elizabeth, "he meets some of the first persons of Europe." If all this preparation came to no avail, Elizabeth assured her father, it would not be due to her neglect. "I spare neither money nor personal exertions to procure for him every possible advantage." She also fretted that his exposure to the Bonapartes, their palaces and extravagant ways, might turn the boy from his studies too early and limit his ambition. "If I were to take the child to a palace, he would naturally prefer pleasure to study," she worried.[32] Yet, she wanted her boy in a palace, married to a princess, titled and noble. For a child whose identity was already conflicted, this kind of parenting could only have enhanced Bo's disjointed sense of his place in the world, America or Europe, palace or law office.

Despite Elizabeth's efforts to expose Bo to the finest European education and society, he continually looked across the sea to America. "Since I have been in Europe I have dined with princes and princesses and all the great people of Europe, but I have never tasted a dish as much to my taste as the roast beef and beef-steaks I ate on South Street [in Baltimore]."[33] Unwittingly, Elizabeth had let her son become an American who missed "roast beef."

His attachment to America aside, Bo took pride in the Bonaparte name and, in later years, fought for recognition by his French family. Yet, his life-long ties to the European Bonapartes were accompanied by frustration over that family's lack of financial support and their ultimate unwillingness to acknowledge the legitimacy of his birth. His relationship to his imperial legacy was complex and must be viewed through more than the lens of Elizabeth's desire that her son be made a king, for Jérôme was also important in shaping the boy's dual identity.

Bo's earliest surviving letter to his father, written when he was sixteen, reveals the complicated emotional relationship he maintained with this absent figure in his life. "*Je n'ai jamais été si heureux que ce jour que Ma Mére vient de me dire que je puis vous écrire*" ("I was never so happy as I am this day when my mother just told me that I could write to you.") Eager to know more about and be closer to his "true father," he complained that he had been in Geneva for two years before learning that Jérôme was nearby in Rome. Despite his youth, he then expressed a sentiment far beyond his sixteen years and one that echoed the mantra Elizabeth had worked into her son's psyche from his earliest years and one his father had expressed when Bo was first born: "*Le nom j'hérite que est immortel; je ne négligerai aucun des moyens dans mon pouvoir de ne pas m'en rendre tout à fait indigne.*"[34] ("The name I inherit is immortal; I will neglect no means in my power in order not to make myself unworthy of it.") Whether Bo saw himself becoming the ruler of France remains unknown, but this letter shows that the teenager knew himself to be a Bonaparte and looked at his family connections with clarity and purpose. Only later, when life taught him otherwise, would he realize that bearing the Bonaparte name did not make him a French Bonaparte.

In Bo's papers, a slim notebook written by Elizabeth provides more evidence of her belief that the Bonaparte name imposed specific expectations on those who bore it. Unfortunately, it is undated, but Elizabeth may have sent it to Bo while she was still in Europe and he in Maryland. One day he would travel abroad, and she wanted him to have the benefit of the many lessons she had learned. "If any one, capable of advising, had taken any Pains with me, I should have shunned many follies, which all undirected young People run into," she lamented. "My Father was neither desirous or able to advise me."[35] In fact, Patterson's advice to his daughter had been unstinting. She had simply chosen not to follow it.

"I repeat to you, Be proud of your name & of your connexion with an illustrious family; but do not suppose that these distinctions are a little Deed to Sloth, & consequent ignorance; on the contrary they should be your incentives to exertion," she wrote.

> An illustrious name depreciates, instead of elevating those who know not how to act up to it. It becomes sun shine on a Dung Hill—Sense, knowledge, Education & good manners should accompany a great name; the want of these advantages is more conspicuous in an individual of Rank, than in a Bourgeois—You must be well acquainted with History ancient & modern; your own name is historical therefore it is more incumbent upon you to read attentively History & Memoirs.

To merely rest upon being a Bonaparte was not enough. Bo must earn the associations that name carried. "Should you fancy that because you have the honor of being called a Bonaparte, talent & knowledge will not be exacted to you, the sooner you lose this fatal illusion the more fortunate it will be for yourself," she scolded, as if Bo's behavior necessitated such a rebuke. "I assure you that infinitely more accomplishments are expected from you than if you were the son of an enriched Upstart." In fact, Bo had been a dutiful student in Emmitsburg, and, despite an initial unwillingness to learn Latin, he had shown himself to be well mannered and intelligent. Just like her father, Elizabeth possessed a judgmental streak that often led her to criticize her son without reason. Such was the case when she repeatedly cautioned him against idleness and laziness. "What would the Emperor Napoleon have been had he spent his time in idleness? A Zero, altho' his family was one of the Best in Italy." The implication was that Bo's role model in the Bonaparte family should not be his father but his uncle, the emperor himself. "Endeavor to live with your Superiors. The companionship of those greater or Better than yourself will do you good." In Bo's case, his superiors would only be found among the highest ranks of European society. He must know how to interact with royalty.

> Were you to converse with a King you ought to be unembarrassed, but every Look, word & action should imply the utmost respect—what would be proper & well bred with others, much your superior, would be absurd & ill bred with one so very much so. You must (with Royalty) wait until you are spoken to. You must receive not give the conversation.[36]

As a Catholic who would be privileged to meet the pope, Bo must know, "The Title given to a cardinal is 'your Eminence' & to the Pope 'your Holiness' (*votre sainteté*)." Kings would receive him, popes would receive him, he would need his mother's guidance to be worthy. She had learned that "*Les manières nobles* [noble manners] are . . . only to be acquired in highest society." To associate with inferiors "can only degrade your mind, your manners & your habits." Her little book offered more than advice: it was a warning.

It was also a guide to becoming less American. "Do not speak through your nose "*à l'Américaine*," Elizabeth exhorted and then listed "vulgarities to be avoided." Those included the difference between American English and that spoken abroad.

Window shutter not Vinder shetter

Coachman not Driver

Housemaid not Chamber maid

Sitting room or Drawing Room not Parlour

Dining Room not Parlour

Glass of Water not Drink of water

He doesn't *not He don't*

Just so not Jest so

Lie down not to Lay down

It is very steady not very study

Shut the Door not *shet* the Door

A Chair not a cheer

He said (for *the past*) not say*s* he, or he says

Tomorrow *will* be Sunday not *is* Sunday

He did—she did not he *done*

Eating Food, but never victuals

Dashing, Elegant Genteel are not said & Females (unless speaking of female monkeys, Dogs, or any of the inferior animals) can not be said—say women, Ladies any thing but Females

Endeavour to live with your Superiors. The Companionship of those greater, or Better than yourself will do you good. Get rid of Envy (should you possess this characteristic of of vulgar minds) & instead of vainly trying to drag down the Excellence of those above you resolve on equalling, & if possible Surpassing, them in Merit. Recollect that Emulation is the quality of a great mind, & that Envy is peculiar to mean contracted base, grovelling ones. & that, whilst it tortures, it prevents the possibility of reaching that superiority which is the object of its hatred. Groundlings are purse proud & Envious, incapable of comprehending the Superiority of intellect which they however know how to hate. Great minds are incapable of this mean Sentiment. Emulation is not envy. Instead of Shirking the Company of those who possess a higher degree of intelligence than yourself, let it be your endeavour to render yourself either useful or agreeable enough to them, to be able enjoy the advantages of their Society. If you have any intellect you will however admire the possession of it in others — Take care how you offend Persons of Sense — Remember the Onion "my mordens { "Plangit {

Vulgarities to be avoided
Window Shutter — not — Vinder shelter
Shooting — not — Gunning
Coachman — not — Driver
Housemaid — not Chamber maid
Sitting room or Drawing Room — not Parlour
Dining Room — not Parlour
Glass of Water — not a Drink of water
He does'nt — not He d'ont
Just so — not Jest so
Lie down — not to Lay down
It is very steady — not very study
Shut the Door — not shet the Door
a chair — not a cheer
He said (for the past) not says he, or he says
Tomorow will be Sunday — not is Sunday
He did — She did — not he done
Eating Food, but never Victuals —
Dashing, Elegant Genteel are not said & Females (unless speaking of Female monkeys, Dogs or any of the inferior animals but women) can not be said — Say women, Ladies any thing but Females.
Bad Room — not Chamber
You cannot say either Syrup, or reckon, or right for very — do right well

Elizabeth penned these reminders of proper conduct for Bo.
Box 5, MS 144, JNB Papers

In 1820, Elizabeth received the first invitation to visit Pauline Borghese, Napoléon's sister, but she had concerns about the princess's "capriciousness" and the reliability of the Bonaparte family as a whole. Lady Sydney Morgan, Elizabeth's friend, exhorted her not to send Bo to Princess Borghese, remarking that under the influence of the Bonapartes, "his education would be sacrificed . . . he would adopt the most absurd ideas of his own greatness, as they call themselves Majesty and Highness." Elizabeth admitted to her father, "I do not think there is any confidence to be placed in expectations from his father's family." Socially positioned as she was, Elizabeth had learned that Madame Mère, Bo's grandmother, remained burdened by the extravagances of her children and that the "King of W[estphalia] spends everything he can get hold of, and will keep up a kingly state until his expended means leave him a beggar."[37] She wanted to use her Bonaparte relations to advantage, but not to the detriment of her son's education.

By the fall of 1821, after much hesitation, she and Bo traveled to Rome to meet the Bonaparte family. She bemoaned the expense as well as Bo's break from his studies but wrote to her father shortly before Christmas: "Bo has been well received by his family. . . . I am rejoiced at having brought him here, although I feared the experiment might prove a dangerous one. At all events, there will be no loss except of a few months from his education."[38] Bo's fluency in French, coupled with the strikingly Napoleonic features that had prevented him from entering France, were his greatest advantages during this interlude. Pauline Borghese, Napoléon's sister; Madame Mère, his grandmother (Letizia Bonaparte); and Cardinal Joseph Fesch, Madame Mère's half-brother, all embraced the boy, giving him gifts and money.

Madame Mère, Maria Letizia Ramolino Bonaparte (1750–1836)
Attributed to Anna Pecchioli
Circa 1825
Watercolor on ivory, gold and glass
Maryland Historical Society
Gift of Mrs. Charles J. Bonaparte
xx.5.61

In 1821, when Bo was sixteen years old, Elizabeth took him to Rome for an introduction to his grandmother, Maria Letizia Ramolino Bonaparte.

Rome with St. Peter's and the Castel Sant'Angelo
John Glover (1769–1849)
Circa 1821
Oil on oak panel
National Gallery of Australia, Canberra

Although Bo's relationships with the Bonapartes proved emotionally gratifying, they did not yield the long-term monetary support Elizabeth and even young Bo had hoped to gain. Pauline, in particular, "treated him exactly as she has done all her other nephews—this is promised, and then retracted. . . . She chooses a new heir every week."[39] During this visit, Bo formed enduring attachments to the Bonaparte family, but his attachment to America, particularly his family in Baltimore, did not diminish. Like his mother and grandfather, Bo gradually recognized that financial comfort would not be found with the European Bonapartes and that his prospects in Baltimore, back at his grandfather's South Street home, might well remain his best option financially, and perhaps emotionally, too.

Suspecting Bo's attachment to the city she despised, Elizabeth made it clear to her son that Baltimore represented the epicenter of vulgarity. "Baltimore is not the seat of refined & polished manners," she had cautioned in her book of advice, it was a place where vulgarity was commonplace and acceptable. "You cannot crowd different things on your Plate, or Eat, as I have seen at Baltimore, Beef steak & Turkey together—Fish & cabbage idem." There were worse offenses. "Persons of good company are not prodigal of gesticulations; such as . . . plucking Hairs out of the Face, or Ears (the latter often practiced at Baltimore, as well as other vulgarities)." Table manners ranked among the most important signs of breeding and what you ate, as well as how you ate it, communicated your social standing. "Vulgar foods," according to Elizabeth, were—unsurprisingly—American and included, "indian-meal Cakes . . . apple dumpling . . . pork and beans."[40] "Low persons" drank whiskey, an American beverage. It was fortunate Elizabeth did not know of Bo's longing for "beef-steaks" on South Street. His palate, shaped at Patterson tables, remained decidedly American.

Elizabeth's advice concerning marriage is perhaps the most perplexing of all the sentiments in the notebook. Long before Bo reached marriageable age, she contemplated a European union for him. James Gallatin remarked in 1816, "Her son seems to be her one thought. . . . she is most ambitious for him. She even has a list of different princesses who will be available for him to marry: as he is only ten years old, it is looking far ahead."[41] To her mind, Bo was the true successor to the French throne, therefore his wife ought to possess an aristocratic position to match. Her lists of possible brides do not survive among her papers, but her aspirations for her son are well documented in her correspondence.

Madame Mère thought the young man should marry his cousin, Charlotte Bonaparte, the daughter of Joseph, who had self-exiled on his estate, Point Breeze, in Bordentown, New Jersey. The idea for this union, according to Elizabeth, sprang from the Bonapartes themselves. "She [Pauline] and Madame [Mère] wish Joseph to marry him to his youngest daughter," Elizabeth wrote to her father in the fall of 1821. From her letters, it seems her enthusiasm for this union overflowed. Patterson, though, felt differently and explained,

> It is more than probable that the match first talked of with his cousin [Charlotte] may be renewed, & should this be the case, I told him unless the family would make up a fortune of two hundred thousand Dollars at the least, placed unconditionally at his own disposal, & that the young Lady & her family would Consent to their living in this Country, that it would not answer for him to engage in the Business & of this he seemed fully sensible himself.

The Sisters, Zenaide and Charlotte Bonaparte
Jacques-Louis David (1748–1825)
1821
Oil on Canvas
Museo Napoleonico, Rome

Charlotte Bonaparte with her sister Zenaide, Bo's cousins. Bonaparte family members thought marriage to Charlotte would enhance Bo's future.

Elizabeth saw the marriage as an opportunity for a title and wealth. Not only would Bo marry a Bonaparte, thereby further strengthening his family ties, he might also receive a legacy from his quixotic aunt Pauline, who, despite her nature, promised him $8,000 when he married.[42]

It is curious, then, that in her book of advice Elizabeth wrote, "I advise you never to marry, because I consider matrimony as the most irreparable folly a man can commit—The choice is difficult; the success doubtful & the engagement Perpetual. *Should you* be so unwary as to impose the chains of marriage on yourself avoid large families or poor *Females* if you do not wish your House

& Fame & your Purse to be tortured—Indignant [sic] relatives (on the wife's side) are mill stones to drag down a man's fortunes however solid, or extended—tongues of adders."[43] Elizabeth's view was simple: marriage brings misery, and jeopardizes both fame and fortune. Unless he could marry a suitable woman like his cousin Charlotte, it was not a step worth taking. "Early marriages are misery—imprudent marriages idiotism. Marriage at the Best is the Devil—nothing is less becoming to a wise man than matrimony." When Elizabeth wrote of "early marriages," she must have remembered her own at eighteen, her groom then only nineteen but claiming to be twenty-five. Moreover, from an early age, Elizabeth had watched her mother endure a marriage overburdened by a controlling husband, thirteen pregnancies, and repeated infidelities carried on within her own home.

Elizabeth's own *mésalliance* surely strengthened her negative opinion of marriage. In a journal, she wrote a poem that summarized her union with Jérôme. "The Bargain must be / That when I chase I am perfectly free / For this is a sort of Engagement you see, / Which is binding on you, but not Binding on me."[44] Her "engagement" had been anything but "Perpetual," but the effects of her marriage, good and bad, lingered over her life. Elizabeth saw marriage as a sacrifice worth making only if the social and economic benefits far outweighed the burden. "There is one advantage from the connection, which is, that he is placed by it in the first circles of Europe, that his acquaintance has been sought by persons of the highest rank, and that, with very little money, he can always live with them. This I consider a great point."[45] The "connection" Elizabeth referred to was, of course, the Bonaparte family. Her own "imprudent marriage," which brought misery, also made her a Bonaparte, in legacy if not in name, and her son an heir to the French throne. Had she never married a Bonaparte, it is unlikely her son would have needed such advice.

Despite Elizabeth's guidance, Bo decided his future rested in America, a conclusion largely motivated by financial interests. Like his father, Bo enjoyed spending money and showed little inclination to work for a living. When discussions about his marrying Charlotte suggested it might be a possibility, Bo wrote to his grandfather from Europe, "I hope it may take place, for then I would return immediately to America to pass the rest of my life among my relatives and relations." Joseph Bonaparte, Charlotte's father, was rumored to be among the wealthiest Bonapartes, a prospect that made such a union appealing. Elizabeth viewed it as "the only probable way of ever getting anything

like pecuniary aid for the boy from any of the family."[46] Bo, in contrast, saw the marriage as a means of returning to America and securing a life of ease for himself. The fact that his own Bonaparte legacy would be strengthened was not foremost in his mind. Upon his arrival from Europe in 1822, he went directly to Point Breeze to spend time with Charlotte. Numerous letters between them attest to the fact that they became friends, but romance never materialized.

Patterson, always eager to advance his grandson's fortune, investigated the possible match, and, like his grandson, his curiosity was purely mercenary. He had heard rumors about Joseph's wealth that interested him far more than the man's last name. To his dismay, he learned from a Madame Toussard, a friend in Philadelphia who spent time with Joseph and his daughter, that Charlotte was "in size a dwarf and excessively ugly. Jerome is quite too handsome for her; it would be a great sacrifice."[47] More important, Joseph was not as well off as rumors suggested. A Bonaparte marrying a Bonaparte might assure the legacy but would not line Bo's pockets. Elizabeth thought it better for her son to remain unmarried if a suitable bride could not be found, and allowed him to go to Harvard, a continuation of his American education. Such a decision was in keeping with advice she had

Charlotte drew this image of Point Breeze, her family's New Jersey home, for Bo.
Box 9, MS 142, Maryland Historical Society

Joseph Bonaparte
Augustin Challamel and Desire Lacroix, *Grands Hommes et grands faits de la Revolution* [Paris: Jouvet & Cie, editeurs, 1889]

written in her handbook, but, given her commitment to Bo's European life, her decision to send him to an American university is yet another contradiction and an act that helped solidify his attachment to his home country.

In February 1823, Bo was admitted to Harvard, where he studied a range of subjects, including French history. Elizabeth, initially disappointed by the unsuccessful courtship of Charlotte, admitted to her father, "I am now not sorry he is under college discipline." He even studied the rise and fall of his uncle, Napoléon.[48] His father maintained a sporadic but affectionate correspondence with him during this period and sent money to support Bo's education. On January 31, 1824, a frustrated Jérôme wrote to Bo, "*Je suis fâché que tu ne me rendes pas un compte détaillé de tes études*" (I am annoyed that you do not give me a detailed account of your studies), and complained that Bo, whose letter contained only ten lines, did not tell him more about his academic life. "*Ta lettre est beaucoup trop courte; ce n'est pas dix lignes que tu dois écrire à ton Pere, mais dix pages.*"[49] (Your letter is far too short; it is not ten lines that you must write to your father, but *ten pages*.) There seems to have been a loss of intimacy between father and son. Bo's letters, once so adoring, had gradually become terse and unemotional, obligatory missives devoid of information. After seeing the disparity between the life of extravagance and idleness his father lived and his own, Bo's regard for Jérôme diminished.

After Bo's departure in 1822, Elizabeth remained in Europe. Writing to his grandfather, Bo remarked, "Mama's letter is dated April, Paris [1822]. She begins thus 'I am now in Paris looking for an occasion to sail for America, feeling so much anxiety about your concerns there and fearing you require my presence and advice on many subjects. It puts me to great inconvenience to make the voyage but I prefer any personal inconvenience to leaving you without my advice. I shall try to sail from the Havre.'"[50] Elizabeth, who had been enjoying a robust social life in Florence and lavish evenings spent with Prince Nicolas Demidov, was not eager to return to Baltimore. That year she wrote to her father that her finances and her worries about Bo drove her to return. "I consider it my duty . . . to be as near him as possible, for which reason I shall try to establish myself at Cambridge or in Boston. . . . I can be of more use to him at present in New England than I could in Baltimore." After spending several months in Paris, Elizabeth sailed from Le Havre to New York on July 15, 1824. She did visit Bo in Cambridge, meticulously recording her expenses as always, but she did not remain there more than a few months. "The professors of Cambridge do not approve of the mothers of students living in Cambridge," she explained.[51]

Interestingly, that same year Elizabeth happily told her father that Bo had received a letter from Jérôme, who was then the guardian of his nieces, the daughters of Maria Anna Elisa Bonaparte Baciocchi Levoy. "They have large fortunes, and would be excellent matches for any young man with a great name and a slender purse," she wrote enthusiastically, no doubt thinking her son, whose great name came without a fortune, would be a fine match for his cousins. Again, Patterson did not share her enthusiasm and advised his grandson that despite Jérôme and Elizabeth's vision of a European union for him, such a marriage would be incompatible with Bo's "Republican education and habits." Patterson then gave his impressions of the Bonaparte family:

> Your father's family cannot get clear of the notion of what they once were and the brilliant prospects they then had. Their fortunes cannot now be very considerable; they are living in idleness on what they have, and when that property they now possess comes to be divided among their children it will scarcely keep them from want, and the next generation will in all probability be beggars. What prospect, then, would you have by marrying into such a family, as I presume your father means that you should be connected in marriage with some of your relations? . . . Your father's family is all on the decline and going down hill.

In a final blow to thoughts of a European alliance, Patterson concluded, "in Europe you would be nothing, and must come to nothing with the other branches of your family."[52]

After her visit to Harvard in 1825, Elizabeth chose not to return to Baltimore, but to live with Madame Toussard in Philadelphia, before sailing to Paris with her on June 6, 1825. By the time Bo decided to return to Europe in 1826, his mother had already been living abroad almost a year and was then residing in Florence, where her social circle was firmly established. The object of Bo's second trip abroad was to meet his father for the first time. During his first trip to Europe, he had visited other members of the Bonaparte family but had not met his father face to face. Before Bo arrived, Jérôme expressed his worry that their meeting might not please his second family. "I desire to place you in a natural position, without, however, prejudicing in any way the condition of the queen and the princes, our children."[53]

The letter, which never reached Bo, suggests Jérôme's concern for his second family. He wished to establish a fond relationship with Bo and honor him as his son, but not to an extent that would compromise his loyalty to his wife and children. Jérôme's carefully chosen words reveal an important distinction: Bo deserved a "natural position," defined by his biological connection to his father, but Jérôme's other children were entitled to their royal positions and those positions could not be jeopardized by Bo's presence.

That fall, Bo at last met his father and his half siblings, the brother also named Jérôme, together with Napoléon and Mathilde, and he eventually decamped with the Bonapartes to Rome. Little is known about Bo's emotions upon meeting his "true father," the man who had cast a shadow over his childhood in Baltimore and had remained a presence only through letters and newspapers. During this visit and as evidenced in Bo's correspondence, he formed a friendship with Louis-Napoléon Bonaparte, the son of Napoléon's brother Louis and Hortense de Beauharnais, Empress Josephine's daughter from her first marriage. This relationship would later shape the trajectory of Bo's son's life.

Despite the attachments Bo made during his visit, he quickly grew "excessively tired" living at his father's, where "killing time" and lavish spending filled their days. Unlike his mother, who found late dinners and languid conversation scintillating, Bo thought it all dull and depressing. "The more I see, the more firmly I am persuaded of the superiority of my own country," he wrote his grandfather. The young man whose mother referred to America as the "land of nuts and apples" and its inhabitants as nothing more than a "dull, fat, heavy, prejudice[d] race" only wanted to go home. Elizabeth could instill the importance of his Bonaparte name in her son and he could establish fond relationships with his European family, but she could not compel him to make a life abroad. "I cannot think for a moment of settling myself out of America, to whose government, manners, and customs I am too much attached and accustomed," Bo told his grandfather. "America is the only country where I can have an opportunity of getting forward." In contrast, Elizabeth wrote to her father in 1826, "I want to give him enough of Europe to prevent his desiring to leave me in America." In fact, the more Bo saw of Europe, the more determined he became to return to Baltimore. "You have no idea how anxious I am to return home. I was always aware that America was the only country for me, but now I am still more firmly persuaded of it than ever."[54] Despite his boyhood longing to go to Europe with his mother and his desire to know his "true father," Bo now thought his destiny lay in America.

Other than strengthening his relationships with Louis-Napoléon and his half-siblings, Bo's visit proved unproductive. Once he realized that his father did not intend to provide for him financially, he saw no reason to prolong the visit. In January 1827 he wrote to his grandfather, "I have now been three months with my father. . . . He continues very kind to me; but I see no prospect of his doing anything for me."[55] Bo's reaction raises a question that will return in later years: Was his interest in the Bonapartes primarily driven by money rather than the desire for a title?

With the uncertainties surrounding his citizenship and whether he would be acknowledged as a Bonaparte, it is little wonder that Bo turned his thoughts to the more practical advantage afforded by his lineage—money. Neither the society of the Bonapartes nor a love of European culture tethered him to the continent. His experiences only confirmed his desire to return to America, where a fortune might be gained with greater ease. Patterson wrote to Elizabeth in April 1827, "I perceive that he is tired of Europe & expresses his anxiety of returning to this Country, this I do not wonder at for no one of an independent spirit could think of living in Europe after having seen & experienced the happy state of this country compared with any other in the world." Father and daughter would never agree when it came to the value of Europe over America, particularly as it related to Bo. Patterson continued:

> I do not see that *Bo* can promise himself anything from his family in Europe & the sooner you & him returns perhaps it will be the better for both, should you find it agreeable you & him may live with me as long as all of us find it convenient, so to do or until you can look round you and fix some permanent plan of life. As to your idea that it might be useful for *Bo* to spend another year in Europe for the sake of seeing company, I am quite of a contrary opinion & I think he has too much good sense not to think with me. This is the only country in which he can live with any satisfaction to himself & the less he sees or knows of the follies of Europe the better.[56]

Jerome Napoleon (Bo)
Bonaparte
(1805–1870)
Unknown artist
Circa 1829
Watercolor on ivory
Private collection, photograph by
Elizabeth Moltke-Huitfeldt

Susan May Williams Bonaparte
(1812–1881)
Unknown artist
Circa 1829
Watercolor on ivory
Private collection, photograph by
Elizabeth Moltke-Huitfeldt

Like Bo, Patterson saw the merits of the Bonapartes in pecuniary terms. If they had no money to offer his grandson, Bo might as well return to Baltimore.

Although Bo hoped his mother would return with him, Elizabeth saw no opportunities for herself in Baltimore and remained abroad for seven more years. Bo sailed for home in 1827, eager to pursue a path more profitable than life with the Bonapartes offered. Like his mother and grandfather, he was unmovable when he settled on a plan. He soon stopped writing so frequently to Jérôme, who complained in 1827 that he had only received one letter from his son and warned that one day he would be a father himself and understand the pain a child's neglect causes a parent.[57]

Bo now focused his attention on building his American life. From 1827 to 1829, he made a feeble attempt to study law in Baltimore—a venture for which he showed no natural inclination. Reflecting on his grandson's efforts, William Patterson wrote to Elizabeth on July 24, 1829, "After Jeromes last return to this country I endeavored to get him to study law, not intended as a profession, but as a useful part of his Education & together with other Reading to qualify him for public life if such should happen to be his Lot hereafter. He went once through Blackston[e]s Commentaries & attended some few Law Lectures & here he made a full stop, & has neither read Law or History ever since."

Regretfully Patterson added, "He has . . . a rooted aversion to study or reading of any kind," and confessed that he had stopped urging Bo to continue his academic pursuits. Despite this, Patterson admitted that Bo was a tremendous social success, "esteemed and caressed" by many.[58] Elizabeth, still in Europe, continued to entertain visions of a life abroad for him. A diplomatic career might be suitable, and the Swedish minister to the Court of Tuscany thought there might be an opportunity for Bo in his country.

But in Baltimore, after struggling with the study of law, Bo pursued a different course, one that would forge a rift between mother and son that would never fully mend. While Elizabeth schemed to tether her son to Europe, Bo decided to marry an American heiress, Susan May Williams, whose wealth alone made her an ideal wife. Elizabeth's letters of protest reveal much about her hopes for her son. "He ought never to marry unless it be into some of the great European families if I can prevent it, if the authority of a Mother can prevail, he never shall degrade himself & destroy his

Mrs Bonaparte-Patterson   Florence 5 September
                                                    1829

D.r Sir.

I rec.d your letter of the 24 July.
I am at present too unwell to reply to it at any
length not being able to write more than three words at a
time. You & the son of Prince Jerôme Bonaparte
have been told so often by me that I considered a
marriage between him and any american woman
so much beneath him that I would never for
any consideration consent to it —
                                        I can only
repeat that if it takes place I shall declare
publicly that I was not consulted; that my
consent was not asked — & that my opinion
always was, & always will be that
he ought to live single unless he marries
suitably to his connexions in Europe —

He has only to put off this marriage for a year
& by that time he will be sensible of the folly of
marrying Miss Williams.   E Patterson

P. S. I shall not mention this subject to any one
here — If it really takes place, it will then be time
enough for me to justify myself from all the
blame of it — He is now of age, therefore I have
no legal controul over his actions —

Elizabeth's vitriolic response on learning of Bo's plans to marry American heiress Susan May Williams.
Collection of Mark B. Letzer

prospects. . . . The nephew of Napoleon has no equal in America," she raged to her father in September 1829. In another letter she fumed, "I have told you and my son so often of my intention that he should never marry an American." She had chosen not to remarry in order to preserve the dignity of a royal alliance. "[I] might have made twenty marriages," she ranted, ". . . but I never forgot that I had the honor having made one that rendered it impossible for me to marry a low person." No one other than an aristocrat, or rather, a Bonaparte, would do. Unfortunately, by the time her damning letters arrived in Baltimore, it was too late. On October 17, a defeated Elizabeth wrote, "If he thinks he can be happy by this marriage I shall no longer oppose it."[59]

Patterson later confessed to his daughter that had her letters arrived in time, he would have put a stop to the marriage. That was easy to say after the fact, and probably not true. He was pleased enough with the marriage to give his grandson $50,000 as a wedding gift, and he encouraged his daughter to

Marble busts of Bo's grandparents, Charles and Letizia Bonaparte, were a wedding gift from Joseph Bonaparte.

rethink her opposition to the union, of which even Bo's uncle, Joseph Bonaparte, approved. Though in poor health, Joseph had attended the wedding bearing as gifts busts of Bo's grandparents, Charles Bonaparte and Madame Mère (Letizia), and jewels for Williams, the newest American Bonaparte. Madame Mère, Bo's grandmother, exclaimed, *"J'ai appris avec plaisir votre marriage, puisque la personne que vous avez choisie réunit tous les avantages que l'on peut désirer."* (I learned of your marriage with pleasure, since the person whom you have chosen unites all the advantages that one could desire.")[60] Other congratulations came from the Bonapartes, including invitations to visit the family in Europe. As a matter of politics, they might be unwilling to acknowledge Bo as family, but they willingly gave their affection. It was a pattern to be repeated again and again in later decades.

Elizabeth, still furious, had tried to reconcile herself to her son's unsuitable marriage but could not. Patterson tried to explain. Bo, he told her,

> altho of fine capacity is by nature rather indolent without much ambition, therefore not calculated for the kind of life that you would wish him to figure in Europe; he is however amiable & sensible, & will always be esteemed & respected, with a much better prospect of happiness in this country than he could promise himself in Europe. [Y]ou call to mind Lord Chesterfields disapointment with his son with whom he had taken so much pains, to prove that nature cannot be changed under any circumstances.[61]

Elizabeth, like Chesterfield, had indeed taken "great pains" with Bo's education, even creating a book of advice for him, but she had failed. Her attempts to shape Bo's future had turned him back to America and a marriage prompted by desire for wealth rather than a title. His childhood in America, spent largely in the care of the Pattersons, and his years at Harvard had made him comfortable in the ways of American society. More significantly, his grandfather's generosity far outstripped anything he might find in Europe.

As Charlene Boyer Lewis has recently observed, "Perhaps more than any other episode from this period of her life, her son's marriage forced Elizabeth to look back at the choices she made and evaluate them."[62] In her mind, she had made great sacrifices to establish a different destiny for her son, yet he had rejected what she offered him. With time, she came to recognize that it was "unreasonable to expect him to place his happiness in the only things that can make me happy. . . . He has neither my pride, my ambition, nor my love of good company." Ambition, as Elizabeth defined it, was not hereditary. Despite her proclamation that "The Dignity of a great name must be served up to by activity, diligence, & persevering," her son chose to rise through marriage rather than hard work. Like the elder Patterson, Edward, Bo's uncle, recognized in his nephew a "total want of ambition . . . and inordinate desire of wealth." Bo's priorities were simply different. Elizabeth had reared him to marry a princess or no one at all, but that was not his natural inclination. Nor did he have any desire to work. As his great aunt, Nancy Spear, explained to Elizabeth, Bo "was unhappy because he was not independent [but] born with an unbounded love of money."[63]

Patterson, who could not abide his daughter's ambitious "nature," could with cold economic reasoning fully accept his grandson's lack of it. As far as his

Entrée Dishes with coronet finials
Samuel Kirk
1837
Silver, stamped on underside
"S.M.B./1837" for
Susan May Bonaparte
Maryland Historical Society
Gift of Mr. and Mrs. John J. Neubauer Jr..
1987.133.156.1.1a,b; 1987.133.156.1.2a,b

Detail, entrée dish's coronet finial
Samuel Kirk
Silver
Maryland Historical Society
Gift of Mr. and Mrs. John J. Neubauer Jr..
1987.133.156.1

Detail, entrée dishes
Samuel Kirk
Silver
Maryland Historical Society
Gift of Mr. and Mrs. John J. Neubauer Jr.
1987.133.156.1_1

grandfather was concerned, Bo had made the right choice, "for what could he have promised himself by forming connexions in Europe where his family were all on the decline and must in all probability be reduced to poverty," Patterson wondered.[64] The marriage to Williams ensured his future, which the spend-thrift Bonapartes could not have done. The bride's wealth made Bo's lack of ambition irrelevant.

Elizabeth saw Bo's marriage as a rejection of his Bonaparte legacy and, more significantly, as a conspiracy driven by her father. Five months later, her brother Edward confirmed this suspicion. "The whole business was managed by Jerome [Bo] & his grand-father with George [Patterson, their brother] to advise." Patterson, who had never approved of Europe, knew Elizabeth's intentions for her son and engineered an outcome he knew would anger her. As Edward observed, "it was a purely *mercenary transaction* . . . carried through in a purely mercantile spirit and admits of *no palliation*." To add to the insult, Edward reassured Elizabeth that she should not "fear seeing the couple in Europe," because Bo "must have sense enough to see that [Williams] is not in any respect qualified for a trip of that kind."[65] Bo had chosen a woman ill-equipped to travel in the European social circles his mother believed superior to all others. The marriage represented the ultimate rejection of all Elizabeth's values and aspirations.

Edward's and Elizabeth's conclusions notwithstanding, Susan possessed many of the same qualities that had made her mother-in-law a success in European society. She "has the finest figure you ever saw, with a beautiful complexion

[and] has great ambition & industry," Nancy Spear remarked. "She was born rich & her education has been attended to."[66] Furthermore, surviving books owned by Williams in the Bonaparte collection suggest that she could indeed read French if not speak it fluently. She also fully embraced the Bonaparte connection, commissioning silver with coronets and raising her sons to speak French and know their Bonaparte relatives in Europe. A surviving portrait shows her draped in ermine, the fur of royalty. This was not a woman who devalued her Bonaparte name or her "royal" connections.

There was little Elizabeth could do after the marriage but revoke Bo's allowance and write her will.[67] Given Patterson's generous gift to his grandson of $50,000 and Williams's wealth, that was a negligible chastisement. As for her will, Elizabeth did not disinherit her son or his future offspring, but she did tell her father, "strangers must not profit by my sacrifices," meaning outsiders like Williams should not inherit her wealth.

She also asked that her possessions in Baltimore be returned to her in Europe, "My instructions to Miss Spear (if he has married [Williams]) will be to send me by the first vessel sailing to Leghorn all the house Linen, plate & wearing apparel left in Baltimore," she told her father. "The box of jewels to which Jerome [Bo] has the Key could be sent by someone coming here with an inventory of its contents."[68] She wanted to make certain that none of the material things that represented her link to the Bonapartes would fall into the hands of this American daughter-in-law. Spear, who continued to manage Elizabeth's affairs while she was abroad, dutifully sent her possessions to Europe. During her lifetime, with some exceptions, she would deprive the son who had betrayed her and the daughter-in-law she thought unworthy of the possessions that documented the imperial legacy.

Susan May Williams Bonaparte (1812–1881)
George D'Almaine (?–1892)
1856
Pastel on paper
Maryland Historical Society
Gift of Mrs. Charles J. Bonaparte
x.x.5.76

Susan May Bonaparte embraced the royal connection, commissioning silver with coronets and coats of arms.

French Dressing Box with Silver Equipage owned by Susan May Williams Bonaparte
1839
Private collection, photograph by Elizabeth Moltke–Huitfeldt

Bo probably gave this dressing box to his wife, an example of the luxurious gifts he bought.

Elizabeth's anger did not prevent Bo from materially embracing his Bonaparte heritage after marriage brought him a fortune. Whereas once he had expressed disdain for the idleness and extravagance of the Bonapartes, he now constructed for himself an aristocratic existence that consisted mainly of managing investments, acquiring elegant furnishings and fashionable clothing, and raising horses. That which Elizabeth had strongly advised him against became what Bo preferred. In her book of advice, Elizabeth had written, "Money is more profitably expended on Education than on large Houses or Horses. . . . one of the most useless usages of money is to spend it on Horse feed & on Horse shoes," yet that is precisely what Bo did. Elizabeth also believed that Americans made up for the dullness of life with "superfluous expense in [the] furnishing of Houses & Table equippages."[69] Life in the

Bonaparte house, Park Avenue,
Baltimore, circa 1865
svf, Maryland Historical Society

Livery buttons, circa 1835
Silver
Maryland Historical Society
Gift of Mrs. Charles J. Bonaparte
xx.5.315 a-c

Bonaparte home on Park Avenue could not have been dull, laden with fine objects as it was.

Bo emblazoned the Bonaparte coat of arms on his possessions. A small, undated piece of paper, with a sketch and Bo's handwriting, survives in Elizabeth's papers. It reads: "My arms to be cut on a seal with the statue of the Emperor for handle."[70] The "handle" in the form of Napoléon was to be part of a silver piece that is not known to have survived, but the coat of arms and the coronet finials of the Samuel Kirk silver dinner service he and Susan commissioned told all who looked upon them that they were in the home of a Bonaparte. His liveried servants sported pins in the shape of crowns on their coats and buttons with the Bonaparte coat of arms.

A collection of household receipts in Bo's papers at the Maryland Historical Society gives evidence of a life filled with luxurious possessions, extensive household redecoration projects, and expensive cigars. Bo's extravagance, a contentious point between mother and son, began while a young man at Harvard and continued throughout his lifetime. On every trip to Paris, Bo purchased household furnishings from ormolu clocks to leopard-patterned rugs. When he died in 1870, he owned five carriages—a phaeton, a carryall, a family carriage, a coupe, and a Victoria—plus four horses valued at almost one thousand dollars. His probate inventory is that of a man who did not heed his mother's advice. The list of household furnishings in the city house and the "country mansion" comprises more than eight pages.[71]

Bo's life in Maryland bore little resemblance to what she had envisioned for the son of Jérôme, but in some ways it was the leisured, social life of an American "aristocrat." His adoption of the Bonaparte coat of arms followed the fashion of other wealthy Americans whose use of heraldic arms proclaimed their long and distinguished lineage. His own grandfather emblazoned the Patterson coat of arms—a pelican in her piety—on his possessions. Bo and Susan maintained the Baltimore townhouse but spent most of their time at Pleasant View, the country estate northeast of the city that his grandfather had given him.[72]

Bonaparte coat of arms
Box 11, MS 142, EPB Papers

Bo ordered servant livery with the Bonaparte coat of arms on the buttons.

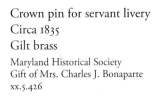

Crown pin for servant livery
Circa 1835
Gilt brass
Maryland Historical Society
Gift of Mrs. Charles J. Bonaparte
xx.5.426

William Patterson (1752–1835)
Gilbert Stuart (1755–1828)
1820
Oil on canvas
Collection of Stiles Tuttle Colwill

With the birth of Bo's son, Jerome Napoleon Bonaparte Jr., in 1830, the second generation of American Bonapartes began. Still resentful over Bo's marriage, Elizabeth did not immediately return to see her first grandchild but remained in Europe until he was four. When she did arrive in Baltimore, in 1834, she visited with her son and his family, but one historian suggests that she never developed a relationship with Susan, her American daughter-in-law.[73] Among the hundreds of letters she wrote to her family, not one survives addressed to Susan.

The birth of her first grandson, though, renewed Elizabeth's hope for the Bonaparte legacy. Her account book notes numerous gifts of cash to the little boy, and her affection for him grew as his achievements mounted. Late in life she told a friend that Jerome Jr. was "the idol of my heart." What began as small gifts during his childhood became more substantial as he matured, at times surprising him. Referring to her always as "The Madame," a habit begun by his father, twenty-two-year-old Jerome Jr. told Bo, "I wrote to the Madame the other day & thanked her for her Christmas gift. She has been unusually generous this year." Elizabeth went on to offer her grandson a $3,000 annual allowance, although later she claimed to have given him $5,000 annually for twenty years. When he eventually found himself in France, the place where she hoped he would make his life, her gifts became more lavish.[74]

Elizabeth and Bo remained distant. The many years mother and son had spent apart, together with Elizabeth's harsh criticism of his marriage, forever changed the affection that once existed between them. The boy who felt he would be "a forlorn creature" without his mother was now a man with his own priorities. Only at moments when events threatened Bo's wealth and Bonaparte legacy did mother and son unite in a common cause.

Such was the case in 1835, when William Patterson's will shocked and disappointed them both. Elizabeth's share of the vast Patterson estate was a mere four properties. This small inheritance for her ultimately meant less for Bo, who, ever eager to increase his fortunes, traveled to Philadelphia to meet with the law firm of John Sargeant and Horace Binney, whom Elizabeth had engaged to contest the will. In her wedding contract with Jérôme, Patterson had promised "a share of his estate equal to that given to his other children," but the will redacted that promise with an epic castigation of her behavior. She had, he claimed, cost him great sums of money as well as emotional distress, and had "spent" her inheritance before his death.[75] As for the lawyers, "both say, that in their lives they never read so singular a document as the will," Bo observed. "They both asked if his mind had not been very much weakened by old age." For the first time, he advised his mother. "They say it is all important, that neither you, nor myself should yet take anything under the will, as that might void the contract so be very particular not to receive any rents or exercise any act of ownership over the property bequeathed to you by the Will, as that might destroy the value of your marriage contract."[76] Contesting the will could lead to her complete disinheritance because of a clause Patterson had shrewdly inserted into the document:

> Should any of my heirs be so far dissatisfied and unreasonable as to attempt to break and undo this will, then in that case I do hereby withdraw, revoke, and annul all and every my bequests and devises, that all and every share or shares of my property here intended for him, her, or them shall be forfeited and that the same shall be divided equally among such of my other heirs who may be ready and willing to abide by and comply with this my last Will and Testament.[77]

Elizabeth relied on former U.S. attorney general Roger B. Taney for additional advice. Taney along with Sergeant and Binney agreed the will was unjust and the words "break and undo" in the disinheritance clauses, as well as the use of the term "shares," were not legal terms. Despite their opinion that the will was unjust, they all believed adjudication of claims, even if the penalty clause proved invalid, would be very difficult to pursue.[78] According to promises made in Elizabeth's 1803 marriage agreement, she was entitled to a share of her father's estate equal to that of her brothers. This contract remained enforceable, but invoking it meant forfeiting the right to protest the terms of the will. Elizabeth and Bo had to choose which legal document to fight, but to do that they would have to petition the Court of Equity "to enable them to obtain such knowledge of their rights and interests." In the meantime, neither Bo nor Elizabeth could collect on their settlements. It was a Gordian knot of legalities that produced extensive correspondence between Bo, Elizabeth, and the lawyers. Bo, whose contact with his mother appears to have been minimal after his marriage, was now central to all the correspondence regarding the matter. Where money was concerned, he was his mother's son and would fight to win what was theirs.

In later years, Elizabeth wrote extensively and angrily about the will and subsequent lawsuit. "The moral leprosy engendered in the Stagnant Trough of Avarice & mad selfishness of my horrible Father & his true representatives his precious sons was for me a plague & pestilence never to be driven off, never to be purified from."[79] Her brothers, Joseph, Edward, and Henry, joined forces against her in the suit, bribing her aunt Nancy Spear to give them Elizabeth's letters and using the threat of blackmail. Only her brother George shared his portion of their mother's estate with Elizabeth and stepped out of the suit.[80] To fight Patterson's last blow seemed to Elizabeth to be a hopeless endeavor, one that ultimately cost her a lifelong closeness with Spear and her long-time ally, her brother Edward. She had depended on both for personal and financial advice, but their loyalty, in her mind, ended when they defended Patterson's will.

Her father's final affront represented a loss of more than his love and money, both of which she had lived without most of her life. She now felt she had lost her son as well. In one of her account books, Elizabeth wrote, "It will be proved that certain unnamed persons loved my inheritance better than they did my company." Her son stopped writing to her with affection. "He never says 'Dear Mama' any more. He doesn't end with anything," she observed regretfully.[81] Bo's relationship with her became businesslike, nothing more. To others, he called her simply, "Madame." Although Elizabeth attributed this behavior to the lawsuit, she never recognized that Bo's coldness probably began when she condemned him for his marriage and rejected his wife.

On May 6, 1835, Taney wrote to the lawyers and officially terminated the suit, but Elizabeth's bitterness toward her father, aunt, and brothers festered for the rest of her life. Acting upon this hatred for her relations, in 1840 she purchased a lot in Green Mount Cemetery for one hundred dollars. She recorded it in her account book with the remark, "I hope never to be buried at Cold Stream because my Father & Robert & Edward & John his sons are there interred."[82] More than twenty years later, Elizabeth was still seething over the injustices of the will and in 1857 wrote, "The burden, which the cold iron hearted stolid tempered Father had laid upon me, still & will ever cast a deep

black shadow even from his grave."[83] She filled the pages of her notebooks with resentments and affronts, most of them originating from her father's actions.

Throughout the 1830s, instead of shifting his life entirely to America as Elizabeth feared he would, Bo actively maintained ties with his French relatives. When in 1837 he learned that his cousin, Louis-Napoléon Bonaparte, intended to visit the United States, he invited him to stay with the family at Pleasant View.[84] Unfortunately, Bo's letter arrived too late for Louis-Napoléon to travel to Baltimore and the men did not see one another until a year later in Paris. Born only three years apart, the two had first met during Bo's visit to Rome in 1826 and from that point onward maintained a regular and affectionate correspondence.

By the spring of 1838, despite Edward Patterson's assurance to Elizabeth that she should not "fear seeing the couple in Europe," Bo began planning a trip to the Continent with Susan and their son. Travel abroad continued to be difficult, because, despite his American citizenship, he was still a Bonaparte and Bonaparte family members were banned from entering France. On June 23, 1838, Bo wrote to Lewis Cass, the American ambassador to France, letting him know his wish to travel to Paris with his wife, her mother, his son, Jerome Jr., and "one coloured man servant." The family planned to sail on the packet to London, stay in Britain for a short time, and then make their way

Elizabeth's parents and many of her siblings are buried in this now abandoned family cemetery where her father's Cold Stream estate once stood.
Maryland Historical Society

to Belgium and Italy. Their final destination would be Paris. To travel to France, Bo's only choice was to use the Patterson name on his passport. His connections to his father's family and particularly to Louis-Napoléon, who had staged an uprising against the French government in 1836, made obtaining visas a challenge. On October 20, 1838, he wrote to Cass:

> I am a citizen of the United States about to go to Italy and anxious to pass through Paris and such other parts of France as would form part of the route. I find myself unable to obtain the necessary passports for that purpose on account of my connexion with (being a nephew of) the late emperor Napoleon. The whole of the Bonaparte family are prohibited to enter France by a special law enacted for that purpose. As however, I am aware that many members of my family have at different times by making the necessary request been furnished with passports for the purpose of going to France, and as I am advised that such a request would be readily granted in my case, I take the liberty of addressing myself to you, begging that you will be good enough to procure from the proper authorities in Paris a passport which will enable me to pass through France. I shall be accompanied by my son (8 years old) & one servant & as I wish to attract no attention whatever during my stay in Paris (which will be very short) nor during my passage thro' France (which will be very rapid) I should prefer that the passport should be made out in the name of Edward Patterson rather than in my own name.[85]

Five days later, Bo received word from Cass that "the government [is] disposed to accommodate you, but at the same time it has been intimated that it would be desirable to restrict your residence in Paris to as short a time as may comport with your convenience." Shrewdly, Bo pointed out to Cass, "A *few* weeks in Paris will suit my purpose very well, the more so as *few* being a relative and indefinite term may be made to apply to almost any number."[86] On December 7, Bo received the welcome news that permission had been granted for the family to eventually travel to Paris. Tongue-in-cheek, Cass asked Bo for his solemn promise "not to excite a revolution" during his stay in that city and informed him that the family needed separate authorization to bring a carriage and baggage into France and would have to submit to a full inspection of all their possessions. In Geneva, Bo had difficulty securing the necessary visas from the Austrian government to enter Italy. "I am a citizen of the United States, married to a citizen of the United States, the greater part of my property is there," he wrote to Ambassador Henry Muhlenberg. "I live there. I have never meddled either directly or indirectly with European politics."[87]

Despite Cass's assurance that the family could travel to Paris, their visas were denied. On September 3, 1839, after more weeks of frustration, the family was finally granted visas to travel to Marseilles, the closest Cass could get them to Paris. This trip, plagued with difficulties, undoubtedly brought back memories of Bo's first attempt to enter Paris in June 1819. Finally, on October 20, 1839, the necessary visas were granted and the family could travel to their long-sought destination.[88]

After Bo had briefly returned to Baltimore, the Bonaparte family drew him back to Europe. On August 26, 1839, writing from Geneva, Bo explained to Cass that he needed his assistance once again because he had "some business in Italy connected with the will of Cardinal Fesch."[89] This time, he and Elizabeth joined forces and returned to claim his inheritance from Cardinal Joseph Fesch. He also took the opportunity to see his cousin, Louis-Napoléon, having missed seeing him in Baltimore. Bo had met his uncle, Fesch, during that first trip to meet Madame Mère and now stood to collect 50,000 francs in inheritance; the estate would also benefit his son, Jerome Jr., who was then nine. As late as 1845, Bo remained unable to collect the legacy. Writing to his Italian lawyers on September 8 of that year, he noted that "seeing that the residuary legatee (the prince of Canino) does not think that I have any rights under the will, it appears to me that the only course left is the one you point out, viz. to take

Joseph Fesch (1763–1839)
Charles Meynier (1768–1832)
1806
Oil on canvas
Ministére de Finance, France

Bo's great-uncle, Cardinal Joseph Fesch.

competent legal advice concerning my rights."[90] The Bonapartes, always cordial and welcoming in their communication with Bo, consistently resisted any financial acknowledgment of him as a legitimate descendant of Jérôme, a "true" Bonaparte. This attempt to secure the legacy failed amidst a tangle of legal impediments in large part created by the Bonapartes and the ongoing dispute about Bo's identity.

Twelve years later, in 1857, Bo continued to engage lawyers regarding the settlement of the Fesch estate. Bo's half-brother, Prince Napoléon, obtained an official decree in 1857 that all the funds for "tous les enfants Bonaparte" from eight to eighteen would be sent to France and managed by the Imperial family, effectively nullifying the part of the legacy Fesch intended for Bo's sons.[91] Although Jerome Jr., at twenty-seven, was now too old to receive anything from the Fesch estate, Bo's second son, Charles, born in 1851, was young enough that this ruling made him a rightful heir. Despite his eligibility, Charles never received a settlement from his great-uncle's estate. For almost four decades, Bo, sometimes with his mother and sometimes without, waged a battle with the Bonapartes. On one hand, Bo was motivated by a sincere desire for recognition of his identity, but this was also a struggle to receive the financial remuneration that would accompany his acknowledgment as a legitimate member of the family. It was the latest phase in the battle Elizabeth had begun in 1809 when she wrote to the emperor Napoléon, demanding acknowledgment for her son, and it was not to be the last.

Jerome Jr.

The protracted legal issues with the Fesch estate stand as one of the many incidents in the lives of Bo and Jerome Jr. that illustrate the nature of the Bonaparte family's relationship with their American relatives. Just as Elizabeth once facilitated Bo's connections to the family, so did Bo for Jerome Jr. By maintaining cordial relations with his French family, he was laying the groundwork for his son's future. Despite his decision to reside in America, Bo's attention to the Bonaparte legacy was no less focused and determined than that of his mother. He did, however, express it in different, perhaps more direct ways.

Although she was devoted to Jerome Jr., Elizabeth remained on the sidelines of her grandson's life. For much of his childhood and youth, she stayed in Europe and let his Bonaparte legacy come to him primarily through his father.

His surroundings in the family's Baltimore home reinforced that Bonaparte identity. Coats of arms and
crown finials, portraits and marble busts of
Bonapartes, and miniatures of his Bonaparte
cousins reminded the boy of who he was and
what his name meant.

Beginning in young adulthood, Jerome Jr. displayed a pride in that legacy.
When he was eighteen he wrote to his
grandmother, complaining about Elizabeth's friend, Harriet Stewart, who repeatedly sent him letters addressed to,
"Jerome Bonaparte Patterson," which he
found annoying. "You might also say
that I do not annex the name of Patterson
to mine as I am quite satisfied with the
name Bonaparte."[92] He went on to warn that
the letters likely would not reach him, and
that if they did he would not accept them because that was not who he was. The desire to affix
Patterson to Jerome Jr.'s named plagued him years later
and always drew the same reaction: he was a Bonaparte and
that last name was all he required.

In 1847, Jerome Jr. entered Harvard, his father's alma mater, but the
school did not suit him and he remained there only two years. From an early
age, his interest was in the military, and his experience at Harvard only
strengthened his desire to attend West Point. That he staged a cockfight in his
room hastened his departure from Cambridge. Fortunately, Bo had begun a
letter-writing campaign to his friend and former Baltimore neighbor, Robert
E. Lee, then the superintendent of West Point, and on April 1, 1848 received
a letter from J. W. Ligon informing him that his son had received an appointment.[93] Life at the military academy agreed with Jerome Jr., and reports to
his father about both his comportment and achievement brimmed with
praise. On June 18, 1851, a senior officer wrote to Bo, "The examination of the
second class closed today with their examination in Chemistry & I am much
pleased to say your son acquitted himself in a manner very highly creditable

Jerome Napoleon Bonaparte Jr.
(1830–1893)
George D'Almaine (?–1892)
1850–1852
Pastel on paper
Maryland Historical Society
Gift of Mrs. Charles Joseph Bonaparte
xx.5.74

to him. I have taken every opportunity since I have been here of enquiring not only of the professors & assistant professors but of his fellow cadets as to his standing & without hesitation, or any exception, my information is most satisfactory in every respect."[94] Jerome Jr. soon began teaching the other cadets French and eventually was appointed assistant professor of French in 1850.

Despite the favorable reports, Bo exerted pressure on his son to do better, achieve more. His expectations at times seemed unreasonable to the boy, just as Elizabeth's demands on Bo had once appeared to him. Bo, an obsessive horseman, expressed particular distress when his son's grades in horsemanship were less than perfect. A frustrated Jerome Jr. replied, "I observe you say something about the marks in riding—as they do not count in stand[ing], they are not of much importance, except perhaps in getting an office in the cavalry department in the first class year."[95] Ironically, in later years Jerome Jr.'s career in the French cavalry won him honors and recognition.

On February 3, 1850, the winter of his second year at West Point, Jerome Jr. informed his father that he was not going to be one of the top five cadets in his class. He confessed,

> There is one portion of your letter which really gave me great pain. . . .
> My intention was anything but what you seem to think, for I merely
> meant to save you the disappointment which you must necessarily
> experience if you set your heart upon my having a place among the
> five. Since I have been here I have made quite as great an exertion as I
> am capable of & you see the result. I do believe my talents are suffi-
> cient to raise me a file or two if I had more industry, but it would be
> impossible for me to get into the five if I were to study from morning
> to night, for the five men who are there now are far superior to me in
> every respect; and there are several others who have the advantage of
> untiring perseverance. Now I don't want you to misunderstand me &
> think that I am not making you a proper return for your affection,
> anxiety & care towards me for I have already made a greater effort
> than I ever thought it possible for me & I can with perfect truth say
> that it has been almost entirely on your account; for *like you* I am
> somewhat wanting in ambition. I only hope that I may be able to
> keep it up, but I must say that I look forward with something like

dread to the two long years after furlough, as the application which I have given to my studies for the last eighteen months has been far from increasing my taste for study."[96]

Jerome Jr.'s attitude toward ambition differed markedly from his grandmother's. In one of her journals she wrote, "Every Man ought to endeavour at Eminence (not) by pulling others down but by raising himself & enjoy that pleasure of his own Superiority without interrupting others in the same felicity."[97] She had pummeled Bo with exhortations to be ambitious, yet she appears not to have done the same to Jerome Jr. Instead it was Bo who prodded his son to aim higher.

But Jerome Jr. had acquired a sense of his own goals and a recognition of his limits. He also saw in his father what others, including William Patterson, had seen. Bo never had tremendous ambition, and like father, like son. "You may observe that I have underscored 'like you' above, & you may think it rather strange that I should accuse you of want of ambition after your expressing such a desire that I should take a high stand in my class," Jerome Jr. explained. "But I don't consider ambition the desire that those connected with us should be distinguished. I have plenty of that desire myself. . . . What I call ambition is the desire of superiority for oneself and I know that *neither of us* has much of that. I don't know what is the reason with you, but with me it comes from a sort of feeling that '*le jeu n'en vaut pas la chandelle*' [The game is not worth the candle] as Ma expressed it in one of her letters."[98] In other words, possessing great ambition and making great efforts are not always sufficiently rewarded. Jerome Jr.'s definition of ambition did not match his father's, just as his father's had not matched Elizabeth's. He would pursue things he deemed to be important. He measured accomplishment for its value to one's self.

Despite the fact that he was not the highest-ranking cadet in his class, he experienced the "notoriety" his name alone brought. In 1851, he told his father,

> It amuses me to hear . . . all the . . . foreigners, who come here, talking about me. They think that you have every much the same power in this country that Louis has in France & that if I want anything done, all I have to do is to mention it. These French people are very anxious that I should get a leave next winter, as they want to

give me a dinner & ball & all sorts of things. I explained to them that I could not get a leave unless upon my urgent business, but I found that I might as well try to kick down a stone wall as persuade them that I could not do just as I please.[99]

To those on the outside, the Bonaparte name meant absolute power. The young cadet found that amusing.

Although Elizabeth was an absent figure in her young grandson's life, her devotion to him increased as he matured. During his brief time at Harvard she often sent him gifts of $25, $50, and $100 and later, during his tenure at West Point, she sent him letters and more money. Elizabeth visited West Point on at least one occasion, his graduation, where her appearance is said to have caused a stir, but the cadet never mentioned that in his letters. She also gave him "a present of the white heron feather which Murat gave the King [Jérôme], when 'both these worthies' were young."[100] Although Jérôme, his grandfather, had only been king of Westphalia for a few years before becoming prince of Montfort after 1816, he had once been a king, something Elizabeth wanted her grandson to remember. To her, he was the future of the Bonaparte legacy and the feather was to remind him that his grandfather, if ever so briefly, had ruled a kingdom.

Bo and Susan's second child, Charles Joseph Bonaparte, was born on June 9, 1851. Bo wanted Jerome Jr. to be the godfather and wrote to Captain Breverton at West Point to ask that his son be given leave. "It has always been my intention and desire that Jerome my eldest son should stand as Godfather of his infant brother, in the ministrations of the sacrament of Baptism."[101] Jerome Jr. did receive permission to return to Baltimore and the family delayed the baptism. On January 11, 1852, Jerome Jr. wrote to his father,

> I should have liked very much to have passed the holidays with you all, so that Charlie could have been christened. Has Ma determined to have the ceremony performed by a catholic priest, for that is a sine qua non if I am to be the God father. I am not a religious person mais je tiens beaucoup à la religion catholique [I am very attached to the Catholic religion] on account of my having been brought up in it & also on account of its being that of my forefathers, to say nothing of my really believing it to be the true one. Seriously speaking, I hope Ma will excuse me if she intends to have the ceremony performed by a protestant."[102]

Susan and Bo raised their sons in the Catholic tradition, despite Susan's Protestant faith. As Jerome Jr. pointed out, he believed in Catholicism not only for its religious meaning but because it was the religion of his "forefathers," the Catholic Bonapartes, not the Protestant Pattersons.

Young Charles Joseph received an education similar to that of his father and brother. Elizabeth thought her new grandson a "prodigy" and told her friend, Martha Custis Williams Carter, "he was born religious, was fond of reading his Bible as early as age eight." She recalled a conversation with her young grandson in which his pride in his name impressed her. Elizabeth explained how she had said, "Charles, it is a grand thing to have a grand historic name." To which, she recalled, "He replied yes grandma if one lives up to it, it is."[103] At six, Charles began attending a French school, Tusculum, directed by Monsieur and Madam Bujac. By the time he was ten and his brother and father were in Paris, he was writing to them in French, showing off his knowledge of grammar and vocabulary just as his father had once done at about the same age. Even as a young boy, his proficiency was striking, yet as an adult, he never corresponded in French or mentioned his mastery of the language.

While Charles was learning to walk and talk at his parents' Park Avenue home, Jerome Jr. continued his studies at West Point. On April 29, 1852, publishers Edwards Lester and Edwin Williams wrote to Cadet Bonaparte, explaining that they were preparing a "new historical work," and wanted "all the information" he could provide on his branch of the Bonaparte family. They then asked for a portrait of Elizabeth "in her youth," one of Jérôme at about the same time, and one of himself. "We are all proud of having a grandson in this country of the only brother of Napoleon now living and we wished to have a short sketch of your life and insert your portrait near that of the 'King of Rome.'"[104] His legacy as the grandson of the former King Jérôme had not escaped public notice.

In a self-effacing manner, Jerome Jr. replied, "My life as you may suppose has been very uneventful so far. I was born at Baltimore on the 5. Nov. 1830 and entered the military Academy as a cadet in June 1848. I expect to graduate next month and obtain a commission in the army. I have no portraits of myself or any of my family here, but my Father has them all in his possession." Bo, the keeper of the Bonaparte history and the material objects and images that documented it, was happy to share them, but with a proviso. He wrote to Lester and Williams, "It will give me great pleasure to afford you any information I may

Jerome Napoleon Bonaparte Jr.
(1830–1893)
Ernst Fischer
1850
Oil on canvas
Maryland Historical Society
Gift of Mrs. Charles J. Bonaparte
xx.5.73

Jerome Jr. in his West Point uniform

possess about my family whether of the American or European branch, with most of the elder members of which I have been well acquainted. . . . I have no disposition to keep back any fact concerning the family. My only desire being that what is published should be strictly conformable to the truth." Whether Bo permitted his son "to run down to New York and allow Mr. [Mathew] Brady (205 Broadway) to take a superb daguerreotype of him at our expense," as Lester and Williams requested, remains unknown. One daguerreotype of Jerome Jr. in uniform survives in the Maryland Historical Society's collection. While he was at West Point, his parents also commissioned a portrait of him in uniform. In 1856, Elizabeth had George D'Almaine of Baltimore copy the painting into a pastel portrait that was still in her possession at the time of her death.[105]

Jerome Jr. graduated in 1852, ranked eleventh in his class, and held in high esteem by his superiors. Prior to graduation, he expressed a desire to go to Europe before beginning his service. His grandmother, who had asked him repeatedly to go abroad with her, offered to pay for the trip. Bo and Susan were well aware of Elizabeth's manipulation, particularly with regard to money, and worried that in Europe she could set her grandson on a path he did not wish to follow simply by bribing him with gifts.

Jerome Jr.'s responses indicate that he understood their concerns and, more importantly, Elizabeth's ambitions for him. In January, before his graduation, he tried to put the matter to rest. "You seem to think I have some insane idea of living on the Madame & entering into her schemes for legations & all that nonsense, but I can assure you that I am well aware she has no idea of supporting me & as for the legations, I would not have one if I could get it," he told his father. "I must either be in the army or do nothing—well the latter alternative I can't take, so I must take the former." His reference to "legations" suggests that Bo and Susan thought Elizabeth might attempt to place the boy in a diplomatic post as part of a scheme to link her grandson to Europe, just as she had tried to do with Bo years earlier. Jerome Jr. went on to explain the reasons behind his desire to go abroad.

I never had the slightest idea of asking any favor of Louis [Louis-Napoléon Bonaparte]. All I wanted was to go to Europe on leave of absence for a year after I graduate—pass the winter in Paris & in the spring go to Germany & Italy—reach England about the summer & after travelling over that country come home and join my regiment. The reasons why I wanted to go as soon as I graduate were first, because it would certainly be much more agreeable to me to be in France while Louis is in power – 2d – because there is nothing in the world for me to do here & I could consequently be very well spared & ideally because I thought the Madam might possibly give me some kippies [money] for the trip now that she is in the humor of it, & I know she will not give me any if I wait two years, and lastly because the younger I shall be better able to enjoy all the sights than after two years when I may possibly have a chronic diarrhea to bear company during the journey.[106]

Jerome Jr., n.d.
pvf, Maryland Historical Society

His explanation is revealing on several accounts. The first is that he recognized this as an opportune time to visit France because Louis-Napoléon Bonaparte had assumed the role of president of France in December 1848. Given Bo's close relationship with his cousin, now President Bonaparte (later emperor), it seemed an ideal time to visit Paris. Secondly, Jerome Jr. remained unsure of his future role in the military; he leaned toward the cavalry but was not certain he could obtain a desirable position. Thirdly, he knew his grandmother's changeable nature and wanted to take advantage of her generosity while it was still offered. Even Susan and Bo could not dispute that observation about "The Madame." But Bo and Susan prevailed. "Since you consider [the European trip] premature I am satisfied to go out West & hunt buffalo for a couple of years & then get the leave of absence," he told them, and ordered his dragoon uniform. It would consist of "a shell jacket & a pair of black pants. I am only going to be extravagant in one particular & that is the shell jacket, which is to be the handsomest thing of the kind that can be turned out."[107] Like his father and grandmother, Jerome Jr. knew that the finest attire made the best impression.

Shortly after graduation, Jerome Jr. was commissioned a second lieutenant in the U.S. Army and joined the Texas Mounted Artillery. He began running scouting missions along the Rio Grande. Conditions at Fort Ewall and Fort Inge, the two posts where he spent much of his two-year tenure, were in sharp contrast with the harsh winters of West Point. In 1853, he wrote to his mother from Fort Inge, "I was sent out in pursuit of a party of Indians, who had committed depredations on the Rio Grande. . . . we were in the saddle . . . 14 hours. . . . We had not tents, nothing but the wide canopy of heaven to cover us. My bed consisted of my india rubber cloth, a pair of blankets & my horse blanket with my saddle for a pillow." Life in Texas, far removed from the privileges of Baltimore, suited him. "I was old as a child, but the life at West Point & out here has made me young as a man," the twenty-three-year-old philosophized. Despite temperatures in excess of one hundred degrees, swarms of mosquitoes, and flies in his food, he did not ask for leave to go to Europe at the end of 1853. At first, he requested only two months away from service. If his application was unsuccessful, "I cannot think of throwing off my commission. It will be the fortune of war & I must endeavor to bear it . . . for it shall never be said of me that I resigned to get off of duty. . . . In case of refusal, I shall feel it my duty to serve at least another year with the regiment before thinking of resigning." As always, Jerome Jr.'s ambition came from a sense of duty, his standard for himself. "I do not think I shall ever regret having come out here. . . . I have seen more real service than I should have done in ten years in the States," he said of his time in Texas.[108]

Jerome Jr.'s request was not honored and, in April 1854, he wrote to Secretary of War Jefferson Davis, explaining, "My application for leave of absence of 12 months not having been approved, I have the honor to ask permission to leave the United States for six months for the purpose of accompanying my Father on a visit to my family in France. I would respectfully state that I have never seen my Grandfather, who is now advanced in years." Advised by Robert E. Lee, Bo told his son he must give a single reason for his request: he wished to see the emperor of France. This second request could not be denied and, in fact, by the spring of that year, father and son made plans to depart for Europe. Lee, pleased with the outcome of his advice, remarked to Bo, "I am very glad to hear that you and Jerome are about to embark for France. It would be as agreeable to you as beneficial to him and I think you can fairly take great pleasure in comparing him with his princely relations. When worth makes the man and rank is but the stamp, his head can tower as lofty as the best."[109] Jerome Jr.'s "princely relations" provided full justification for his time away from the army.

Little did Lee know, but his time in France would re-direct the young man's military career for the next two decades.

It is in the letters Bo and Jerome Jr. wrote during this trip to Europe that a picture of the complex relationship between the French and American Bonapartes fully emerges. Rather than viewing this relationship through the lens of Elizabeth's disappointments and regrets, Bo's letterbook and the letters sent to Susan by her son reveal the inherent contrast between the private attitude of the Bonapartes toward Bo and Jerome Jr. and their publicly projected affection for them.

Arriving in Paris on June 18, 1854, Bo immediately wrote to his father, whom he referred to exclusively as "the King." In 1854, Jérôme's fortunes had risen with the success of Napoléon III, Louis-Napoléon Bonaparte, who had served as the first president of the Second Republic and, when denied a second term, engineered a coup d' état to become emperor. Appointed governor of the Hôtel des Invalides in Paris with an annual salary of 45,000 francs, the former King of Westphalia resumed living well at the Palais Royale.[110] Bo found his father "*tendre* & affectionate, verily engaged, having an appartement prepared for our use, the rooms very handsome . . . but I respectfully declined." On their second night in Paris, Bo and his son dined with Emperor Louis-Napoléon and Empress Eugénie at St. Cloud. "If I had made my reception myself, nothing would have added to its kindness and cordiality both from the Emperor and Empress," Bo observed to Susan with pleasure. Jerome Jr., wearing his uniform, was met with great interest and particularly enchanted the empress. "The King, & in fact all of the family, are as kind as possible to both of us," he informed his mother. "I get along remarkably well, for not being excitable in my temperment, I do not feel in the least embarassed. . . . I talked to [Empress Eugénie] fully an hour the night I was presented. . . . She admired my uniform very much."[111]

LEFT: Jérôme Bonaparte, former king of Westphalia, secured a government post when Louis-Napoléon engineered a coup-d'etat and became emperor of France.
Photograph by Pierre-Louis Pierson
undated
Private collection

Empress Eugénie (1826–1920), wife of Napoléon III.
Library of Congress

Mathilde Bonaparte Demidov
(1820–1904) financially supported
her father.
French, undated
Private collection

Bo and Jerome Jr. found themselves navigating an ever-shifting landscape of Bonaparte family resentments and intrigues. Tensions lurked just beneath the surface of cordial dinners at the Palais Royal and St. Cloud. Jérôme's children from his marriage to Catherine of Württemburg—Princess Mathilde and Prince Napoléon Joseph—greeted their American relatives with a mixture of concern and pleasure. "We dined at Mathilde's . . . she and the king, not being on speaking terms, which I very much regret," Bo observed. Jérôme's lifelong habit of extravagance made him, for several years, financially dependent on his daughter, Princess Mathilde. For a time, Mathilde provided him with an allowance of 40,000 francs from the annual 200,000 pension she received from her former husband, Prince Anatole Demidov. The break between Mathilde and her father stemmed, in large part, from her refusal to continue his allowance once he was receiving a generous salary from Napoléon III.

Bo expressed delight when he saw that his half-brother, Prince Napoléon, was not well liked, especially by the empress. "Everyone abuses Plomplon dreadfully and I am most happy he is not here," he remarked.[112] The derogatory nickname, "Plon Plon," "Plomplon," or "Plomb plomb," originated among the troops he commanded during the Crimean War, when they discovered he was afraid of the sound of exploding bombs—"plon." Bo's disdain for his half-brother grew as the events of the visit unfolded.

Shortly after their arrival in Paris, Bo presented the emperor with papers to establish his legitimacy, one of the main reasons for his visit. Louis-Napoléon looked over them and, according to Bo, said, "if they [the details of the case] were so . . . that the 1st Napoleon for the purpose of founding a dynasty had dissolved the 1st marriage of my father, but never had had any idea of committing an injustice or making me illegitimate, that he believed me to be perfectly legitimate to the laws of France as well as those of every other country; that it would not suit his views at all to have my son about him, except comme mon cousin [like my cousin]. . . . we had a full interchange of ideas about the King and entirely agree in opinion."[113]

The cousins may have agreed about Jérôme and where he stood in that matter, but months later the emperor and particularly Plon Plon would not. Bo's resentment of his half-brother grew by the day. "Plomplon has the worst character of any one I ever knew," he told Susan, "I never knew a human being so . . . detested by every one great and little as Plomplon."[114] Plon Plon saw a threat in Bo and Jerome Jr. Standing next in line to the throne, he feared that the emperor's acknowledgment of their legitimacy might mean they would usurp his future power. Bo, though, saw establishing his legitimacy less as a way of attaining the throne than as a means of finally defining his identity as a Bonaparte. After decades of dispute about who he was, Bonaparte or Patterson, legitimate or not, American or French, he wanted the matter settled publicly. "I have no desire nor idea of interfering with others, I only want to establish my rights." Unlike Elizabeth, who focused on Bo's right to the throne, her son never wrote about wanting any such thing: "All I wished was to have my own rights & not in any way directly or indirectly interfere with theirs," meaning Mathilde and Plon Plon, he reiterated in a letter to Susan.[115]

Bo's perception and Plon Plon's could not have been more opposed, but Jérôme made matters worse when, pressured by Plon Plon to turn Bo away from France, he began to object to Bo and Jerome Jr.'s presence in France. "He [Jérôme] is the only person here who gives me any embarrassment as he is the only one who is not sincere," Bo told Susan. Once again his father proved to be a disappointment. Just as Jérôme had expressed kindness to his son in the 1820s, and later sent him away in favor of Plon Plon, now once again he wanted his American family out of the way. By July, Bo was spending less and less time with his father. Where once they had dined together regularly, he explained, "I am dropping off gradually, now my dinners are reduced to two per week, as soon as I can do it without being observed, I will reduce them to one a week." In that same letter, Bo told his wife how "The Director des affairs civiles . . . told him [the emperor] signed the decree . . . that this admission into his *civil family* entitled me to 100000 francs a year, which he proposed dividing between Jerome & myself in the following proportions viz 70000 frs to me and 30000 francs to Jerome & asked me if I would be satisfied with the amount and the division." Bo felt strongly that he had accomplished his purpose and obtained a "plain, open, truthful statement of facts, bearing honesty & firmness on its face."[116] He could also now see his relationship with his father for what it was, insincere and based on obligation. "He wishes for the public to appear very kind to me, and we are to all appearances very well together, but our feelings are unchanged, and if it

Napoléon Joseph Charles Paul (Plon Plon) (1822–1891), Bo's half-brother, with sons Louis and Victor.
French, undated

were not for my own purposes I would not go near him, and if [it] were not for his own purposes he would not receive me."[117] Linked in name, but nothing more, father and son danced a dance of affection in public while privately disdaining one another.

Although Bo devoted himself to the matter of his legitimacy, he also poured considerable energy and money into buying large quantities of clothing for himself, his wife, and his young son, Charles. Turning to his half-sister Mathilde for advice about the linen he wished to buy for Susan, he made a seemingly bizarre request, "[I] . . . asked her to shew me her linen, or under-clothes, which she did. . . . I told her the reason was simple I wished to have a complete set of linen made up for you & wanted to see hers to know what was necessary."[118] Susan was to have linen fit for a princess at an expense of several thousand francs. In addition, Bo commissioned a number of dresses, all modeled on examples worn by the empress and Mathilde. For Charles, then only four, Bo commissioned a "small red cap with gold lace . . . exactly like the cipi [kepi] of a 2d. Lieut. dragoons such as Jerome Jr. wears in undress."[119] Much as his mother did throughout her life, the wardrobe worn by the next generations of American Bonapartes signified their ties to French royalty. Bo might not want to be king, but he would dress his family as if he were.

During this visit, the emperor and empress developed strong ties to Jerome Jr. and wanted him to remain in France. Aware of his military accomplishments in the United States, the emperor offered the young American officer a position in the French army. Jerome Jr. delighted in the offer but prudently informed the emperor that he could not accept a position unless it was one equal or better to the one he held in America and that he would only serve in the cavalry. Furthermore, like his grandmother, he wanted to know what "the kippies"—his salary—would be. Writing to his mother, he explained that Louis-Napoléon "had been thinking over the matter & come to the conclusion that the best would be to give me a place as 2d lieutenant. As a member of the 'famille civile,' I would receive 30,000 francs [$6,000] annually in addition to my pay." Tellingly, the emperor "remarked that he thought it would have a very good effect on the army to have *one* of his family among them & one who could bien faire son métier [do well in his profession]." The emperor went on the say that Joachim Murat, though a successful second lieutenant in the Imperial Guard, might do well, but "ça n'a pas le nom de B—" (but he was not a Bonaparte).[120] This distinction reinforced what Bo wanted most for himself and his sons, full acknowledgment as members of the Bonaparte family.

On learning of the emperor's decision, Jérôme wrote to him in outrage about the presence of the American Bonapartes in their midst, claiming their residence in Paris made bastards of his children.[121] Despite this, the emperor and empress remained unchanged in their feelings toward Jerome Jr., and their loyalty to the young man infuriated Jérôme, who saw it as a betrayal. Eugénie fretted over how hard the young officer was working while learning the French military commands at Versailles. As Bo related it, she said Jerome, Jr. "is working very hard, so hard that he has again become very thin. . . . his aunt who told him on Saturday last, that he looked starved '*et quand on est gentil, joli garçon, bien placé dans le monde, et son nom est Bonaparte, vraiment mon cher neveu, ce n'est pas la peine se lever à quatre heures du matin*'" (and when one is a nice, handsome lad, well placed in the world, and his surname is Bonaparte, really my dear nephew, it is not worth getting up at 4 in the morning).[122] Bo told Susan that their son did not share this sentiment and worked harder than any of the Bonapartes in the army.

Locket, engraved, containing photographs of the Bonaparte family
Circa 1870
Brass
Prince Murat
Maryland Historical Society
Gift of Mrs. Imogene Anderson
1959.117.3

Joachim Murat (1878–1901), Second Lieutenant in the Imperial Guard and close friend of Jerome Jr.

While in Paris, Jerome Jr. fully embraced his status as a Bonaparte and ordered livery for his groom that consisted of a "green coat, silver buttons with a B on them." Bo and Jerome Jr. were allowed to adopt this livery, which differed from the emperor's only in its silver trim. "I believe I am the only person (except sovereigns & royal princes) to whom he ever lent it," Bo added with obvious pleasure.[123] Bo consistently placed great importance on these outward signs, more than his son would later. He also considered such material gestures from the family to be proof of the Bonaparte link, yet, as events unfolded, symbols of the Bonaparte legacy did not reflect reality within the French Bonaparte family.

By the fall of 1854, Jerome Jr. was in Sebastopol on the Black Sea, a second lieutenant in the 7th Dragoons. The empress, whom he referred to as "*ma tante*" ("my aunt") wrote to him frequently. While many of the soldiers were suffering "a great deal—numbers of frozen feet," he enjoyed "the pelisse . . . fur cap . . . fur gloves and a sac lit en peau de mouton"—a bed sack of wool she sent him.[124] He could work as diligently as any soldier, but *his* gifts from home came from the empress herself.

When he spent a leave in Paris the following year, he and his father encountered yet another attempt to separate them from the Bonaparte name. In an effort to placate Plon Plon and Jérôme, the emperor offered Bo and Jerome Jr. the titles of Duke and Count of Sartène in Corsica. They refused. "I have come from a long private audience with the Emperor where I explained to him fully my views," Bo wrote Susan. "I do not think there will be any more talk about a title." A month later, he told Susan that the emperor confessed to him that he was "urged" by Jérôme and Plon Plon "to *make* Jerome [Jr.] and myself take the titles, simply with the insane idea of sinking (or obliterating) our name." He continued, "The Emperor does not think it would have that or any other injurious effect; I differ with him and think I gave him so many unanswerable arguments against any title at this moment, that he will not return to the subject, but I regretted to find that he ever had seriously entertained the thought."[125] Sorely disappointed by this conversation with the emperor, Bo now knew he had one less ally in his struggle for acknowledgment as a Bonaparte.

Jerome Jr.'s service in the Crimea won him a promotion to first lieutenant in less than a year. As Bo told Susan, "the minister of war & all the French army are enraptured with Jerome's conduct." Jerome Jr. told his mother about Plon Plon's declining reputation in the Crimea. After Plon Plon was accused of avoiding the bloody battle at Inkerman, the people of Paris "no longer call the Prince Plon Plon . . . but Craint Plomb meaning "fears lead." Amused, he added, "There is another bon mot about him which is attributed to my aunt [Empress Eugénie]; when he left here he had all his beard & it is said she remarked on his return, '*Il est revenu d'Inkerman avec une barbe de sa peur.*'" (He has returned from Inkerman with the beard of a sapper.) This was a play on the word "sapeur," soldiers who were permitted to wear a beard into battle.[126] Even Empress Eugénie mocked Plon Plon with this word-play, saying, "sa peur," or "his fear." The news not only delighted Bo and Jerome Jr., it thrilled Elizabeth, who took great pleasure in Plon Plon's failures despite keeping a miniature of the boy with her until her death.[127] A few years later, reflecting on her grandson's time in the Crimea, Elizabeth wrote to a friend, "the Crimean War had shewn that Sous Lieutenant Bonaparte, my grand son, had evinced that courage under fire demanded by the military name of his family & by the blood of an American."[128] In a moment of uncharacteristic patriotism, Elizabeth attributed his remarkable bravery to the duality of her grandson's identity: his name was French, but his courage was American.

Elizabeth pasted notes and cartoons in her scrapbooks, including these mocking Plon Plon's marriage and his reported cowardice on the battlefield.
Box 16, MS 142, Maryland Historical Society

Furthermore, his fame brought attention back to her story, something that pleased Elizabeth's continued desire for celebrity.

Although the emperor and empress, Jérôme, and members of the Bonaparte family continued to receive Bo and his son in Paris, the warm feelings of their visit in 1854 had cooled considerably a year later. Mathilde, once so attentive to Bo, no longer wrote to him. "The gossip in Paris is that Plon Plon frightened Mathilde so much when he saw her about Jerome & myself, that she joined the coalition against us." He also noted, "The King's [Jérôme's] opposition has been unceasing & open since my absence from Paris." When Mathilde did invite Bo to dine, the situation became clear to him. Although "her feelings are unchanged," he thought, Jérôme had successfully allied the family against him and his son. Undaunted, Bo summarized the situation. "They [the Bonapartes] play their game & I play mine, the future alone can develop who will be the winner, but for the moment, the King seems to have united them."

Siege of Sevastopol
Franz Alekseyevich Roubaud
(1856–1928)
1904
Sevastopol Rotunda, Crimea

Jerome Jr. consistently earned praise and commendations for his military prowess. Plon Plon's continued anxiety and fear of explosions resulted in his demeaning nickname.

The crux of the issue was Jerome Jr.'s military prowess, which inspired considerable jealousy, especially after he received the Order of the Mejidie from the Sultan of Turkey in 1855 and the Crimean medal from Queen Victoria in 1856. While in the Crimea, he fought at Balaklava, Inkerman, Tchernia, and Sebastopol, as well as in numerous small engagements and skirmishes.[129] In every instance, his conduct won him praise. In contrast, Plon Plon bore his demeaning nickname for the rest of his life.

As Paris celebrated the fall of Sebastopol on September 11, 1855 with a "te deum" sung at Notre Dame and "an illumination," Jerome Jr. grew concerned about his position in the army. His uneasiness stemmed from the situation in Paris. The emperor's attempt to force titles on him and his father, coupled with Jérôme's growing antipathy and Plon Plon's anxiety, made him wonder if he would have to resign his commission and return to Baltimore. Susan thought it certain the emperor would send her husband and son home, but her son

Jerome Jr.'s medals: the Legion of Honor, Mejidie, Decoration of Military Valor, Médaille d'Italie, and Crimean Medal

Image courtesy of Stack's, Bowers, and Ponterio

wondered, "What do you suppose induced him [the emperor] to give me a place in the army? I did not ask him for it—it was his proposition & if his desire was that I should remain here, the way he went to work . . . was novel certainly."[130] When he reflected upon the emperor's actions, he was mystified. Once again, messages from the Bonaparte family were mixed.

Not wanting to abandon his military career, but preferring to avoid the Bonapartes' intrigues in Paris, Jerome Jr. wrote to the emperor on April 14, 1856, requesting a post in the cavalry in Africa, and ten days later the minister of war informed him that he would join the 1st Regiment de Chausseurs d'Afrique. He immediately ordered his uniform in the striking Zoauve style and made plans to leave Paris for an assignment that was "next to Paris the most agreeable one in the army." He described Algiers to his mother as "on the seaboard, only 24 hours by steam from Marseille & the residence of the Governor General of Algeria." Far from the days of using his saddle as a pillow in Texas and Spartan living conditions in the Crimea, Jerome Jr. now found himself living in a style more befitting a Bonaparte. He rented a sizeable house with a "*salon, chambre à coucher, cuisine et deux petite pieces*" (parlor, bedroom, kitchen and two small rooms). In addition, he now had a stable for his horses and a shed for his carriage. He bought French furniture for his rooms, including a "*table de jeu*" *en acajou*" (a mahogany gaming table), and ordered "worsted damask" curtains for his "salon." Despite spending lavishly on his accommodations, he nevertheless considered his status uncertain. "If all is up, my trip to

Jerome Jr. in the Zouave uniform
of the 1st Regiment de Chaussers
d'Afrique, circa 1856.
Collection of Denis Gaubert

this place will have been attended with great expense & not a little trouble. . . . if I am to leave here to return to the land of the free & home of the brave, I confess that I do not care to work quite so hard." In the same letter, he told his father to use his influence in Paris to get him a promotion. His fate in France might be undecided, but if he remained in the cavalry, he wanted to be captain.[131]

Jerome Jr.'s anxiety about his commission was not unfounded. At Jérôme's urging, the emperor consented to assemble a Conseil de la famille to determine the status of the American Bonapartes: could they use the Bonaparte name or not? Name alone was not the issue—if Bo and Jerome Jr. were Bonapartes, they could be considered in the line of succession, and therein rested the debate. The Conseil de la famille, composed of members of the Bonaparte family, the minister of state, the minister of justice, the presidents of the senate and the assembly, a member of the council of state, the president of the Court of Cassation, and a marshal of France, would decide the question. For months, Jerome Jr. hoped that the weekly steamer would bring news of the council's ruling. In August he confessed to his father, "I am able to take things very coolly. No one here has an idea of the state of the case. . . . I manage to preserve a charmingly calm exterior. I confess however that the wrenchings in my stomach in the morning are frightful."[132] Bo, who suffered from the same stomach ailments as his son, must have felt great sympathy.

Then, on June 13, 1856, Jerome Jr.'s Medal of the Medjidie arrived with the name "Patterson" affixed to Bonaparte. It was not the first time such a "mistake" had occurred, but he could not dismiss it with mild irritation, as he had when Harriet Stewart wrote to him under that name. "The letter that accompanied it [the medal] is signed Mr. B.[onaparte] simply. I signed the receipt B., after having remarked to the officer that they had added a name which did not belong to me." In his mind, this affront clearly indicated what his fate would be. He feared that his name would now be published in *The Monitor* with "Patterson" for everyone to see. Disheartened he wrote to his father, "We might as well bring things to a close at once & retire in exile."[133]

164 ⚜

If fate was going to send him back to the United States, he intended to spend his last days in Algeria in royal style. He threw a dinner for ten, complete with "champagne frappé, sherry & burgundy," vowing to "economize in the U.S." later. Unlike his father, who continued to believe the ruling would favor him, Jerome Jr. formed his own opinion. "You always regard him [Plon Plon] in the same light as he appeared to you as a boy in Florence, but I have studied him as a man, & I discover new traits every day in conversing with people, which only tend to confirm my belief. He is universally detested by every one."[134] His pessimism proved justified. The Conseil de la famille ruled that, although Bo and his *descendants* could use the Bonaparte name, they would not be considered members of the *famille civile*. What the emperor had given to Bo and his *descendants* in 1854 was now reversed. They were Bonapartes in name only.

Elizabeth was not surprised by the ruling. She penned in her red journal, "To those who believe in Divine Justice & in its participation in the Events of this world the Conseil de la famille was a punishment devised by God for the wickedness & treachery of old Jerome Malaparte, who grudges us even the Candle ends & cheese parings of the party now in Power & which he may thank [us] for enabling him to dance with glee to the tune of 'Money in Both Pockets.'" She also wrote to her grandson, who remarked to his mother, "She [Elizabeth] is very much excited about the Conseil de la famille & her letter abounds in invective against the King."[135] Elizabeth poured out her vitriol in letters to her son and grandson, and decades later continued to rage about this decision.

In a letter to his cousin, Emperor Louis-Napoléon, Bo was unusually direct in rejecting the conseil's decision. "Since my birth is legitimate and has always been so recognized by my family, by the laws of all countries and by the whole world, it would be the height of cowardice and of dishonor to accept a warrant of bastardy." Jerome Jr., too, was frank when he spoke to the emperor. With the matter of the Medal of the Medjidie still on his mind, he wrote to his father, "I told him . . . it was impossible for me to change my name during your life. I put it on your shoulders."[136] Bo did not protest. In fact the emperor did not want one of his more talented cavalry officers to resign, but he left Jerome Jr.'s position nebulous and allowed him to return to Algiers.

The ruling by the Conseil de la famille, which Elizabeth followed with intense interest, pasting articles about it in her scrapbook and writing about it

Louis-Napoléon Bonaparte, le Prince Impérial et Son Chien Néro
Jean-Baptiste Carpeaux (1827–1875)
1865
Bronze
Maryland Historical Society
Gift of Mrs. Charles J. Bonaparte
xx.5.48

Louis-Napoléon Bonaparte (1856-1879) was the only child of Napoléon III and Empress Eugénie. This line of descent ended with his death and the title went to Plon Plon's son Louis.

Bataille de Solférino
Adolfe Yvon (1817–1893)
Undated
Andreas Praefcke

Jerome Jr. led a victorious cavalry charge directly into Franz Joseph I's Austrian army at the battle of Solferino in June 1859.

in letters and in her journal, inspired her to investigate once again the legal issue of her marriage. In 1857 she sent her 1803 marriage contract to Pierre Antoine Berryer, the Paris lawyer Bo had engaged to continue investigating his case. Recognizing the decline in Jérôme's health, Bo thought his father's death might allow him to overturn the Conseil's ruling. Elizabeth agreed.

Meanwhile, Jerome Jr. added to his military reputation, thereby further elevating the French people's opinion of the American Bonaparte. In June 1859, as captain of his regiment during the fierce battle of Solferino, when French and Sardinian forces led an assault against the Austrian army of Franz Joseph I, he led a cavalry charge directly into the "Austrian squares." A day after the battle he told his father, "My regt. led the charge & suffered terribly—10 officers & about 100 men killed." The next day he wrote a four-page account of the engagement, confessing, "The battle was on such an immense scale that I only know what took place in the right wing where we were." He did not, at that point, even know what the battle would be called, but he said it "would make

LEFT: Jerome Napoleon Bonaparte, Jr. in uniform of the Cuirassiers, unknown artist, circa 1870, oil on canvas. Private collection, photograph by Elizabeth Moltke-Huitfeldt

a page in history."[137] Bo proudly informed Susan that their son "made one of the most brilliant & affective charges of cavalry ever known without receiving injury—his regiment lost in killed & wounded about one man in seven." At his club in Paris, Bo heard gossip that "the King has withdrawn his opposition & asks the E[mperor] to reward him for his gallant conduct." Whether or not that was true, the emperor awarded Jerome Jr. the Médaille d'Italie for his gallantry at Solferino. Bo also gleefully reported to Susan that the battle had resulted in yet another example of Plon Plon's cowardice.[138]

When Bo returned to Paris in the spring of 1859 to meet with Berryer and contend with his legal case, he found the Bonapartes to be more than just cold. "The King [Jérôme] has taken no notice of my desire to see him." Mathilde, then residing several hours outside of Paris, told Bo he must come to her, but Bo declined. "I am perfectly indifferent to seeing her & seeing the King would be unpleasant to me," he told Susan, adding that he had written to both of them just to "put them in the wrong."[139] In addition to investigating the Conseil de la famille's judgment, Berryer assisted Bo with the fight for Cardinal Fesch's legacy, a nine-year struggle that thus far had been unsuccessful.

Despite his difficulties with the Bonapartes, Bo commissioned a bust of Napoléon. Like Elizabeth, he separated current reality from his desire to materially preserve his legacy. On July 18, 1859, he enthusiastically wrote to Susan, "Lately the French government has discovered in Egypt & purchased a magnificent plaister cast of General Bonaparte, made by a very great sculptor of the day. . . . The E[mperor] has had a marble bust made for it, the only one yet, [and] I am having one made by Iselin. . . . the cast remained forgotten for over 60 years in Egypt." He went on to predict, "[it] will produce a great effect in the US as nothing like it has ever been seen." From this statement it is clear that Bo wanted those at home who saw the sculpture to be impressed by its beauty and rarity—and by its significance.[140] Bo also commissioned a bust of his son, done much in the same manner, which to date has not been located.

Le General Bonaparte
(1764–1821)
Iselin after Corbet
1859
Marble

Maryland Historical Society
Gift of Mrs. Charles J. Bonaparte
xx.5.49

Bo ordered this marble bust of Napoléon, made from a sixty-year-old plaster cast the French army found in Egypt.

In August 1859, Jerome Jr. returned to Paris and marched in the triumphal parade to celebrate the empire's recent victory at Solferino. After seven years of hard service in the American and French cavalry, he wanted to step back from front-line service. He wrote to his mother, "Life is too short to persist in these distant parts."[141] By distant parts he did not mean France. His intention, supported by Bo, was to join the Imperial Guard and return permanently to Paris. Always suspicious of the Bonapartes, Jerome Jr. did not trust that his desire would be satisfied, but in 1860 the emperor granted him a position in an elite cavalry regiment, the 1st Carabiniers-à-Cheval. He took a large apartment in Versailles and began decorating it with Parisian furnishings.[142]

Tea Caddy
Jean-Baptiste Odiot
Circa 1816
Silver, monogrammed "EP" for
Edward Patterson
Maryland Historical Society
Gift of Mrs. Andrew Robeson Jr.
1959.118.34

Elizabeth bought this silver tea caddy for her brother Edward from Jean-Baptiste Claude Odiot, silversmith to Napoléon I. Bo patronized the same company during his 1860 trip to Paris.

Bo, too, turned his attention away from legal matters and ordered "a leopard carpet . . . a Christolphe [silver] soup tureen for 6 persons, price $17.50, two large dishes extra size for $35 each, 2 butter boats, $11 each, an egg boiler, $11."[143] In patronizing the silver company used by Napoleon III, Bo once again made the same choice Elizabeth had made when she bought silver from Odiot, silversmith to Napoléon I. The American Bonapartes would live with furnishings fit for royalty.

Bo again added to Susan's wardrobe. "Mrs. Burns [the milliner] is attending to your things. . . . she has found out that a new kind of square cashmere shawl trimmed with guipere lace . . . [is] being gotten up for the Empress, the Princess, Mathilde and Clothilde [Plon Plon's wife]. Of course," he explained, "they cannot be worn in Paris until after they appeared on them, when they will become very fashionable next winter. . . . I asked her to try & get you one in green."[144] When Bo returned to Baltimore and his wife wore this new cashmere shawl, she could say it was just like that worn by the Bonapartes in France; perhaps she would even wear it sooner than the women of Paris. When she used her silver tureen, she could say it came from the silversmith to Napoléon III. Like the bust of Napoléon he had recently commissioned, material possessions acquired in Paris represented more than just aesthetic choices. They symbolized the Bonaparte legacy in cashmere, silver, and marble. Visitors to the Bonaparte home in Baltimore would have no idea that the relationship with the European Bonapartes remained tenuous at best; the objects in the Park Avenue house told another story.

Shortly after Bo's return to Maryland in 1860, Jerome Jr. wrote to his father about the ever-evolving politics of the Bonapartes. With Jérôme's failing health and imminent death becoming apparent, "Plon Plon is all powerful at present. Ses idées triompant sure la ligne [His ideas triumph on the line]." Where Bo and Elizabeth had seen Jérôme's impending death as their opportunity, Jerome Jr. saw it as the rise of Plon Plon to great power and influence over the Bonapartes, Emperor Louis-Napoléon and Empress Eugénie included. On June 26, 1860, he told his father, "The King died on Sunday last at 5 1/4 pm at Villegenis."[145] Jerome Jr., no longer part of the family circle and refused access to his grandfather before his death, was not present. "As I was not informed of his death, I have just written to the Emperor a letter and asked to be allowed to attend the funeral." In that letter, Jerome Jr. expressed his hope that, as Jérôme's grandson, he would be allowed to assume his rightful place among the mourners.[146] Bo, who was back in Baltimore, would be unable to attend, but Jerome Jr., residing in Paris, saw the effect that Jérôme's death had on the populace. Though not well loved, "His death has broken the last link which bound the present with the past. He was the last man who took a prominent part in the gigantic events of the first empire & his name was surrounded by a certain prestige and respect as the only remaining brother of the great Emperor."[147] Bo and his son may have remembered Jérôme as a disappointment, but Jerome Jr. was objective enough to recognize the lingering attachment to the former King of Westphalia. Removed by two generations from the many disappointments Jérôme had inflicted upon his grandmother and his father, he could see the situation in Paris more clearly.

Locket, circa 1870
Brass
Engraved locket containing photographs of the Bonaparte family
Princess Clothilde
Maryland Historical Society
Gift of Mrs. Imogene Anderson
1959.117.3

Princess Clothilde of Savoy, Plon Plon's wife

Although he expected to be denied a place at the funeral, he was granted a spot in the "tribune de la famille" or family tribunal. Seated with "those who have no rank, I was of course in the last [tribune]." He wore "full uniform" and was given a chair, which was a compliment considering that some associated with the emperor were relegated to benches. He told his father, "As usual [my cousins] were all delighted to see me & I am convinced the public think us a united family."[148] The harmony of the family remained part of the show, and he participated in it knowing full well the truth that lay beneath the spectacle.

The empress expressed her regret that he and his father would not "accede to the wishes of the Emperor" because, as Jerome Jr. explained, "She thinks that even now, if we would be reasonable, the Emperor would feel disposed to do as he promised."[149] That promise—to keep them in the "famille civile "—had been made six years earlier and been vacated long ago due to the efforts of King Jérôme and Plon Plon. But the family did not want a lawsuit because of the scandal it would occasion. Eager to step out of the proceedings, Jerome Jr. urged his father to come to Paris quickly. "Your presence is absolutely necessary here. . . . It is utterly impossible for me to attend to . . . my military duties."[150] He added, "it produces a very bad effect for me to meddle with these affairs, as I appear to push myself forward in things over which I have no control." This was his father's fight and, just as he had once put it on his father's "shoulders" when he defended his name to the emperor, he now stepped back from the suit.

Elizabeth's bitterness about her annulled marriage had never abated, and her resentments only grew as she followed Bo's efforts to gain acknowledgment from the Bonapartes. She vented her spleen in her journal, proclaiming Bo, "The grand Son of Jerôme the great, yes the Legitimate descendant of Jérôme Le Grand old Père Malaparte." She was outraged when her use of the pension from Napoleon was called into question during the lawsuit. "Let them chew the curd of Sweet & bitter fancy. We interfered not with his [Jérôme's] inglorious Past – his prosperous Present or his promising Future. . . . The brutal & ill Judged Effort to bastardize you has, in the opinion of Everyone, proved to be a palpable failure, & has inflicted upon its authors a heavy Damage, from which they can never recover. It has recoiled upon those whom old Jerome extended to benefit by perjury."[151] Like her son, Elizabeth wanted to right a wrong that had long ago been committed and endured; blinded by that desire, she ignored developments in Paris that pointed against the future success of Bo's case.

Jerome Jr. was caught in the middle. While his father was in Baltimore, he traveled back and forth between Paris and his post in Tours to deal with the lawyers. He also spent considerable time with the Murats, longtime allies, who shared with him their insights into the palace's stance on the matter. In a letter to his father, he explained the Bonapartes' perspective regarding the marriage and pension. "If she [Elizabeth] rec'd it for herself as stated by the Palais Royal it might be considered that she acknowledged the nullity of the marriage & recd. it as a compensation, whereas if it was for you, it was acknowledgment of your existence."[152] He told his father to gather any relevant correspondence and documents that could bolster the argument that Elizabeth had only used the pension to support her son. In fact, her meticulous management of the pension and use of only the interest it generated was well documented. Jerome Jr. also informed his father of the status of Cardinal Fesch's long disputed legacy. It "has been divided among the Emperor, the King, the children of Lucien [Murat] and the Canino children as they are the heirs of Joseph [Bonaparte]."[153] The Fesch settlement would never come to them.

With Jérôme's death, Bo promptly returned to Paris, not to mourn his father but to bring all his energies to bear on his court case. His mother went, too. Together, they first gathered all the relevant documents, including birth certificates and Elizabeth's marriage contract with Jérôme. Mother and son, estranged since Bo's 1829 marriage but briefly united in 1835 and again in 1839, now joined forces once more, as they had against the Pattersons. Berryer filed his suit against Prince Napoléon ("Plon Plon") on September 6, 1860.

The crux of the suit, stated by Berryer and his associate, Charles Legrand, demanded "an accounting, liquidation, and distribution of the assets constituting the estate of His Imperial Highness, Prince Jérôme."[154] The French defense, led by M. Allou, articulated many of the old arguments against the validity of the marriage, embellishing them to include accusations concerning Elizabeth's character. He also cited Patterson's will, and the criticisms of his daughter found in it. Allou contended that the pension from Napoléon was proof that the marriage had been nullified, and insisted that the 1856 ruling of the Conseil de la famille decisively invalidated it. On this last point, he argued that the same issue could not be brought back to the court again and again.

Elizabeth cut out several articles on the case for her scrapbook, including one entitled, "The Best of the Bonapartes." "Now in Paris," it read, "There is, in fact, no reasonable question about the insufficiency of the pretenses urged by the EUROPEAN BONAPARTES. Whatever the decision may be, the case offers some points so honorable to the American branch of the family as to deserve mention." The French court could disparage her character, but, the reporter maintained, albeit inaccurately, despite the bribes of the Bonapartes, "To none of these seductions did this noble American lady for a moment listen." Furthermore, even if the court ruled against Bo, "the moral stature of this man will greatly and always out-tower the grandest of the Bonapartes." Another article observed, "a century ago the Pattersons were as important as the Bonapartes and a quarter of a century ago the Bonapartes were in exile, [and] were glad to claim the kindred they now refuse to acknowledge. No one imagines that the dynasty which now controls France will last longer than the life of its present head and . . . many will live long enough to see the Bonapartes again in exile."[155]

On February 15, 1861, the court ruled in favor of Plon Plon. Encouraged by M. Duvigne, who acted as a "friend to the court" and represented the French attorney general, Bo and Elizabeth appealed the case. It is not clear whether Elizabeth was as certain as Bo was that the courts would decide in their favor, but in July 1861 the court rejected their appeal. Jerome Jr. wrote to his father, saying,

> I saw Legrand yesterday at the Madame's immediately after the judgment had been rendered. It was as every one (except yourself) supposed it would be, a confirmation of that of the first tribunal. . . . The Madame is determined not to appeal to the Cour de Cassation [Court of Appeals] & says that if you wish to do so, you will have to do it alone. . . . I think it would be useless to go any further, as every one agrees in saying that you have affaire à trop forte partie (You are dealing with too strong an opponent). . . . In the cour de cassation . . . none of the judges are sufficiently independent to go against Plon Plon whose power increases daily. You have public opinion in your favor, but it is useless to hope for an instant that you will have the decision of the tribunals in your favor. Don't fancy that I think you ought not to have brought the suit. On the contrary I am strongly of opinion that you could not do otherwise, but you have now done everything in your power & it would be injurious to struggle any longer in the case when you have all the power against you.[156]

Although she was concerned about the money they had spent, Elizabeth nevertheless paid half the expense of the suit and turned to her letters and journals to vent her anger. On July 18, 1861, she wrote to her son, "There existed no one single individual in France, who ever supposed we should have justice done us by the French Tribunal—because Plon Plon reigns triumphant, & is, no one knows exactly why, Master of the situation. . . . I will not be dupe enough ever to try Justice in France under their dynasty."[157] For the rest of her life, she replayed this injustice in words that grew ever more severe with time.

Elizabeth departed Paris in July and landed at New York in early August, regretting that she had had to leave her grandson. "Were I to remain here I

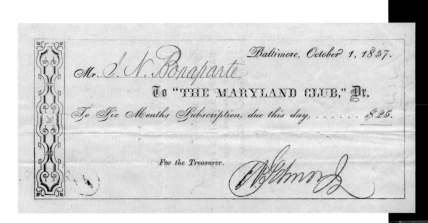

should be able to tell Jerome quantities of things useful to him, which his present position renders it impossible for him to learn from any other person," she told Bo. "My greatest talent is diving & divining."[158] Jerome Jr. was not advancing in the Carabiniers as she had hoped, and she blamed Plon Plon and the family conspiracy for denying him a promotion.

Having abandoned any further attempts to fight the Bonapartes, Bo returned to Baltimore in 1861 and resumed his life of leisure, at his home in Baltimore and Chestnut Wood, his country estate, occupied by his young son Charles and his horses and carriages. He and Susan navigated the Civil War, siding with the Union and separating themselves from many of his fellow Baltimoreans, who allied themselves with the South. The Maryland Club, a private gentlemen's club in Baltimore's Mount Vernon neighborhood of which Bo was the first president, supported the Confederate cause so ardently that he no longer felt capable of maintaining his membership. Following the Pratt Street Riot of 1861, when Massachusetts troops passing through Baltimore opened fire on a violent mob, Baltimore became an occupied city, and many suspected Southern sympathizers found themselves thrown into prison. Jerome Jr., who followed the events in his hometown, joked with his parents, "I imagine that the whole of you had been seized as conspirators against the government." Jerome Jr. found the resistance of some Baltimoreans to the Federal cause puzzling. Like his grandmother, he thought of the fiscal advantages the war offered Union sympathizers and observed to his father, "What I do not understand is why there should be so many secessionists in the Monumental city. . . . What strikes an unbiased mind is that by remaining quiet Baltimore was destined to profit immensely by the war from the simple fact of the passage of so many troops & the necessary apparatus which they must have made."[159]

LEFT: Membership receipt for the Maryland Club
Box 6, MS 144, JNB Papers, Maryland Historical Society

ABOVE: Jerome Napoleon Bonaparte (1805–1870)
John Dabour (1837–1905)
1876
Oil on canvas
Image courtesy of the Maryland Club

Posthumous portrait of Bo, first president of the Maryland Club, a social club whose members included some of the most prominent men in business and politics.

Chest on Stand
Unknown cabinetmaker
1783–1880
Red cedar with applied walnut panels
Maryland Historical Society
Gift of Robert A. Fisher
1928.7.1

Bo served as first president of the Union Club, a group of prominent Baltimore unionists organized in 1863. The chest was built to hold the thirty-five star flag that flew daily from the club's headquarters during the Civil War.

Calling card for Bibi, Jerome Jr.'s dog
Box 11, MS 142, EPB Papers

Given their sympathies, Bo and Susan found their social life radically altered. In 1861, Bo formed the Union Club, an organization supportive of the Federal cause. Susan, with her New England roots, remained more staunchly Unionist than her husband and often paid her husband's lapsed membership dues to the club. Some believed she also worked for the Union cause by spying on her neighbors and reporting them to the Federal authorities. J. Thomas Scharf, a historian of early Baltimore, recorded an "exact copy" of a letter Susan wrote to General Nathaniel P. Banks in Annapolis, on July 1, 1861, shortly after Federal troops had taken up positions in the city. "I enclose a few names from a source entirely reliable in every respect. I am waiting to add some others for another direction, but as Mr. Bonaparte thinks these will answer your present purpose, I beg leave to submit them to you."[160]

While the United States struggled through four years of war, the tides of French politics continued to shift. Napoléon III's Second Empire had begun to show signs of decline. In 1861, France allied with England and Spain against Mexico, hoping to seize that country and thereby gain access to trade with Latin America. Although Jerome Jr. was not sent to Mexico, those events turned attention back to the American Bonaparte in Paris. On July 3, 1863, the *Baltimore Sun* reported rumors that Jerome Jr. would assume "the diadem of the Montezumas" and rule Mexico for France. He, of all the Bonapartes, had attained the military honors to prepare him for the role; even some French newspapers agreed.[161]

Although the accounts proved untrue, Jerome Jr. continued his military career in France while maintaining his relationship with the emperor and empress. In 1865, Louis-Napoléon promoted him to the Cuirassiers, the senior branch of the cavalry. Two years later, the emperor elevated him again, appointing him to the Dragoons de L'Imperatrice. During this period, Jerome Jr.'s service was nothing like the hard duty of his early career. His letters home, often written from Paris, talk of theater with Murat and even his dog, "Bibi Bonaparte." "Bibi was asked in marriage by one of my friends," he joked. "He returned today, but did not say whether he was pleased or not. If his children resemble him, I might send the Madame one of them." His grandmother possessed a great fondness for dogs, once writing in the margins of a book: "The more I know of dogs and cats, the less I think of men."[162]

Inkwell
Circa 1861–1865
Bronze
Maryland Historical Society
Gift of Mrs Charles Joseph Bonaparte
xx.5.372

General John A. Dix, commander of Union troops in Maryland early in the war, gave this sarcophagus-form inkwell to Bo. Dix and Bo maintained a friendship throughout the war and, when he could, the general spent time at the Bonaparte house.

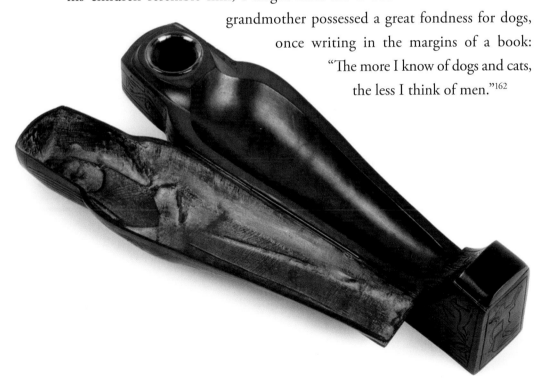

After the failed lawsuit of 1861, mother and son united only one more time. Following Bo's return to Baltimore in 1861, he and Susan found themselves embroiled in marital strife. The cause is not evident in surviving correspondence. Perhaps Bo's prolonged absences in Europe had begun to wear on Susan, who was left to care for their young son Charles without her husband's assistance. Faced with the possible dissolution of his marriage and domestic life in Baltimore, Bo returned to the other "home" he had come to know, Europe, and, surprisingly, brought Elizabeth with him. On November 10, 1863, Jerome Jr., on learning of this breach between his parents, wrote to his mother:

> I was much surprised to hear through the Madame that she & Pa were to sail on the *Persia*. I was in Paris to receive them. . . . On Saturday morning he announced to me your determination not to live together for the future. As you may suppose I was much distressed at this unfortunate termination of 30 years of marriage, but I have asked no details as to the cause, for I do not wish to be the judge between my parents. I still hope that this separation is not definitive & that by mature concessions, you will arrive at a more suitable termination of past difficulties. I do not consider it the part of a son to give counsel in such a case & the more so from the fact that I am completely at a loss to comprehend how people who have lived happily together for as long a period should be obliged when old age is coming, to separate. . . . the result of such decision must be most disastrous to us all.[163]

Divorce meant scandal in 1863, and all the American Bonapartes, being members of a socially prominent family, would suffer in the press if the separation became public. Jerome Jr. recognized as much when he noted that such a thing would be "disastrous to us all." Like Elizabeth, he knew that reputation in society mattered. Bo and his mother stayed only a few months in Paris. At seventy-eight, Elizabeth found the trip more arduous than expected and suffered a fall on board ship during the trip. When Bo returned to Baltimore, he reconciled with Susan, but the terms of their reconciliation are not known.

By 1870, Bo's lifelong indulgence in spirits and cigars exacted its toll, and he suffered from throat cancer for months prior to his death on June 17, 1870. In 1876, Elizabeth recalled his last days to her confidante, Martha Custis Williams Carter. Upon learning how serious Bo's condition was, she ventured to the Park Avenue house. She thought herself "the most natural person to be there" and "determined to go every day" to tend to her ailing son.[164] She was not welcomed. Susan was not at home, and a Mrs. Hoffman, who appears to have been the housekeeper, greeted her as "Madame Patterson," something Elizabeth construed as a deliberate insult, even though she had legally returned to her name of Patterson and used it frequently. She explained to Carter, "You observe [this was said] before the *dying Bonaparte*, she insinuating that [Bo] was a bastard by calling me Madame Patterson!" Hoffman commanded: "Leave this house you are not wanted here—leave this house!" Elizabeth refused and, as she told the story, remained with her dying son, whose last words to her were, "My children!" She interpreted this as "an appeal & . . . understood that he commended them to me." She believed he had asked her to look after their legacy, the one they had fought together to uphold.

Whether factual or embellished for effect, this scene touches on the troubled relationship between mother and son as the result of Elizabeth's lingering resentment toward Susan. Elizabeth concluded her story by telling Carter that before Bo died she "got him to sign a check for a thousand dollars for each of them [her grandsons] & the next day thinking to gratify the poor fellow still more, I brought another check and asked him to sign that." After years of emotional separation from her only son, in his last hours she could only reassure him of her affection by giving money to his sons.

Overcome by shock and grief after Bo's death, Elizabeth told her grandson Charles, "It would be impossible for me to view the remains of my unfortunate child—I shall be incapable of attending any of the Ceremonies or the funeral—The death of your father is harder to bear than all the other fatalities of my life." She signed the letter, "your affectionate & reliable Grand Mother Mme Bonaparte."[165] She added the word "reliable" to assure him of her continued devotion. It was the only time she signed a letter that way.

Bo's obituary in the *Baltimore Sun* described a life occupied by "business interests and agricultural pursuits," which was accurate so far as it went. If he devoted himself to anything beside his houses and his horses, it was his quest to be acknowledged by the Bonapartes as a member of the family. The obituary recounted in detail the story of his mother's marriage and listed Jerome Jr.'s accomplishments with particular emphasis on his service to Napoléon III. It acknowledged the ruling of the Conseil de la famille and pointed out that, should the ruling have been in Bo's favor, it would have given "Jerome of

The Bonaparte family lot at Loudon Park Cemetery, Baltimore; note the coat of arms and coronet on the obelisk.
Maryland Historical Society

Baltimore precedence over his half-brother and the Princess Mathilde." The author noted that "He resembled Napoleon more than any of his family" and added, "His mother, who is now 90 years of age . . . cherishes the belief, it is said, that her grandson may yet attain the position of Emperor of France."[166] The obituary did more to revive Elizabeth's story than tell her son's, but its tone reinforced his legacy, the one his mother had maintained for him. It is also carved in perpetuity on his gravestone at Baltimore's Loudon Park Cemetery. Written in Latin, it reads, "Under this stone/are deposited the remains of Jerome Napoleon Bonaparte/son of Jerome Bonaparte/He died at sixty five years of age/on the 17th of June A.D. 1870,/conspicuous of fidelity to friends, affection of his family and reverence for God. He inherited a distinguished name and transmitted it unstained to his *descendants*."[167] Absent from the inscription on the stone is any mention of Elizabeth. Perhaps that was Susan's lasting gesture toward the mother-in-law who once referred to her daughter-in-law's "dirty blood."[168]

Bo's probate inventory, comprising furnishings and possessions at the Park Avenue house and Chestnut Wood, creates a picture of two well-furnished, heavily carpeted homes. His passion for fine wines, particularly Madeira, was evident in the twenty gallons of fortified wine in the cellar at the time of his death. Valued at $1,600, the Madeira was worth almost three hundred dollars more than his 1,003 ounces of silver flat- and tableware. Nine carriages of various types, as well as the three horses he kept, were further evidence of his "agricultural pursuits," which consisted chiefly of driving his horses.

Charles, his younger son, served as his executor. Given Jerome Jr.'s absence in France, this unorthodox choice appears to have been pragmatic, but is also an early example of the role Charles assumed as caretaker for the family after his father's death.

The year 1870 undoubtedly left Susan more than unnerved. On the same day Bo died, her mother, Sarah C. Williams, also died. Jerome Jr., in Tours, France, at the time of his father's death, made only a brief visit back to Baltimore. Upon his return to France, he found himself caught up in another war and a political shift. With the commencement of the Franco-Prussian War in July 1870, Napoléon III's eroded power slipped further. After several devastating losses, culminating at the Battle of Sedan on September 1, 1870, the empire fell. Jerome Jr., a Dragoon de l'Imperatrice, aided the empress in her flight to exile in England.

With the end of the Second Empire, Jerome Jr. turned his thoughts to life as a civilian. His brother Charles, then twenty and attending Harvard, assured his mother that his brother would soon come home. "He could not as a soldier resign while war was raging, but there is no obligation for him to remain in time of peace and he is [so] thoroughly disgusted with the whole course of events in France that there will be little inducement for him to

Game chest
Burl walnut veneer, metal, ivory, mother-of-pearl
Maryland Historical Society
Gift of Mrs. Charles J. Bonaparte
xx.5.233

Bo purchased this expensive game chest in Paris.

General Reille delivers to King Wilhelm I on the battlefield of Sedan the letter from Emperor Napoleon III, 1884
Carl Steffeck (1818–1890)
Wall painting in the Ruhmeshalle Berlin (destroyed)

In 1870, after Napoléon III's empire fell at the Battle of Sedan, Jerome Jr. helped the Empress Eugénie escape to England.

"Mésalliances are Fatal in Most Families" 179

remain there now." On April 14, 1871, the *New York Times* announced "A Bonaparte Among Us . . . Colonel Jerome Napoleon Bonaparte."[169]

Once back in Baltimore, the forty-year-old retired soldier directed his attention to the one thing he had avoided for more than two decades: marriage. Dating back to his time at West Point, Jerome Jr. had frequently reassured his father that he had no desire to tether himself to a woman before establishing his career. In 1850 he wrote, "Tell Ma not to tremble for me for the older I get the less inclination I have to tie myself to a poet, as the Madame terms it . . . [I am] more circumspect every day in my intercourse with ladies on the lookout for partners." Elizabeth and Susan both worried that he would make an imprudent match. His father advised him to focus on "married women" who could amuse a young man without desiring a union. "Poets," according to Elizabeth, were people without resources, and Jerome Jr. knew enough from his father's shrewd marriage not to find a match among them. A year later, he told Bo frankly, "I would not marry a woman without money."[170] His parents and grandmother had taught him that lesson, but just what kind of bride Elizabeth envisioned for her grandson is not clear from the surviving correspondence. In 1861, when she read a report in an Italian paper that he was betrothed to the daughter of Murat, she wrote to Bo, "The contemptuous & contemptible conduct of the Bonaparte family towards myself renders a Marriage with any Member of the family either near or remote utterly impossible. My veto shall ever be affixed to marriage with any person in whose veins lingers a single drop of Bonaparte blood." Continuing her rant, she added, "I hope that neither of your sons will ever marry & above all, I flatter myself that they never marry any of the Bonapartes."[171] How far Elizabeth now found herself from the days when she hoped Bo would marry Charlotte Bonaparte and solidify the family alliance.

Jerome Jr., like his father, selected his own bride, who turned out to be an unlikely candidate. Caroline LeRoy Appleton Edgar, the granddaughter of senator and former secretary of state Daniel Webster, was a member of the American political aristocracy. Although, like Susan, she had New England roots, the family was concerned because Caroline was not only a widow but one with three children from her first marriage. On January 21, 1871, Charles, who was still in mourning for his father, took out his stationery with its heavy black border and wrote to his mother, "The General's letter was very satisfactory, though I could not make out the name of the person who had given him the information about the Edgars." "The General" may have been

John A. Dix, who commanded Union troops in Baltimore in the summer of 1861 and remained a family friend.[172] Mother and brother did some investigating. Based on several letters from 1871, an "incident" had occurred in a series of "imprudent letters" Caroline had written to Susan. These may have been written when, after the fall of Napoléon III, Caroline feared for Jerome Jr.'s life. Precisely what she wrote remained unstated, but the younger son spoke as if he were the elder, reassuring his mother, "I think the affair may serve as a lesson both to the major [Jerome Jr.] and her."[173]

On September 11, 1871, Jerome Jr. married the former Mrs. Newbold Edgar in a ceremony performed at St. Mary's Catholic Church in Newport, Rhode Island. Described as "a lovely type of American woman . . . a widow for several years," Caroline Edgar owned a substantial home in Newport and possessed sufficient means from her first marriage. Susan and Charles attended the "unostentatious, quiet affair," which was performed after the family sought special dispensation for the Protestant bride, but, as the last line of the *Baltimore Sun*'s account reads, "Madam Patterson Bonaparte was not at her grandson's wedding."[174]

Writing in French and employing the formal, "vous," Jerome Jr. informed his grandmother, "I have had the weakness to engage myself to Mrs. Edgar. C'est une folie—c'est tout ce que vous voudrez, mais je l'aime à la folie, c'est le cas de le dire." (It is madness—it is all that you will want, but I love her madly, I may well say so.) Fearing her wrath, he continued, "You have always been so kind and affectionate to me that I cannot think of letting you hear it from another than myself. I hope that although you may not approve, you will pardon my weakness and allow me to present my wife to you when we go to Baltimore. I do not dare to ask you to take the trouble to come on here to the wedding, as you assured me that you never would go to see a friend make a fool of himself, and I indulge in the fond hope that you will

Caroline LeRoy Appleton Edgar Bonaparte (1840–1911)
Fernand Paillet (1850–1918)
1892
Watercolor on ivory
Image courtesy of the New York Historical Society, gift of the estate of Peter Marié 1905.25

still look upon me in a friendly light." He then provided his grandmother with all the details. "I suppose you know that Mrs. Edgar has three children—two boys and a girl—but it may be some satisfaction for you to know that they are amply provided for by their father. Mrs. Edgar is the granddaughter of Daniel Webster, and I have the weakness to think that she has inherited some of his talent, but of that you will be more capable of judging, as you will not be blinded by your love."[175]

Elizabeth was outraged.

> The humiliating shame of Mortification, heaped on myself by Relations, amount to Fatuity, from which there is no Escape. I pity you because the remainder of your disgraced position will be a lingering remorseful agony. Mésalliances are fatal in most families, & no marriage disapproved by me will escape regret — you have chosen an eternal separation from the Best friend, Myself, whom you ever possessed. Therefore I will never admit Mrs. Edgar or yourself to my presence. The Presence of a child, who has disappointed my expectations & hopes would add to my scathing mortification & grief. The menaced marriage, so entirely beneath your position in the world & your name, fills with astonishment & regret all who take any interest in your future prosperity & happiness. It is considered the act of madness on your fated self.

Claret Pitchers (askos)
Samuel Kirk and Son
1871
Silver, with cast coat of arms and engraved "CLRB" for Caroline LeRoy Appleton Edgar Bonaparte
Maryland Historical Society
Gift of Mr. and Mrs. John J. Neubauer Jr.
1987.133.158.1.1-2

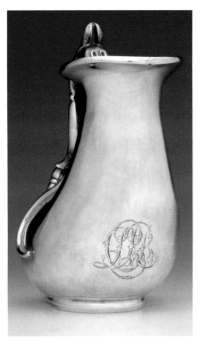

That was not all. She went on to inform him that she would stop his annual allowance of $5,000. "I will never see you after your fatuitous marriage with a widow & her three children; & I wish that you at least had not poured the last drop into the nearly overflowing cup of bitterness, held to my Lips during my Past Life, by my near relations."[176] Her reaction mirrored that which she had directed at Bo when he married Susan, even to cutting off Bo's allowance upon his marriage. Jerome Jr.'s marriage was an affront to her and to her generosity, a rejection of all she had worked to achieve for him. His bride might be wealthy and come from an esteemed American family, but she was no more suitable for a Bonaparte than his mother had been for Bo. For four decades, Elizabeth's last hope for her legacy had rested in her elder grandson, and now he "Trainer un grand nom dans la boue!!"—he had dragged his great name in the mud.

A year later she was still angry. "The report from Boston is that the successor of rich inheritance of widow & children of the Bourgeois, has paid off Mortgage on a house amount $5000," she told Charles.

> The opinion remains unchanged that the Imbecility or Insanity alone could have led any man to commit the error of so preposterous a connexion! Should he recover from insanity to reason his Life will be one long regret. There existed neither Beauty, youth, Position, Wealth to excuse his abdication of Ambition & Pride due to his name & to his Position. My sentiments differ not from Every Individual here or Else where & you know that I learn what is thought & what is said & have ever been kept informed of whatever I may be supposed to ignore.[177]

Her grandson's ambition, the trait she valued above all others, was lost when he married Caroline. Elizabeth continued to believe she knew more than anyone else, despite the fact that those who knew Caroline observed that she "is moving heaven and earth in the Bonapartist cause, and if it ever comes up again, she will be a princess. . . . she is . . . quite capable of playing the part."[178] Elizabeth would never believe it; she forever called Caroline the "Widow Edgar."

But the severity and unfairness with which her father had treated her had taught Elizabeth that a will should not become a lasting punishment for one's descendants. Her own will, first recorded in 1871, a year after Bo's death, provides some insight into her relationships with her grandsons. Although she divided her real estate and investments evenly between the two men, the original will left a third of "the rest, residue, and remainder" to Jerome Jr., but two-thirds to Charles. Her decision to give Charles more was occasioned by two events. The first was Jerome Jr.'s marriage. The second is referred to in the will as "the large sums" Elizabeth had previously given Jerome Jr. during his stay in Europe. She told her friend Carter that she had given her grandson $100,000 total. As her obituary noted, "The ruling passion of this remarkable woman's life seems to have been to regain her rights on behalf of her grandson, and she is believed to have studiously economized that her great wealth might add to his chances for the crown."[179] In 1875 she redistributed her estate with a codicil, so that Jerome Jr. shared in it equally. Much like her father, she had demonstrated her approval or disapproval through largesse. Only after reconciling with Jerome Jr. in her last years did she increase his inheritance.

She entrusted all of her possessions, though, to Charles: "the portraits of King Jerome, his grandfather, and that of myself—three heads on one piece of canvas, painted by Stuart; the cabinet portrait of myself painted at Geneva by Massot, and also the portrait made of me by Kinson . . . the furniture, silverplate, books, clothes and house linen; and also all . . . jewelry." Her writings, the "skeleton" of her autobiography, would also go to Charles. Her youngest grandson would be the keeper of the family legacy and history, not his brother.

In addition, Elizabeth decided to buy Jerome Jr.'s share of Chestnut Wood, left to him by Bo, and give it to Charles. "My desire is that you should own the whole of the country seat & that should you die before myself leaving no children it may be kept out of the possession of strange women."[180] The "strange women" referred to Mrs. Edgar and Elizabeth's daughter-in-law, Susan. This can be interpreted as a punitive judgment about her son's and grandson's marriages, and to some extent it was. After his marriage, Jerome Jr. decided on a life far away from Baltimore and resided primarily at "Harrison House," Caroline's home in Newport that she had inherited from her first husband, Newbold Edgar.

Armed with the infusion of Bonaparte money from the marriage, Caroline redecorated the sprawling cottage that still stands today, transformed into condominiums.[181] Charles frequently visited his brother, a trip made easier by Newport's proximity to Cambridge, where he was attending Harvard. He sent reports to his mother in Baltimore and happily, albeit skeptically, reported that "Carrie," as they called Caroline, thought of becoming a Catholic. Whether this was a gesture undertaken to win favor with the Bonapartes remains unspoken in the surviving letters, but the children of her marriage were all baptized

Catholic, the religion of their French ancestors. When Caroline died in 1911, the family held a requiem mass for her at St. Matthew's Catholic Church in Washington, D.C.[182]

In 1873, Jerome Jr. and Caroline's daughter, Louise Eugenie (1873–1923) was born. They named Empress Eugénie godmother. "I am pleased to learn that the recent acquisition to the family gives promise of beauty and wisdom," Charles wrote to Susan. "The latter quality she gets from her uncle and the former from her great grandmother." According to Charles, his brother was surprised and disappointed that his first child was a girl. Elizabeth responded to the news of her great-granddaughter's birth with hostility. "It does not surprise me to learn that she is very angry at the birth of Louise Eugenie for she has the knack of getting so whenever anything occurs in the family,"

Louise Eugenie Bonaparte de Moltke-Huitfeldt (1873–1923)
1915
Photograph in embroidered and beaded linen frame
Maryland Historical Society
NN1410

Charles observed. He added, "besides, I think she had set her heart on having Carrie die in her 'accouchement' (confinement) and the disappointment must be severe."[183] The family, though not entirely pleased with the marriage, were delighted that the child looked like a Bonaparte rather than Caroline. In another letter Charles remarked, "I am happy to learn that my niece and the Mamma continue to flourish. I see no objection to her [the niece's] resembling her father physically, but I hope her mental qualities are moulded on mine, for it would be a dreadful thing if she were to develop into an idiot when she reached the years of discretion."[184] Letters written by Charles to his mother suggest that the prudent younger brother who once revered his older brother now thought him an "idiot" for having made such an undesirable marriage after a remarkably successful career.

ABOVE: Sugar Dish
Circa 1835–1846
Samuel Kirk
Silver, with Bonaparte coat of arms

Maryland Historical Society
Gift of Mr. and Mrs. John J. Neubauer Jr.
1987.133.157a,b

RIGHT: Covered Sugar Basin
Samuel Kirk and Son
1876
Silver and gold, stamped on underside
"S Kirk & Son," engraved "CLRB" for
Caroline LeRoy Appleton Edgar Bonaparte

Maryland Historical Society
Gift of Mr. and Mrs. John J. Neubauer Jr..
1987.133.154

The order for this covered sugar basin
appears in a Kirk order book dated March
17, 1876, and specifies an "18K gold gallery."

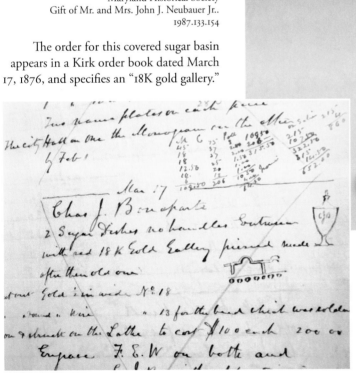

After Louise Eugenie's birth, the family traveled to France and remained in Paris for six years.[185]
Their silver still bears the Paris importation marks
stamped on it when it was shipped from Baltimore
to France.

Soup Tureen
Samuel Kirk and Son
1881
Silver, marked on underside "S Kirk & Son," monogrammed "CJB" for Charles Joseph Bonaparte
Maryland Historical Society
Bequest of Marie Louise de Pozo Rubio
1983.6

Charles Joseph

During the first years of their absence, Charles finished his Harvard law degree and frequently traveled home to assist his mother and see to his ailing grandmother. In 1873 he wrote Susan, "I have continued to think ever since I saw her in December that she was on her last legs, but I am strongly in hopes that the limbs aforesaid may serve to carry her until the summer when her decease will not so horribly inconvenience me as it would at present."[186] Perhaps this unbecoming sentiment was written for his mother's sake, but it also may reflect his weariness with his grandmother's unending bitterness and her constant carping about the injustices done to her family.

Always snide in his use of nicknames—a habit of his grandmother's throughout her life—Charles began to refer to her as the "Queen of Westphalia," knowing how it would have galled her.[187] During the winter of 1873, Elizabeth fell ill and death seemed imminent, but she rallied. "My health has improved however slowly & to the surprise of those who thought me past recovery, which all in this house did, I walk about my room Eat & sleep & expect soon to be able to resume my avocation of looking over my temporal concerns," she informed her grandson. That autumn, she reassured Charles that, "My health is neither better nor worse than when you last saw me. I totter on the streets when the sun permits me, held up by the arm of a kind Friend, who always lends her aid."[188] Earlier that year, Charles had instructed his mother to pay two different women to attend to Elizabeth's needs.[189] His grandmother's lifelong fear of being buried alive preoccupied her, and she wrote to Charles, "I

According to the Kirk order book, Charles Joseph Bonaparte placed the order for this tureen from the Kirk firm on December 3, 1881. The order listed "I Plain Tureen to hold 4 quarts." It is surmounted by the coronet used on earlier pieces commissioned for the Bonaparte dinner service. This style was first made in 1837 for Bo and Susan May and continued to be replicated for the second generation of American Bonapartes. The soup tureen is the only piece Charles ordered for his own use and is the only known instance of him emblazoning an imperial Bonaparte reference on his household goods. While Charles's wife Ellen wore Elizabeth's clothing and jewels and showcased the Bonaparte connection, Charles, as an American patriot, generally shied away from such visual references to his imperial connections. After Charles's death in 1921, Ellen sent the tureen to Louise Eugenie in Denmark. It passed to her daughter, Marie Louise, Marquesa de Pozo Rubio, and was bequeathed to the museum in 1983.

have ever been afraid of being buried alive in Lot 155 Green Mount Cemetery: Deed 691. 3d volume. . . . Take a note of the above & see that I am dead before my Burial."[190] She trusted him above anyone to see that even in death, her wishes would be carried out.

Despite his frustrations with "the Queen of Westphalia," Charles felt protective of her story and the portrayal of the Bonaparte legacy. In 1873, when W. T. R. Saffell's *The Bonaparte-Patterson Marriage in 1803 and the Secret Correspondence on the Subject Never Before Made Public* appeared in print, he found the publication irksome, and told his mother so. "I am very sorry that it has been published, for it is an absurd and indecent compilation and of no utility to any one; but in inducing the publishers to send Beasley's account of his interview with the Madame and to insert an expression of our disapproval of it, I have avoided the more serious evils which I feared from its appearance and I think we may all treat it with contempt."[191] The interview to which Charles referred had appeared in the *New York Herald* on January 17, 1873 entitled, "The Baltimore Bonapartes: Views of Madame Patterson and Col. Jerome Bonaparte on the French Situation," and Saffell had reproduced it in the back of the book.[192] Charles deemed it "the fictitious interview" and told his mother not to buy a copy; unwilling to put more money in the publisher's pocket, he would lend her the copy a friend had given him.

As he feared, both Saffell's work and the interview in the *Herald* continue to be cited by scholars as accurate depictions of Elizabeth's story. Although elements of the article correlate directly with information documented in letters written by Elizabeth, Bo, Jerome Jr., and Charles, the writer's interpretation should be called into question based on Charles's assertion that the interview was fictitious. Two weeks before the article appeared, Elizabeth had informed Charles: "I say nothing of the death of L.N. [Louis-Napoléon]. . . . Emissaries of [the] *New York Herald* called on me to learn my opinion—I refused to tell them."[193] That did not stop the reporter from writing, "She Conversed Freely Upon the Situation in France." The article stated that when discussing the "popular demonstration" at Napoléon III's funeral, Elizabeth said, "This . . . would show that the Bonaparte family were yet admired by the people, and that the empire would yet be re-established, with a Bonaparte at its head."[194] Although she may not have spoken those exact words, she had spent much of her life uttering that sentiment.

Elizabeth died on April 4, 1879, in Mrs. Gwinn's boarding house, at the age of ninety-four. Jerome Jr. had returned to Baltimore from Paris on March 26. On the thirty-first, the *New York Times* reported: "The arrival of her grandson, Col. Jerome Bonaparte, whom she desired so much to see, did not seem to have much effect upon her. She received him without any particular demonstration. . . . It had been hoped that the arrival of Col. Bonaparte would rouse her, and be a decided benefit, but in this her physician was disappointed."[195] Both grandsons were with her in her last hours. "The Madame has just expired, 1:20 P.M. C.J.B.," Charles informed his wife.[196] Knowing her fear of being buried alive, he saw that she was placed in an ice coffin for several days before her burial at Green Mount Cemetery. Charles's wife, Ellen, told Elizabeth's confidante Carter, "I wish you might have seen it, for the sweetest noblest traits of her character seemed to have been drawn out through the last suffering days."[197]

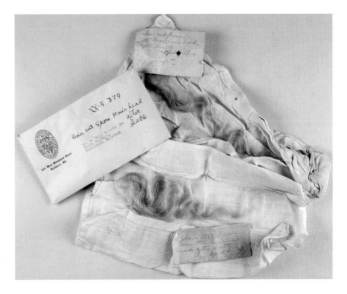

Hair cut from Elizabeth Patterson Bonaparte after death 1879
Maryland Historical Society
Gift of Mrs. Charles J. Bonaparte
xx.5.379

Elizabeth's obituary, printed in the *Baltimore Sun*, paid particular attention not only to her history but that of Jerome Jr. The grandson who "poured the last drop into the nearly overflowing cup of bitterness" she drank, remained her legacy in France. In the retelling, his military triumphs under Napoléon III seamlessly comingled with his grandmother's story. To the press, both were the story of France. The obituary writer concluded: "The

Elizabeth Patterson Bonaparte's solitary grave at Green Mount Cemetery, Baltimore.
Maryland Historical Society

Chateau Bonaparte,
home of Jerome Jr.
undated
Image courtesy of Kiplinger
Library, Historical Society of
Washington, D.C.

Medallion originally on an
oval mahogany mirror
Maryland Historical Society
Gift of Mrs. Charles J. Bonaparte
xx.5.99b

ruling passion of this remarkable woman's life seems to have been to regain her rights on behalf of her grandson."[198] Although that is an oversimplification, for more than three decades she had planned for her grandson to rule France.

After her death, Jerome Jr.'s family, including another son, Jerome Napoleon Charles Bonaparte III (1878–1945), returned to the United States. In 1880, Jerome Jr. began work on a mansion at 1627 K Street in Washington, D.C. An article in the *New York Times* in July 1881, reprinted from the *Baltimore Gazette,* described it as a Louis XIV-style three-story mansion, costing $30,000.[199] Another account noted that the "interior arrangements follow the fashion of the period in France." The furnishings were French and included "hand-carved brass chandeliers, marble and bronze mantels and mirrors . . . imported from that country as were most of the house furnishings." Jerome Jr.'s taste, formed largely by his time in Paris, was fully manifest in the house that came to be known as "Chateau Bonaparte." Even the interior bore the Bonaparte arms; the stairway was "painted in bronze and gold and bears the escutcheon of the Bonaparte family."[200] Two pieces of furniture from the 1870s survive in the collection of the Maryland Historical Society, both with polychrome cartouches painted with the Bonaparte coat of arms. Although neither the mirror nor the armoire are French, they may have come from Chateau Bonaparte. Several pieces of the home's French furniture survive, including an opulent suite of bedroom furniture dating to the Napoleonic period.

It is clear from Jerome Jr.'s choice of furnishings and architecture that, in the end, Elizabeth had succeeded in passing the Bonaparte tradition down to her son, her grandsons, and beyond. When Louise Eugenie hung portraits of Empress Eugénie and Napoléon III in the entry hall of her Denmark home, Glorup, she made her legacy clear to all who entered that her family was Bonaparte. Jerome Jr.'s life, and later the life of his daughter, wove themselves into the last relics of the Second Empire. They were entangled with the Bonapartes to the end.

Embittered throughout most of her life, Elizabeth could not see the

Armoire with Bonaparte
coat of arms
1845–1870
Mahogany
Maryland Historical Society
Gift of Mrs. Charles J. Bonaparte
xx.5.553

Napoléon III (1808–1873)
Unknown, after Franz Xavier
Winterhalter
Circa 1875
Oil on canvas
Maryland Historical Society
Gift of Mrs. Charles J. Bonaparte
xx.5.70

Empress Eugénie (1826–1920)
Unknown, after Franz Xavier
Winterhalter
Circa 1875
Oil on canvas
Maryland Historical Society
Gift of Mrs. Charles J. Bonaparte
xx.5.71

connection she had helped to forge between the Bonapartes and her descendants. "I had a letter from the Madame this week, containing no news of importance, and pitched in rather a dolorous key," Charles told his mother in 1873. "She laments that she has not the consolations possessed by most persons her age, and says it shows the ingratitude of her relatives to whom she has done much good." In Elizabeth's mind, she had amassed her fortune and secured connections in Europe for the good of future generations—and no one appreciated it. Her only living legacy was in the objects she had saved and the portraits she had hung. They alone remained, long after her son and grandsons had disappointed her. Charles recognized as much. "The Madame's letter is amusing but it is also sad. It is a melancholy sight to see this proud lady with one foot in the grave occupied not with the eternity she is so soon about to enter, but with the gratification of her malice and vanity in the world."[201] Elizabeth's family chuckled over her words, so full of resentment and laments for the past, yet Charles understood the tragedy of his grandmother more profoundly than anyone else. She would go to her grave with no faith in the history she had created.

It is ironic that the grandson who pleased her most was Charles. Despite the fact that he ultimately became the most American of all the American Bonapartes, he was her favorite. Born in 1851, two decades after his brother, he had little proximity to Elizabeth's history. During his first decade, while his father and older brother navigated the Bonapartes' world in Paris, he was learning to walk and write, and taking fencing and riding lessons. His grandmother doted on him, sometimes traveling with him to the spa at White Sulphur Springs in West Virginia. By the time Charles was a teenager, Elizabeth no longer went to Europe or continued the fight with the Bonapartes. His life would be different. His father and brother brought him presents from Paris, even King Jérôme sent him clothes when he was a baby, but his connections to that distant place and people cannot be compared to those felt by his grandmother, father, and brother. His biographer recalled a conversation Charles was said to have had as a little boy. His uncle, "grandfather Patterson's brother," said, "You are a French boy, Charlie." To this, Charles replied, "No, I am an American boy," and he remained one for the rest of his life.[202]

Charles Joseph Bonaparte (1851–1921)
Circa 1860
Sketchbook of
Charles Joseph Bonaparte
Box 5, MS 144, JNB Papers

Although Charles thought of himself as "an American boy," at ten, perhaps with his older brother in mind, he was drawing pictures of French soldiers in battle.

C. J. Bonaparte

Elizabeth's disappointment when Bo went to Harvard instead of remaining with her in Europe did not replay itself when Charles set off for his father's alma mater. As the child who remained in Baltimore, and the young man who handled financial affairs for both his mother and grandmother, Charles was less subject to Elizabeth's bitterness over the past. After graduating from Harvard and its law school, he established a practice in Baltimore, and Elizabeth relied on him for professional advice.

In 1871, at a party in Cambridge, he met nineteen-year-old Ellen Channing Day, the daughter of an accomplished American lawyer. Their brief courtship resulted in a three-year engagement during which time Charles moved back to Baltimore. When they married on September 1, 1875, their union drew no protest from Elizabeth. "I had a long drive yesterday," Ellen told her mother that October. "The Dr. says these drives are doing her [Elizabeth] much good & she is evidently pleased with my frequent attentions, for she told Miss Florence Patterson, a niece, who has tried in vain to gain favor in her eyes that I was not only quite pretty, but had very good manners, and a great deal of tact, the latter point being one which the Mde. greatly prides herself." She added with much relief, "It is such a blessing that the Madame is not an enemy; she tells people she is much pleased with me *to her great surprise!*"[203] Despite herself Elizabeth grew fond of her grandson's American wife. After decades of scorning her daughter-in-law Susan, and Jerome, Jr.'s wife Caroline, she found an American wife she could like.

In 1893, Jerome Jr. died of stomach cancer in a rented house in Pride's Crossing, Massachusetts. Obituaries recounted his military successes under Napoléon III in great detail, and the *Chicago Daily Tribune* recalled him as "the hope of the Bonapartist party." His life after the military was described as quiet and genteel. All but a few obituaries noted the Bonaparte house on K Street, which the *Washington Post* described as "filled with relics of the

Charles Joseph and Ellen Channing Day Bonaparte, 1875
pvf, Maryland Historical Society

house of Napoleon, paintings and busts, besides numbers of personal heirlooms of the distinguished line."[204] At the end of his life, his Bonaparte legacy, his close ties to Napoléon III, and his identity as a "citizen of France" distinguished him among Elizabeth's descendants. Although his grandmother's history found its way into his memorials, his story in some ways outshone hers.

Shortly after Jerome Jr.'s death, his daughter Louise Eugenie took the family's legacy back to Europe, where Elizabeth had always wanted it to be. In yet another irony, the descendant who became a European aristocrat was the great-grandchild she had scorned as an infant and probably never met. Shortly after Louise Eugenie's birth, the family left the United States, and no known letters suggest a meeting between Elizabeth and Jerome Jr.'s family prior to her death. Elizabeth definitely never met Jerome III, her great-grandson born in Paris in 1878, a year before her death. Louise Eugenie spent her childhood moving among residences in Paris, Chateau Bonaparte in Washington, D.C., and Harrison House in Newport. Her upbringing, strongly influenced by her father's connections to the French Bonapartes, prepared her for a future in Europe.

In 1896, while she was staying in Paris with her mother and brother, Prince Joachim Murat (1878–1901) introduced Louise Eugenie to her future husband. Prince Murat, a Bonaparte relative whom she called "Uncle," ranked among Jerome Jr.'s more constant friends during his military service in France. Both men had served in the Imperial Cavalry Guard and in 1870 fought in the war with Prussia. In a 1912 memoir, Louise Eugenie remembered the evening when she discovered that Count Adam de Moltke-Huitfeldt had "found [me] to his liking." A Danish count, Moltke-Huitfeldt descended from one of the most important families in Denmark. His ancestry traces back to Adam Gottlob Moltke (1710–1792), the Lord High Chamberlain under Frederick V, who, in large part, spearheaded the golden age of architecture in Copenhagen and founded the Danish Academy of Fine Arts. The family's ancestral estate, Glorup in Orbæk, Denmark, was known as one of the finest in the country. As Louise Eugenie recalled it, upon learning of Murat's plan to introduce the pair, Caroline wept to think her daughter might have an arranged marriage, a tradition she regarded as un-American. Although the couple's initial meeting was arranged by Murat, they found one another agreeable and, a week and a day after they first met, Louise Eugenie accepted the count's proposal. He was a Protestant, but she consented to marry him so long as their children would be Catholics, the religion of the Bonapartes. Two weeks later, she returned to the

United States to prepare for one of the most celebrated weddings Washington society had ever seen.

On December 30, 1896, a "distinguished assemblage" gathered in St. Paul's Cathedral on 15th and V Streets to witness a brilliant union, a marriage between two aristocrats, one American and the other European. The bride, "tall . . . with an aristocratic bearing" and bedecked with diamonds, wore a pin, a gift from the "ex-Empress," Eugénie, her godmother. Guests included the most illustrious members of Baltimore and Washington society, as well as European dignitaries. Charles served in his late brother's stead and walked Louise Eugenie down the aisle. Had Elizabeth Patterson Bonaparte been alive, this was a wedding she would have attended.

Despite the celebration the event inspired, the story of Elizabeth's own *mésalliance* with the bride's great-grandfather, Jérôme, found its way into the marriage announcement.

Louise Eugenie's wedding portrait, December 30, 1896
Private collection, photograph by Elizabeth Moltke-Huitfeldt

> The beautiful bride . . . is the great-granddaughter of the famous beauty "Betsy" Patterson of Baltimore, the story of whose beauty and belleship and romantic life is known almost the world over. She was the daughter of William Patterson, of Baltimore, and became the wife of Jerome Bonaparte, the youngest of the brothers of Napoleon, Christmas Eve, 1803. The wedding which gave every promise of being happy proved to be one of the saddest ever recorded upon the pages of history for the Emperor, never having recognized it, forced Jerome to a union with Princess Catharina Frederica of Württemberg.[205]

The money Elizabeth saved should Jerome Jr. ever assume the French throne remained behind to benefit the next generation. In 1896, when Louise Eugenie married Count Adam de Moltke-Huitfeldt, Charles became the trustee of the estate she inherited from his brother. Newspapers reported that "Mrs. Bonaparte [Caroline, Jerome Jr.'s widow] will pay $7,000 a year" to Louise

Bella Vista, Charles Joseph and Ellen's country home
MS 3152, Maryland Historical Society

BELOW: Louise Eugenie family portrait, undated. Her brother, Jerome III, is in the background.
Private collection, photograph by Elizabeth Moltke-Huitfeldt

Eugenie after the wedding, but the rest of her income continued to be managed by her uncle.[206] After the wedding, the couple stayed at Bella Vista, Charles and Ellen's country house in Harford County, then sailed to France. Shortly after their arrival, they traveled to Monte Carlo "for Adam to be presented to the Empress Eugenie." Just as her grandfather and father had done decades before, Louise Eugenie visited the empress and paid homage to her family history. Thereafter, her life followed an outline her great-grandmother would have envied. She and her new husband established a residence in Paris, the city Elizabeth revered as a center of culture. Thanks to Elizabeth's wealth, Louise Eugenie lived without the concerns about money that had plagued her great-grandmother. The growing family, eventually including five children, summered at Glorup.

Louise Eugenie was the first of Elizabeth's descendants to build her entire life abroad. After Jerome Jr.'s death, Caroline spent long periods in Paris and

many summers in Denmark, visiting with her daughter. She also maintained a relationship with the empress. In 1905 she reported to her sister-in-law Ellen, "Adam & the children go to Glorup next month & I shall follow them in course of time. . . . I have seen the Empress who inquired assiduously after you. She is well & strong."[207] The empress never met Ellen; she knew of her only in name as an American Bonaparte, but she knew Jerome Jr.'s wife and children well, and gave numerous gifts of jewelry to Louise Eugenie throughout her lifetime.[208]

Bonaparte bedroom at Glorup, Denmark
Private collection, photograph by
Elizabeth Moltke-Huitfeldt

Glorup Hall, Denmark. Note the Winterhalter portraits of Napoléon III and Empress Eugénie, smaller copies of which (seen on page 191) hung in the Bonaparte house on Park Avenue for years.

Private collection, photograph by Elizabeth Moltke-Huitfeldt

Caroline's death in 1911 largely severed Louise Eugenie's ties to America. Only her brother Jerome III remained in the United States after their mother's death, residing in Chateau Bonaparte. Caroline left Harrison House in Newport to her sons from her first marriage, but left Chateau Bonaparte to Louise and Jerome III. She also divided the "Napoleonic relics" and Bonaparte jewels between them.[209] Louise Eugenie took some things from Chateau Bonaparte to Glorup in Denmark. In her memoir she mentioned some of them, including a "Clock with Napoleon on horseback," and a "Clock with Napoleon's Head." She also placed "the big sofa [that] had belonged to my great grandmother, the beautiful Betsy Patterson Bonaparte" in her bedroom.[210] Her Danish home was filled with the Napoleonic relics collected by her grandfather and father. Portraits of Napoléon III and the Empress Eugénie greeted visitors who entered Glorup's front hall, and perceptions of Louise Eugenie as a Bonaparte remained strong throughout her life.

Maurice Francis Egan, the U.S. minister to Denmark, described in his memoir a reception given in 1908 by the queen at the Palace of Amalienborg in honor of the visiting French president, Armand Fallières, that Louise Eugenie's husband attended alone. "Count Moltke-Huitfeldt, married to Louise Eugénie Bonaparte, is almost as French in his sentiments as his wife, and, for her, when the United States joined hands with France, it was a very happy day." He continued,

> One of the events that made the fine castle of Glorup, the seat of the Moltke-Huitfeldts, interesting was the visit of the ex-Empress Eugénie. The Empress Eugénie, like all the Bonapartes, acknowledged the validity of the Patterson-Bonaparte marriage. She has always shown a special affection and esteem for the Countess Moltke-Huitfeldt. The estate of Glorup . . . was at its best during the visit of the empress,

Count Adam and Louise Eugenie de Moltke-Huitfeldt
undated

Private collection, photographs by Elizabeth Moltke-Huitfeldt

who was the most considerate of guests. The American Bonapartes were not ranked as royal highnesses for fear . . . of raising unpleasant questions as to the succession.[211]

The story of the Bonaparte legacy, beginning with Elizabeth and continuing through to the legal battles of 1861, entwined itself around the story of Louise Eugenie. Egan lamented, "The presence of the Countess Moltke-Huitfeldt would have added another interesting touch to the assemblage in Amalienborg Palace, a touch which would have served for a footnote to history. In spite of the name 'Moltke,' Count Adam and his wife are as French as the French themselves. Names in Denmark are very deceptive."[212] In Egan's eyes, such was the power of Louise Eugenie's Bonaparte heritage that it had taken one of the most distinguished Danish names and made it French. Louise Eugenie died in Biarritz in 1923, the vacation spot she often frequented. She is buried in the French Riviera town where her godmother, the Empress Eugénie, built her beachfront palace, the Hôtel du Palais. It is perhaps no coincidence that she rests in a place with a strong Bonaparte history.

The history of Louise Eugenie's brother is less striking in its link to the Bonapartes. For him, the social prestige of his name ranked far above its historical significance. In 1914, Jerome III married divorcée Blanche Pierce Stenbiegh. Their marriage, unlike those of the other American Bonapartes, was a civil union and took place in a basement office of Manhattan's City Hall. "It is a dingy little room and as a rule only the Jacks and Jills of the humbler sort are united there," the reporter from the *Baltimore Sun* commented. Their wedding announcement neglected to mention that he was the great-grandson of Elizabeth Bonaparte, but it did note, "He is much larger than his illustrious uncle, but his head and features suggest those of the Emperor [Napoléon I]."[213] Jerome III attended Harvard and Georgetown University, but he never worked, preferring the life of a socialite. His Bonaparte name brought him attention in the press when he socialized in New York, Newport, and throughout Europe, but most often he is associated with Napoléon I or his uncle, Charles Bonaparte, the American statesman. A 1906 article in the *Washington Post* proclaimed him "An American at Heart" and compared him to Charles, his uncle. In 1924, unfounded rumors circulated in the press that he would be made king of Albania. Much like his father Jerome Jr. did when rumors suggested he would rule

Mexico, Jerome III denied the erroneous reports.[214] In 1945, he died after tripping over a leash while walking his dog in New York's Central Park.

Despite the fascination the Bonaparte name continued to inspire, one of the greatest ironies in the history of Elizabeth's descendants concerns Charles. The grandchild Elizabeth relied upon most and to whom she entrusted her treasured Bonaparte objects and documents ultimately styled himself an American patriot. From his early college days at Harvard, he sought to reform student government and wrote to his mother at length about its "injustices" and lack of protocol.[215] After graduating from Harvard Law School in 1874, his wealth allowed him to take on cases of his own choosing, and his famous name attracted clients.

Charles's interest in politics began when he recognized the corruption prevalent in Baltimore's elections. In 1881 he joined the National Civil Service Reform League, where he made the acquaintance of Theodore Roosevelt. The two men, patrician and wealthy by birth and committed to reform, soon formed a close friendship that ultimately shaped Charles's career. When Roosevelt became president in 1901, he continued to rely on Bonaparte's advice. In

Jerome III (1878–1945) and his wife, New York socialite Blanche Pierce Stenbeigh (1872–1950)
Library of Congress

President Theodore Roosevelt's cabinet. Charles Joseph Bonaparte is third from left, 1909.

M.A. DeWolfe Howe, *George von Lengerke Meyer: His Life and Public Service* [New York: Dodd, Mead, and Co., 1919]

1902 he appointed Charles to the Board of Indian Commissioners and, in 1903, charged him with investigating corruption within one of the local commissions. Roosevelt also appointed him as special counsel in an investigation of fraud in the postal service. When Charles recommended W. Hall Harris, a prominent Baltimore attorney, for the position of postmaster general, the press retaliated. A Baltimore newspaper ran a cartoon of him entitled, "A New Boss in Town," that depicted Charles wearing a crown and surrounded by portraits of the corrupt city officials he had successfully overthrown. Throughout his career, when his popularity waned, his Bonaparte legacy became a vulnerability because it ran counter to his identity as a progressive American reformer. Political enemies in Baltimore called him "The Imperial Peacock of Park Avenue," a reference to his heritage and his Baltimore mansion.[216]

In the press, Charles distanced himself from that legacy as much as possible. Although Ellen chose to wear Bonaparte jewels and gowns handed down to her by Elizabeth herself, Charles emphasized his patriotism rather than his aristocratic connections. In 1905, when Roosevelt made Charles secretary of the navy, the appointment inspired countless cartoons. In one, Napoléon receives a telegram from President Roosevelt announcing, "I have made your grandnephew Secretary of the Navy," to which Napoléon replies, "I hope he does better with ships than I did." Articles published as far away as Turkey remarked upon his family history. The *Levant Herald*, published in Constantinople, reported, "The repudiated scion of the Imperial Napoleon is to become Cabinet Minister of the greatest Republic the world has ever seen. As Secretary of the United States Navy, Mr. Bonaparte will command a fleet vastly more powerful than that of the great uncle."[217] A *Washington Post* reporter, after noting Elizabeth's history, commented, "But this is one of the least things for which Charles J. Bonaparte is famous and he is said to dislike too frequent mentions of his distinguished forebears." When the press viewed him favorably, they separated him from his Bonaparte history, remarking upon his dissimilarity to Napoléon. One article, entitled "Charles Joseph Bonaparte . . . Totally Unlike the Corsican Man of Destiny," mentioned his Patterson lineage in far greater detail, highlighting his great-grandfather William Patterson's story and his mother's Puritan New England lineage.[218]

After reading about Charles's appointment, Caroline, Jerome Jr.'s wife, wrote from Paris, "I see by the *New York Herald* of today that you are to be our new Secretary of the Navy. . . . How proud & happy your Mother would be."[219] Ellen wrote to her cousin, Mabel Whitney Wheeler,

> It has been a complete surprise to us & we are altogether jubilant . . . that his unselfish, constant labors for his country are to be recognized in a lasting way & proud that his name should go down to posterity, linked with such a man as Theodore Roosevelt. He said he had long been wanting such a type of man in his official family & I think him braver than ever to call a Bonaparte & a reformer of very pronounced characteristics![220]

Roosevelt himself enjoyed having a Bonaparte as his secretary of the navy. "I could not help smiling to myself in thinking that here was the British Admiral seated beside the American Secretary of the Navy—the American Secretary of the Navy being the grand-nephew of Napoleon and the grandson of Jerome, King of Westphalia," he mused, "while the British Admiral was the grandson of a Hessian general who was the subject of King Jerome and served under Napoleon, and then . . . deserted him in the middle of the Battle of Leipsig."[221]

The Bonaparte room in Charles Joseph and Ellen's Park Avenue house. Many of the objects seen in this view are now at the Maryland Historical Society, including the portrait of Charles Bonaparte, the portraits of the Empress Eugénie and Napoléon III, and the busts of Madame Mére and Charles Bonaparte given to Bo as wedding presents.

svf, Maryland Historical Society

In 1906, Roosevelt appointed Charles U.S. attorney general, a position he held until 1909. During that period, Charles founded the Bureau of Investigation (later the Federal Bureau of Investigation) and aggressively looked into fraud and corruption in the government and industry. He often invoked the fury of the press, who again used his name as a weapon. Charles, grandson of Elizabeth, who believed ambition and hard work ranked among a person's greatest accomplishments, replied with humor. Shortly before leaving office, he sent the press his "official will," which included a list of anti-trust cases he wished to leave to his successor. These included, "Action against the Anthracite Coal Carriers—a hot case" and "Action against the Harriman railroads—not asleep at the switch." The Brooklyn *Eagle* responded on March 3, 1909, mocking his flippancy in verse. The poem's last lines read, "If he would soar there's a chance galore / He'll maybe run for Governor / As just a Bonapartist!"[222] Punctuating this dig at rumors he would run for the governorship of Maryland was the suggestion that he was a "Bonapartist," a member of the French party that continued to call for the rise of a Third Empire in France.

After Charles left office, he returned to his Baltimore law practice. He maintained a room filled with Bonaparte relics—a shrine Bo had created to the Bonaparte family—on the second floor of his Baltimore townhouse, complete with portraits of Empress Eugénie and his much-celebrated grandmother. Although he continued to exhibit the material pieces of his Bonaparte legacy, he did not actively acquire objects to enhance the room, declined many offers of more artifacts, and in fact spent as much time as possible at Bella Vista (see page 196). The public nevertheless celebrated the Park Avenue house as a Bonaparte residence. In 1912 a reporter from the *Sunday Evening News* described the Bonaparte room's "aristocratic air" and noted that "Here one finds many fine portraits of the Bonaparte family, including one of Napoleon III. . . . The great Napoleon is quite in evidence everywhere through his bust and by articles connected with his life. There is also a fine collection of miniatures of notable persons of the First Empire."[223] An inventory taken after his death listed the artifacts in the "Bonaparte Room." In addition to its furnishings, it contained:

1 Small Oil Portrait of Elizabeth Patterson Bonaparte at age 40, painted about 1820 by Massot $1500.00

1 Oil Painting of Jerome Napoleon Bonaparte by E. Bisel $50.00

1 Oil Painting of Madame Jerome Bonaparte, nee Patterson by Kinson (at the age of 30) $1000.00

1 Oval Portrait of Napoleon III (copy after Winterhalter) $500.00

Large Portrait of Jerome Napoleon Bonaparte in the Uniform of the Curiassier by May $750.00

Portrait of Empress Eugenie in oval frame $200.00

1 Pastelle of Bessie [*sic*] Patterson $15

1 Bronze of the Prince Imperial by Carpaux $300.00

1 Bronze of Jerome Napoleon $25.00

1 Marble Bust of Napoleon $15.00

1 Marble Bust of Napoleon's Father (Sculptor not known, but done in Canova's studio) $300.00

1 Marble Bust of Napoleon's Mother (Madame Mère) and Pedestal (said to be by Canova) $750.00

1 Bust of Napoleon as First Consul, and pedestal, (sculptor not known) $300.00

1 Marble Bust of Napoleon at the time of the Egyptian Campaign, by Iselin, 1859, from the original by Corbet $350.00

4 Assorted Prints of Bonaparte family $25.00

The "Blue Room," as the family called it, is preserved in a series of photographs now at the Maryland Historical Society that were first published in a biography of Charles Bonaparte's life. Elizabeth's possessions, so carefully inventoried, displayed, packed, and unpacked throughout her life, had found a place where their significance would not be lost, and where her memories and legacy would live on.

References to the Bonapartes were not confined to the Blue Room. In fact, the vestibule of the Park Avenue townhouse held "2 Leather Upholstered Arm Chairs with Bonaparte Crest on Back," probably acquired by Bo, who commissioned several pieces of furniture with the family coat of arms. The walls of the vestibule room were given to the Williams family, including an "Oil Portrait of Mrs. Williams, by Thomas Sully, dated 1821 . . . Oil Portrait of Benjamin Williams . . . 1 Pastelle of Mrs. Williams by D'Amoine [D'Almaine]." The pastel portrait of Susan done by D'Almaine is now in the collections of the Maryland Historical Society. The house contained Second Empire furniture as well as objects bought by his father [Bo] in Paris, including "4 Mahogany Cane-Seat Armchairs with crest back" (Napoléon III's) and a "Three-Piece Clock Set in Bronze (two figures) by Prandier, 1847."[224] The linen closet contained the French miniature cannon either his father or his older brother sent to him during their first trip to Paris. Miniatures of four generations of the Bonaparte family, valued at $2,000, were in an "Iron Cabinet." They included:

Miniature of Louis, King of Holland, by Oldani

Miniature of Laetitia Bonaparte, Mother of Napoleon I

Model cannon
Metal, wood
Maryland Historical Society
Gift of Mrs. Charles J. Bonaparte
xx.5.353

Charles probably received this French miniature cannon from his father or brother during their first trip to Paris.

by Anna Rechioli [Anna Pecchioli]

Miniature of Napoleon Camerata, by [Eulalie] Morin

Miniature of Princess Mathilde [Anna Pecchioli]

Miniature of Napoleon the Younger Son of King Jerome
    [Anna Pecchioli]

Miniature of Napoleanne Bacciochi, Camerata (very good) by T.
    Lecourt [J. Lecourt]

Miniature of Jerome, elder son of King Jerome [Anna Pecchioli]

Miniature of King Jerome, with lock of hair in the back by
    [Francesco Emanuele Scotto]

Miniature of Napoleon I [Jean-Baptiste Isabey]

Miniature of Jerome, King of West Phalia, by
    [Jean-Baptiste Isabey]

Miniature of Jerome, King of West Phalia

Miniature of Princess Elise Bacciochi [J. Lecourt]

Miniature Bronze of Jerome (1805)

Miniature St. Cricy, by [Nicholas] Jacques (1816)

Miniature of Louis Bonaparte, King of Holland, father of Napoleon III, by Isa Bey [Jean-Baptiste Isabey]

The cabinet also contained Elizabeth's "Agate bracelet," (see page 30) valued at $2.00. A trunk at Safe Deposit & Trust Company in Baltimore contained silver and various small objects, including "1 Gold-lined Snuff Box with cameo of Napoleon and Cover (by Berini)" and "1 Lapis Lazuli Snuff Box, gold lined." Both boxes belonged to Elizabeth.[225]

ABOVE: Snuff Box with cameo of
Napoléon Bonaparte
Antonio Bernini (1770–1861)
1815
Stone, shell, metal
Maryland Historical Society
Gift of Mrs. Charles J. Bonaparte
xx.5.254

Snuff Box
19th century
Stone, metal
Maryland Historical Society
Gift of Mrs. Charles J. Bonaparte
xx.5.253

Laetare medal, 1905
Metal, fabric

Maryland Historical Society
Gift of Mrs. Charles J. Bonaparte
xx.5.259

This medal was given to
Charles J. Bonaparte by the
University of Notre Dame to
honor his service to the
Catholic Church.

When Charles died at Bella Vista on June 28, 1921, his death was mourned as the loss of a true American. The Women of the Civil Service Auxiliary of Maryland eulogized him, remarking that he "allowed no foreign lure or element to interfere with the preservation of his individuality, but will ever be known throughout the world as a Christian gentleman, an ardent patriot, an American citizen, pure and simple."[226] The most American of all the Bonapartes never went to France, where so much of his family history took place. Of the American line of Bonapartes, he was the only one who never traveled to Europe at all, preferring to vacation in the United States or Canada. Many of the organizations and institutions Charles supported during his lifetime, including the Bench and Bar of Baltimore, the National Civil Service Reform League, and Harvard University, honored him. Some memorials noted his heritage; his obituary in the *New York Times,* for example, remembered him as the "Grandnephew of Napoleon" and recounted Elizabeth's story in detail. Others made no mention of it. Unlike his brother who proclaimed himself a citizen of France, Charles spent his entire career proclaiming himself an American.

On January 9, 1922, at a meeting of the members of the Maryland Historical Society, Mrs. Charles Bonaparte's gift of her husband's Napoleonic collection received the greatest attention. Vice-President DeCourcy Wright Thom and announced the "gift of exceptional beauty and interest." Thom's presentation included a short description of Elizabeth's marriage, excluding any mention

Ellen Channing Day Bonaparte
(1852–1924)
Circa 1905
Library of Congress

Charles Joseph Bonaparte
(1851–1921)
Cecile Smith de Wentworth
(1853–1921)
1906–1909
Oil on canvas
Maryland Historical Society
Gift of Mrs. Charles J. Bonaparte
xx.5.75

of its denouement, and a discussion of the collection Bo had assembled in the "famous Blue Room" on Park Avenue. He went on to explain that "After the death of Madame Bonaparte and her son and his wife, a part of this collection was removed by the late Colonel Jerome Napoleon Bonaparte, but the remainder continued in the possession of our late member, Attorney-General Charles Joseph Bonaparte." According to the proceedings, Ellen donated the collection for several reasons, including "her interest in our Society" and "her recognition that these memorials of two families so intimately connected with the history of the City, should not pass into the hands of another institution." In addition to the objects and works of art, Ellen donated Elizabeth's library, which included books with "marginal notes expressing her estimate . . . [and] her opinion of the individuals mentioned."

In this presentation to the members, the society's trustees linked its significance to the important role Charles's "civic righteousness" played in history. Phillips Lee Goldsborough remarked, "Every man, woman and child in the city of Baltimore and the State of Maryland knows and respects the name of Charles Joseph Bonaparte." His reputation as an American politician and a defender of citizens' rights "balanced" the European associations of the gift and reinforced its appropriateness for the society's collection.

The objects, paintings, and documents were named the "Bonaparte Collection" and, upon adjournment, members were invited to see them displayed in the Bonaparte Room. Ellen oversaw its installation but was not present for the event. On January 16, 1922, she wrote to J. Appleton Wilson about how delighted she was to learn that the collection was "proving of interest to many visitors." She added, "Trusting it may stimulate the aims for good government to which my husband was so devoted."[227] To Ellen, the relics of Elizabeth's aristocratic life and the memorials to the European Bonapartes now represented the most American of the Bonapartes, her husband. Although for very different reasons, the family's imperial legacy continued to be preserved both at the Maryland Historical Society and in the homes of Bonaparte descendants in Europe. Like the material legacy of the American Bonapartes, Elizabeth's occupies two worlds in perpetuity.

Dinner Napkin with the coats of arms of the Bonaparte and Moltke-Huitfeldt Families
Circa 1896
Cotton

Maryland Historical Society, Gift of Mark B. Letzer in honor of Elizabeth Moltke-Huitfeldt, 2014.6.2

This damask napkin is a rare example of an object bearing both the Bonaparte and Moltke-Huitfeldt crests. It descended in the family of Louise Eugenie Bonaparte Moltke-Huitfeldt and is part of a set of napkins that passed to Louise Eugenie's daughter, Marie Louise Moltke-Huitfeldt (Marie Louise Marquesa de Pozo Rubio).

DRAMATIS PERSONAE

Elizabeth Patterson Bonaparte (1785–1879)—Born to the wealthy merchant William Patterson and Dorcas Spear, Elizabeth married Jérôme Bonaparte in 1803. The emperor Napoléon Bonaparte subsequently annulled the marriage in 1805, and Elizabeth divorced Jérôme in 1813. Although most often referred to as "Betsy" Bonaparte in publications, Elizabeth did not refer to herself by that name. A few letters from her father and Jérôme do refer to her as "Betsy," but this book uses the name she herself used. After her divorce, she legally reverted to the surname of Patterson, but people continued to refer to her as Madame Bonaparte for the remainder of her life. She had one child, Jerome Napoleon Bonaparte, known as "Bo."

Jérôme Napoléon Bonaparte (1784–1860)—The youngest brother of Napoléon Bonaparte, Jérôme briefly served in the French navy. In 1803, he married Elizabeth Patterson in Baltimore. In 1807 after the emperor Napoléon annulled his first marriage, Jérôme married Princess Catherine of Württemberg and became the king of Westphalia. He ruled that German kingdom until 1813. From 1816 to 1860, he was known as the Prince of Montfort. With the rise of the Second French Republic and his cousin, Napoléon III, he was named governor of Les Invalides in Paris. In this book, his name includes the French accents to distinguish him from the American Jeromes in this work. After the couple's estrangement in 1805, Elizabeth referred to him as Prince Jérôme, "PJ," and, in later years, as "Malaparte," a malicious play of his last name. He had one child with Elizabeth, Jerome Napoleon Bonaparte (Bo) (1805–1870), and three children

FACING PAGE: The society maintained a Bonaparte room for years. The current exhibition, "A Woman of Two Worlds," opened at the Maryland Historical Society in 2013, featuring objects from the Bonaparte Collection and other holdings of the museum, many of which are on public view for the first time.

with Catherine of Württemburg, Jérôme Napoléon Charles Bonaparte (1814–1847), Mathilde Bonaparte (1820–1904), and Napoléon Joseph Charles Paul Bonaparte (1822–1891), known as "Plon Plon." Bo and his son, Jerome Jr., referred to Jérôme as "King."

CATHERINE OF WÜRTTEMBERG (1783–1835)—Catherine of Württemberg was the second wife of Jérôme Napoléon Bonaparte and mother of three children.

JÉRÔME NAPOLÉON CHARLES BONAPARTE (1814–1847)—Eldest son of Catherine of Württemberg and Jérôme Napoléon Bonaparte.

MATHILDE LAETITIA WILHELMINE BONAPARTE DEMIDOV (1820–1904)—The daughter of Catherine of Württemberg and Jérôme Napoléon Bonaparte, who maintained a close relationship with her half-brother Jerome Napoleon Bonaparte (Bo).

NAPOLÉON JOSEPH CHARLES PAUL BONAPARTE (1822–1891)—Known in later years as "Plon plon," "Plonplon," or "Plomb plomb," Napoléon Joseph Charles Paul Bonaparte was the youngest son of Catherine of Württemberg and Jérôme Napoléon Bonaparte. In this book, he is referred to as "Plon Plon," the spelling of his nickname most often used by Elizabeth and Bo, but the spelling of his nickname varies throughout the Bonaparte manuscript collections and in print. Plon Plon maintained a bristly relationship with his half-brother (Bo), and Bo's son, Jerome Jr. He married Princess Maria Clothilde of Savoy in 1859 who was twenty-four years younger.

NAPOLÉON III (LOUIS-NAPOLÉON BONAPARTE) (1808–1873)—The son of Louis Bonaparte, Prince of Holland, and nephew and heir of Napoléon I, who was the president of the Second Republic (1848–1852) and Emperor Napoléon III of the Second Empire (1852–1870). He married Eugénie de Montijo in 1853.

EUGÉNIE DE MONTIJO, EMPRESS EUGÉNIE (1826–1920)—The Spanish-born wife of Napoléon III (Louis-Napoléon Bonaparte), she became the

empress of France when they married in 1853. Empress Eugénie felt a
particular fondness for Jerome Jr., Elizabeth's grandson, and was godmother to Jerome Jr.'s daughter, Louise Eugenie Bonaparte.

Jerome Napoleon Bonaparte (1805–1870)—Known as Bo, Jerome
Napoleon Bonaparte was the only son of Elizabeth Patterson Bonaparte
and Jérôme Napoléon Bonaparte. In 1829, he married Susan May
Williams. The couple had two children, Jerome Napoleon Bonaparte Jr.
(1830–1893) and Charles Joseph Bonaparte (1851–1921). In this book, he is
referred to as "Bo." Elizabeth sometimes called him Bo, but also called
him Jerome. Like all the American Bonapartes in this book, his name
is written without French accents.

Susan May Williams Bonaparte (1812–1881)—Daughter of wealthy
Massachusetts-born merchant, Benjamin Williams, Susan May Williams
married Jerome Napoleon Bonaparte (Bo) in 1829. Their sons were
Jerome Napoleon Bonaparte Jr.—"Jerome Jr."—and Charles Joseph
Bonaparte. She is referred to as "Susan" throughout this book.

Jerome Napoleon Bonaparte Jr. (1830–1893)—The first-born son of
Jerome Napoleon Bonaparte (Bo) and Susan May Williams Bonaparte,
Jerome Jr. achieved a notable military career in both America and France.
In 1871, he married Caroline LeRoy Appleton Edgar, a widow with three
children. They had two children, Louise Eugenie Bonaparte and Jerome
Napoleon Bonaparte III. In this book, he is referred to as "Jerome Jr." The
family sometimes called him "Junior" and his younger brother, Charles,
often called him "The Major."

Caroline LeRoy Appleton Edgar Bonaparte (1840–1911)—Grand-
daughter of Senator Daniel Webster, she married Jerome Jr. in 1871.
They had two children, Jerome Napoleon Charles Bonaparte and Louise
Eugenie Bonaparte.

Jerome Napoleon Charles Bonaparte (1878–1945)—The son of Jerome
Jr., Jerome III was a socialite who married Blanche Pierce Stenbeigh, a
divorcée, in 1914. In this book, he is referred to as Jerome III.

Louise Eugenie Bonaparte Moltke-Huitfeldt (1873–1923)—The daughter of Jerome Jr. and Caroline LeRoy Appleton Edgar Bonaparte, Louise Eugenie was named after her godmother, the former Empress Eugenie. She married Danish Count Adam Carl de Moltke-Huitfeldt in 1896. Her five children became the only direct descendants of Elizabeth Patterson Bonaparte, and their descendants continue that line today.

Charles Joseph Bonaparte (1851–1921)—The second son of Jerome Napoleon Bonaparte (Bo) and Susan May Williams Bonaparte who served as the U.S. attorney general and secretary of the navy under President Theodore Roosevelt. In 1875, he married Ellen Channing Day. They had no children.

Ellen Channing Day Bonaparte (1852–1924)—The daughter of an attorney, Ellen Channing Day married Charles Joseph Bonaparte in 1875. The couple had no children. In 1921, after Charles's death, Ellen gave the Bonaparte collection to the Maryland Historical Society.

William Patterson (1752–1835)—The father of Elizabeth Patterson Bonaparte, William Patterson was an Irish immigrant who made a fortune smuggling black powder during the American Revolution and later established himself as one of the most successful merchants in Baltimore.

Dorcas Spear Patterson (1761–1814)—The mother of Elizabeth Patterson Bonaparte, Dorcas Spear Patterson was born into a successful family of merchants in Baltimore.

Edward Patterson (1789–1865)—The brother of Elizabeth Patterson Bonaparte, Edward developed a particularly close relationship with his sister until their father's will provoked a lawsuit which ended their friendship.

Anne Spear (unknown)—The aunt of Elizabeth Patterson Bonaparte, Anne Spear, referred to as "Nancy" in this book, remained unmarried and, until 1835, managed Elizabeth's finances and was her confidante.

CHRONOLOGY
1769–PRESENT

✿

Timeline (1769–Present)

1769  Napoléon Buonaparte (Bonaparte) is born in Corsica to Letizia Ramolino and Carlo Buonaparte.

1784  Jérôme Napoléon Bonaparte, Napoléon's youngest brother, is born in Corsica.

1785 Elizabeth Patterson is born in Baltimore to Dorcas Spear and William Patterson.

1799 Napoléon declares himself 1st Consul of France.

1803 On December 24, Elizabeth Patterson and Jérôme Napoléon Bonaparte are married in Baltimore by Bishop John Carroll.

1804 Napoléon becomes Emperor of the French.

1805 Elizabeth and Jérôme depart for Europe. A pregnant Elizabeth is refused entry to France and Amsterdam. Jérôme returns to Napoléon in France.

1805  Jerome Napoleon Bonaparte (Bo), son of Elizabeth and Jérôme, is born in London.

1806 Elizabeth returns to Baltimore. Elizabeth and Jérôme's marriage is annulled by Napoléon.

1807 Jérôme Napoléon Bonaparte marries Catherine of Württemburg by Napoléon's arrangement.

1808 Jérôme promises Elizabeth an income of 200,000 francs a year and offers the titles of Prince and Princess of Smalkalden for Bo and herself. She refuses his offer.

1808–1809  Elizabeth resides in Washington, D.C., and spends time at the White House with her friends Dolley and James Madison.

1809 Elizabeth receives a pension of 60,000 francs from Napoléon and begins making investments in Baltimore.

1810 Congress approves an amendment to invalidate the citizenship of any American who accepted a title of nobility "from any emperor, king, prince or foreign power."

1811 Elizabeth moves to Washington, D.C.; Margaret Patterson, Elizabeth's sister, dies at age 17.

1812 Napoléon is defeated in Russia.

1812 Elizabeth's lawyer submits a petition for divorce to the Maryland legislature.

1812 The United States declares war on Great Britain and the War of 1812 begins.

1813 Maryland's General Assembly grants Elizabeth's petition for divorce.

1813 Bo attends Mount St. Mary's College in Emmitsburg, Maryland.

1814  Dorcas Spear Patterson, Elizabeth's mother, dies as well as several of her siblings, including her sister Caroline to whom she was very devoted.

1814 Napoléon abdicates, but later returns to France.

1814  British burn the Capitol in Washington, D.C., and attempt to invade Baltimore but withdraw after an unsuccessful bombardment of Fort McHenry.

1815 On June 18, the Duke of Wellington defeats Napoléon at Waterloo. Elizabeth departs for Europe six weeks later.

1816  Elizabeth meets Madame de Staël, Countess Rochefoucauld, Marquise de Villette (Voltaire's ward), and Lady Sydney Morgan.

1816 Elizabeth goes to Geneva to look for schools for Bo and meets John Jacob Astor and Russian and Polish expatriates, including Princess Caroline Gallitzin.

1817 Elizabeth returns to Baltimore.

1819 Bo signs an "Oath of Intention" to become a citizen of the United States.

1819 Elizabeth and Bo arrive in Amsterdam. Bo is refused entry into France, and mother and son are forced to travel through Germany to reach Switzerland. Bo begins his studies in Geneva.

1821  Elizabeth brings Bo to Rome to meet Pauline Bonaparte Borghese and other Bonaparte relatives, including Napoléon's mother, Madame Mère.

1822  Napoléon Joseph Charles Paul Bonaparte (Plon Plon) born to Jérôme Bonaparte and Catherine of Württemberg.

1824 Elizabeth returns to Baltimore.

1825–34 Elizabeth sails to Europe and remains there for nine years.

1829 Bo marries an American, Susan May Williams, against Elizabeth's wishes.

1830  Elizabeth's grandson, Jerome Napoleon Bonaparte (Jerome Jr.), is born in Baltimore.

1835  William Patterson dies and leaves Elizabeth only a small portion of his large estate.

1835 Elizabeth sues her brothers for an equal share of William Patterson's estate and terminates her friendship with Nancy Spear, her aunt.

1839  Elizabeth and Bo travel to France to collect legacy of 50,000 francs left to Jerome Jr. by his great-uncle, Cardinal Fesch.

1840 Elizabeth returns to Baltimore and lives in a boarding house on Lexington Street.

1849–1852 Elizabeth travels to Europe.

1851  Birth of Charles Joseph Bonaparte, Elizabeth's second grandson.

1852–1861 Elizabeth remains in Baltimore.

1860 Jérôme Napoléon Bonaparte, former king of Westphalia, dies; Abraham Lincoln is elected president.

1860 Bo and Elizabeth travel to France to press the suit for the imperial legacy. Bo's right to the line of succession denied by the French court.

1861 The American Civil War begins. Elizabeth's son and grandsons support the Union.

1863 Elizabeth makes her last trip to Europe.

1864 Elizabeth moves into Mrs. Gwinn's boarding house in Baltimore and remains there until her death.

1865 The Civil War ends.

1870 Bo, Elizabeth's son, dies at the age of 65.

1871   Jerome Bonaparte Jr., Elizabeth's grandson, marries Caroline LeRoy Appleton Edgar.

1873   Publication of *The Bonaparte-Patterson Marriage in 1803: and The Secret Correspondence on the Subject Never Before Made Public,* by W. T. R. Saffell.

1873   Louise Eugenie born to Jerome Jr. and Caroline LeRoy Appleton Edgar Bonaparte.

1875   Charles Joseph Bonaparte, Elizabeth's grandson, marries Ellen Channing Day.

1878   Jerome Napoleon Charles born to Jerome Jr. and Caroline LeRoy Appleton Edgar Bonaparte.

1879   Elizabeth Patterson Bonaparte dies and is buried at Green Mount Cemetery. A telegram from her grandson Charles Joseph Bonaparte reads, "The Madame has just expired, 1:20 p.m., CJB."

1893   Jerome Napoleon Bonaparte Jr. dies at the age of 62.

1896   Louise Eugenie Bonaparte marries Count Adam de Moltke-Huitfeldt and becomes Countess Louise Eugenie.

1914   Jerome Napoleon Charles Bonaparte marries Blanche Pierce Stenbiegh

1921   Charles Joseph Bonaparte dies and his widow, Ellen, gives the family's collection of Bonaparte objects and documents to the Maryland Historical Society.

1922   The Bonaparte Room, a recreation of a room in the Bonaparte home on Park Avenue, is installed in the Maryland Historical Society's Enoch Pratt House.

2013   *Woman of Two Worlds: Elizabeth Patterson Bonaparte and Her Imperial Legacy* opens at the Maryland Historical Society, the first exhibition ever devoted entirely to Elizabeth and her descendants.

The Present   Today, Elizabeth's direct descendants reside in Europe.

GENEALOGIES

Carlo Buonoparte (1746–1785)

m. Letizia Ramolino (1750–1836) in 1764

Joseph Bonaparte

(1768–1844)
King of Naples,
1806–1808
King of Spain,
1808–1813

m. *Marie-Julie Clary* (1771–1845), daughter of Françon Clary of Marseilles

d. **Julie Josephine** (1796)

d. **Zenaide Letizia** (1801–1854)
m. *Charles Lucien Bonaparte* [q.v.], in 1822

d. **Charlotte Napoléone** (1802–1839)
m. *Napoléon Louis Bonaparte* [q.v.], in 1826

Napoléon Bonaparte

(1769–1821)
Emperor of France,
1804–1815

m.[1] *Marie Josephe Rose [Tascher de la Pagerie] de Beauharnais* (1763–1814), daughter of Joseph Gaspart Tascher of Martinique, in 1796; divorced in 1810

m.[2] *Marie Louise von Habsburg-Lothringon* (1791–1847), daughter of Emperor Francis II of Austria, in 1810

s.[2] **Napoléon-François-Joseph-Charles** (1811–1830), unmarried

Lucien Bonaparte

(1775–1840)
Prince of Canino,
1814–1840

m.[1] *Christine Boyer* (1771–1800), in 1794
m.[2] *Mme. Alexandine [de Bleschamp] Jouberthon* (1778–1855), ca. 1802

d.[1] **Filistine Charlotte** (1795–1865)
m.[1] *Pr. Mario Gabrielle*, 1815
m.[2] *Settimo Centamori*, 1842

s.[1] **[unnamed]** (1796)
d.[1] **Victoire Gertrude** (1797)
d.[1] **Christine Egypta** (1798–1847)
m.[1] *Ct. Arvid Posse*, 1818; divorced in 1824
m.[2] *Ld Dudley Coutts-Stuart*, in 1824

s.[2] **Charles Lucien** (1803–1857)
m. *Zenaide Letizia Bonaparte* [q.v.], in 1822

d.[2] **Letizia** (180?–1871)
m. *Sir Thos. Wyse*, in 1820

s.[2] **Joseph** (1806–1807)
d.[2] **Jeanne** (1807–1829), unmarried

s.[2] **Pierre Napoléon** (1815–1881)
m. *Justine Elenore Ruffin*, in 1853

s.[2] **Antoine** (1816–1873)
m. *Anna Maria Cardinale*, in 1839

d.[2] **Alexandrine Marie** (1818–1874)
m. *Ct. Vincenzo Valentini di Laviano*, in 1836

d.[2] **Constance** (1823–1876), unmarried

Maria Anna Elisa Bonaparte

(1777–1820)
Princess of Lucca and Piombino,
1805–1809
Grand Duchess of Tuscany,
1809–1815

m. *Felix Baciocchi* (1762–1841), son of François Baciocchi of Corsica, in 1797

s. **Felix Napoléon** (1798)

s. **Napoléon** (1803)

d. **Elisa Napoléone** (1806–1869)
m. *Ct. Filippo Camerata-Passionei di Mazzoleni*, in 1824

s. **Jerome Charles** (1810–1811)

s. **Frederich Napoléon** (1814–1833), unmarried

Louis Bonaparte	[Marie]-Pauline Bonaparte	[Marie-Annunciata] Caroline Bonaparte	Jérôme Napoléon Bonaparte

Louis Bonaparte
(1778–1846)
King of Holland,
1806–1810

m. *Hortense de Beauhar-
nais* (1783–1837),
daughter of Alexandre
de Beauharnais of
Martinique, in 1802
First wife of Napoléon
Bonaparte

s. **Napoléon Louis Charles**
(1802–1807)

s. **Napoléon Louis**
(1804–1831)
m. *Charlotte Napoléone
Bonaparte* [q.v.],
in 1826

s. **Charles Louis Napoléon**
(1808–1873)
m. *Ct. Eugenie de
Montijo*, Ct. de Teba,
in 1853

**[Marie]-Pauline
Bonaparte**
(1780-1825)
Duchess of Guastalla,
1806

m.¹ *Gen. Charles LeClerc*
(1772–1802), in 1797
m.² *Prince Camillo
Borghese* (1775–1852),
son of Marcantonio
III Borghese, in 1803

**[Marie-Annunciata]
Caroline Bonaparte**
(1782–1839)
Grand Duchess of Borg,
1806–1808
Queen Consort of Naples,
1808–1815

m.¹ *Joachim Murat*
(1771–1815), son of
Pierre Murat-Jordy,
in 1800
m.² *Francesco McDonald*
(1777–1837), in 1830

s.¹ **Achille** (1801–1847)
m. *Catherine Willis Gray*,
in 1826

d.¹ **Marie Letizia**
(1802–1859)
m. *Guy Thadee Pepoli di
Castiglione*, in 1823

s.¹ **Napoléon Lucien
Charles** (1803–1878)
m. *Caroline Georgina
Fraser*, in 1831

d.¹ **Louise Julie Caroline**
(1805–1889)
m. *Giulio Rasponi*,
in 1825

**Jérôme Napoléon
Bonaparte**
(1784–1860)
King of Westphalia,
1807–1813

m.¹ *Elizabeth Patterson*
(1785–1879), daughter
of Wm. Patterson of
Maryland, in 1803
m.² *Catharina von Würt-
temburg* (1783–1835),
daughter of Frederich
I Wm Charles, King
of Württemburg,
in 1807
m.³ *Marq. Giustina
Pecori-Suarez*
(1811–1903), in 1853

s.¹ **Jerome Napoleon**
(1805–1870)
m. *Susan May Williams*,
in 1829

s.² **Jérôme Napoléon
Charles** (1814–1847),
unmarried

d.² **Mathilde** (1820–1904)
m. *Anatole Demidov,
Prince of San Donato*,
in 1840

s.² **Napoléon Joseph
Charles Paul**
(1822–1891)
m. *Pr. Maria Clotilde di
Savoia*, in 1859

William Patterson (1752–1835)

m. *Dorcas Spear* (1761–1814)

daughter of William Spear of Baltimore, in 1779

William Patterson (1780–1808) m. *Ann Gittings* (1776-1828), daughter of James Gittings Sr., in 1804 s. **William** (1805–ca. 1851) m. *[Mary] Ann (Tracy?)*, in 1826	**Robert Patterson** (1781–1822) m. *Mary Ann Caton* (1788–1853), daughter of Richard Caton, in 1806 d.s.p.	**John Patterson** (1783–1851) m. *Mary Buchanan Nicholas* (1785–1868), daughter of Wilson Cary Nicholas, in 1806 "Atomasco" d.s.p.	**Elizabeth Patterson** (1785–1879) m. *Jérôme Napoléon Bonaparte* (1784–1860), in 1803 s. **Jerome Napoleon** (1805–1870) m. *Susan May Williams*, in 1829

Joseph Patterson
(1786–1866)
m. *Charlotte Nichols*
(1793–1860),
daughter of James Nichols,
in 1817

"Coldstream" and
"Evesham"

s. **William** (1818–1837)
 unmarried
d. **Charlotte Nichols**
 (1820–1846)
 m. *Charles S. Gilmor*,
 in 1839
s. **Joseph** (1825–1832),
 unmarried
d. **Caroline** (1828–1863)
 m. *Reverdy Johnson Jr.*,
 in 1853

Edward Patterson
(1789–1865)
m. *Sidney Smith*
(1784–1879),
daughter of Samuel Smith,
in 1815

"Bagatelle" and
"Coldstream"

d. **Margaret** (1816–1893)
 m. *Charles Cooke
 Turner*, USN, in 1851
d. **Laura** (1824–1918)
 unmarried
s. **Edward** (1825–1886)
 unmarried
s. **Samuel Smith**
 (1827–1887)
 unmarried
d. **Sidney** (1829–1858)
 m. *William Fauntleroy
 Turner*, in 1857
s. **Robert** (1831–1866)
 unmarried

George Patterson
(1796–1869)
m. *Prudence Ann Brown*
(1816–1883),
daughter of Thomas
Cockey Brown, in 1842

"Springfield"

d. **Mary** (1842–?)
 unmarried
s. **George** (1844–1849)
 unmarried
d. **Florence** (1847–1878)
 m. *James Carroll*, in 1877

Henry Patterson
(1801–1858)
m. *Mary Louise Wilson*
(1810–1884),
daughter of James Wilson,
in 1841

s. **James Wilson**
 (1843–1908)
 m. *Margaret Sherwood*,
 in 1882
s. **William** (1845–1935)
 m. *Emma May Clagett*,
 in 1869
s. **Henry** (1848–1850)
s. **Arthur Melville**
 (1850–1879)
 m. *Alice Gerry*, in 1874
d. **Alice** (1856–1944)
 m. *W. Hall Harris Jr.*,
 in 1876
d. **Mary Louisa** (1851–1858)

NOTES

PREFACE

1 Martha Custis Williams Carter, "Conversations or notations from Madame Bonapart [*sic*] Miss Gwinns, 84 Cathedral St., Baltimore: autograph manuscript diary, 1875-1877," Micro 3504, Maryland Historical Society, original in the collections of the Department of Literary and Historical Manuscripts, Pierpont Morgan Library, New York, N.Y. (hereinafter cited Carter, Diaries). The pages are unnumbered and many are undated.

2 "Elizabeth Patterson Bonaparte: Death of a Celebrated Personage," *Baltimore Sun*, April 5, 1879.

3 Ibid. The nobleman was, I believe, Duc de Crillon, Felix Dorothée François Des Balbes Berton de Crillon (1748–1820). His grand residence was the epicenter of Parisian social life prior to his death, and it is very likely he met Elizabeth during her 1815 trip.

4 Like the letters used in Saffell's book, those used by Didier are "lost."

5 "Madame Bonaparte's Fine Scorn," *Baltimore Sun*, September 27, 1900.

6 "A Betsy Patterson Play: Jerome Napoleon's Romance to be Produced on the Stage," ibid., November 14, 1906.

7 "Elizabeth Patterson Bonaparte: Death of a Celebrated Personage," ibid., April 5, 1879.

CHAPTER I
"To Dress for Admiration"

1 Nancy Spear to Elizabeth Patterson Bonaparte (EPB), September 19, 1816, as quoted in Charlene M. Boyer Lewis, *Elizabeth Patterson Bonaparte: An American Aristocrat in the Early Republic* (Philadelphia: University of Pennsylvania Press, 2012), 149.

2 Bonaparte Commonplace Book, blue and red, undated, pages unnumbered, Box 5, MS 144, Jerome Napoleon Bonaparte Papers, 1805–1893. [Hereinafter JNB Papers.]

3 Carter, Diaries, December 1876

4 Carter, Diaries, 1877.

5 Cynthia D. Earman, "Remember the Ladies: Women, Etiquette, and Diversions in Washington City, 1800–1814," in Kenneth R. Bowling, "Coming into the City: Essays on Early Washington D.C.," *Washington History* (Spring–Summer, 2000): 108–9, as quoted in Helen Jean Burn, *Betsy Bonaparte* (Baltimore, Md.: Maryland Historical Society, 2010), 62.

6 Carter, Diaries, entry dated 1876.

7 Ann Buermann Wass and Michelle Webb Fandrich, *Clothing through American History: The Federal Era through the Antebellum, 1786–1860* (Santa Barbara, Cal.: ABC-CLIO, LLC, 2010), 57–65.

8 Ibid.

9 Ibid., 10.

10 Lewis, *Elizabeth Patterson Bonaparte*, 28.

11 Carter, Diaries, February 8, 1877.

12 EPB mentions "old Jerome's wedding blue satin Coat!" in her "Black High Boy," Blue marbled journal, 1857, Box 13A, MS 142, Elizabeth Patterson Bonaparte Papers, MdHS. [Hereinafter EPB Papers.]

13 Solid green journal, Box 13A, MS 142, EPB Papers.

14 Composition book, ibid.

15 Carter, Diaries, undated.

16 Burn, *Betsy Bonaparte*, 129.

17 Solid green journal, Box 13A, MS 142, EPB Papers.

18 Blue marbled journal, ibid.

19 *Baltimore Sun*, February 7, 1906.

20 Solid red journal, 1857, Box 13A, MS 142, EPB Papers.

21 Carter, Diaries, January 1877.

22 "1 January 1871 At Boarding House of Miss Peters. . . . One red covered Trunk contains a black lace dress &

ditto Mantilla present from P. Jerome." Composition Book, pages unnumbered, Box 13A, MS 142, EPB Papers.

23 In the 1980s, the contents of a Bonaparte trunk of lace and other textile fragments were transferred into a storage box. At that time, the pieces in the box were not fully examined. Most of the lace fragments remained rolled in tight bundles, perhaps by Elizabeth herself. Some were carefully labeled with their lengths and other information. A few lengths of lace were wrapped around Parisian business cards. Thanks to the sleuthing of Barbara Meger, curatorial volunteer at MdHS, this collection of over three hundred pieces of lace is now recorded and identified. Many of the "scraps" are now known to be collars, cuffs, and trim removed from gowns. Quotation from Carter, Diaries.

24 The invoice for the garments sent to Elizabeth reads, "Melles Lolive, de Beuvry et Cie./Rue neuve des Petits Champs, No 463, a Paris vis à vis l'Ad . . . de la Loterie au Grand Balcon. Lingères de sa Majeste l'Empereur, de sa Majeste l'Imperatrice et de leurs maisons/Etat du Objets Contenues dans une Caisse Livrer à Son Altesse Imperiale Monseigneur le Prince Jérôme par les dites le 16 Vendemiaire An 14 (8 octobre 1805)," Box 2, MS 142, EPB Papers.

25 Blue and red marbled journal, ibid.

26 Madame Elgin to Elizabeth Bonaparte, November 5, 1805, Letterbook 1805, MS 142, EPB Papers.

27 Jérôme Bonaparte to Elizabeth Bonaparte, November 21, 1805, MS 143, Jérôme Bonaparte Papers, MdHS.

28 Lewis, *Elizabeth Patterson Bonaparte,* 35.

29 Blue marbled journal, 1821, Box 13A, MS 142, EPB Papers.

30 Burn, *Betsy Bonaparte,* 62.

31 *The National Intelligencer,* February 3, 1804.

32 Carter, Diaries, undated.

33 Rosalie Calvert to H. J. Stier, March 2, 1804, quoted in Margaret Law Callcott, ed., *Mistress of Riversdale: The Plantation Letters of Rosalie Stier Calvert, 1795–1821* (Baltimore: The Johns Hopkins University Press, 1991), 77, and Lewis, *Elizabeth Patterson Bonaparte,* 34.

34 Small blue marbled journal, 1815, Box 13A, MS 142, EPB Papers.

35 Solid red journal, 1842, ibid.

36 Address book, Box 10, MS 142, EPB Papers.

37 Dolley Madison to Elizabeth Patterson Bonaparte, November 4, 1813, Box 2, MS 142, EPB Papers.

38 Dolley Madison Papers, University of Virginia Digital Library. I am thankful to Ann Wass for generously directing me to this reference.

39 Mary Caton to Elizabeth Patterson Bonaparte, December 18, 1815, Box 2, MS 142, EPB Papers.

40 Edward Patterson to Elizabeth Patterson Bonaparte, March 25, 1816, ibid.

41 As quoted in Carol Berkin, *Wondrous Beauty: The Life and Adventures of Elizabeth Patterson Bonaparte* (New York: Alfred A. Knopf, 2013), 93.

42 Wass and Fandrich, *Clothing through American History,* 49. I am indebted to Karen H. Thompson for indentifying the Ispwich lace in the museum's collection.

43 Blue marbled journal, 1839, Box 13A, MS 142, EPB Papers.

44 Blue marbled journal, 1860, ibid.

45 Chart of Elizabeth's shoe purchases, created by Barbara Meger, 2013.

46 Chart compiled by Barbara Meger, 2013. The summary covers only the number of purchases of fabric yardage plus the quantity for a given year. A yard equals 36"; a meter is 39.37"; an ell is 45". Brach is a derivation of "braccio" which is equivalent to the English ell or 45".

47 Small blue marbled journal, 1815, pages unnumbered, Box 13A, MS 142, EPB Papers.

48 Blue marbled journal, 1839, pages unnumbered, ibid.

49 Solid green journal, 1839–1840, ibid.

50 Solid green journal, 1860–1864, ibid.

51 Grey-green journal, 1875, ibid.

52 Blue marbled journal, pages unnumbered, ibid.

53 "Dayly accounts–1826–1827–1828–1829–1830 & part of 1832—Paris—Aix—Geneva—Florence—Geneva—Paris," 1830, Marbled blue-green journal, Box 13A, MS 142, EPB Papers. Hereafter referred to as "Dayly accounts Journal."

54 This inventory lists "a veil point de Bruxelles, a ditto half hankerchief, 4 yds & an eighth of my broadest point de Bruxelle Lace, 6 yds & a half of the neat width of Point de Bruxelles, one yd & a half & an eight of narrow point de Bruxelles with Dots, 2½ yds point, narrow with stars on it, 3 yds point Bruxelles with Stars also but differing from the above/narrow, 2½ yards or 2 ells, of point D'Alençon—Broad Lace, 4 yds & a quarter of old fashioned winter Point Lace, 2 lappetts of ditto old fashioned winter Point, 7½ yds (good measure of old mechlin lace, moderate width, [measures 6 /4 written in pencil], 6 & ¾ yards of Broad Brussels Lace, 4 x ¼ yds of french lace—moderate width, 2 & half yds, or 2 ells, of broad figured inserting Lace." Box 10, MS 142, EPB Papers.

55 Blue marbled journal, Box 13A, MS 142, EPB Papers. Many of the scraps or fragments of garments in the collection were in the process of being altered and the work never completed. Elizabeth never disposed of even the smallest fragment of fabric.

56 Green journal, Box 13A, MS 142, EPB Papers.

57 *Matchett's Baltimore Directories,* 1840–1850, H. Furlong Baldwin Library Microfilm Collection, MdHS.

58 "Mrs. B. I. Cohen's Fancy Dress Party," *Maryland Historical Magazine,* 14 (1919): 354, 357. Queen Caroline of Brunswick lived a life that in one main event paralleled Elizabeth's own troubled history. Her marriage to George IV, Prince of Wales, resulted in a separation within years of the 1806 union. In 1821, George banned Caroline from his coronation and refused to acknowledge her right to the title of Queen despite Caroline's protestation. Only Caroline's death that year prevented further scandal. The parallel between Elizabeth and Caroline is that neither woman, despite marrying men who would become kings, became a queen. It is highly likely that Elizabeth knew Caroline's story and adopted the costume as a reference to it. For more detail about the story of Caroline, see Jane Robbins, *The Trial of Queen Caroline: The Scandalous Affair that Nearly Ended a Monarchy* (New York: Free Press, 2006).

59 Solid green journal, Box 13A, MS 142, EPB Papers.

60 Solid green journal, ibid. The transcription is written as EPB wrote it, observing her spelling and capitalizations.

61 Solid green journal, 1864, ibid.

62 Solid green journal, 1864, ibid.

63 Carter, Diaries.

64 Memorial of Personal Effects, 1875, Box 13A, MS 142, EPB Papers.

65 ibid.

66 *Baltimore Sun,* June 30, 1907.

67 Solid red journal, Box 13A, MS 142, EPB Papers.

CHAPTER 2
"All My Actions Were Calculated"

1 Baltimore *Sunday Herald,* December 30, 1896. The article also states that EPB received 1,000 guineas at the time her son was born, $12,000 a year from Napoléon, and an additional $30,000 as a present. All of these statements were either erroneous or exaggerated.

2 Harriet Stewart to EPB, September 26, 1842, Box 7, MS 142, EPB Papers.

3 Figure taken from the probate record. See Probate Records of Elizabeth Patterson Bonaparte, October 1, 1879, Administration Accounts, Box 92, MSA T627-66, 2-36-8-4, Maryland State Archives.

4 This figure, as well as the 4,500 guineas, comes from an undated document in Elizabeth's own hand in Box 11, MS 142, EPB Papers.

5 Burn, *Betsy Bonaparte,* 111. Burn translates the sum of all three to be the equivalent of $1,400.

6 Letterbook, 1805, MS 142, EPB Papers. On November 24, 1807, Kuhn wrote to EPB that she had dined with Jérôme and, "you Madam was no less frequent the Topic of our conversation—he speaks of you as the only woman he ever Loved or even shall Love tho' united to another much against his Inclination which the Emperor his brother cruelly imposed on him."

7 In an undated document in Elizabeth's hand that lists the money she received from the French government, she noted, Jérôme "remitted me through England 1000 guineas of which guineas Mr. W Patterson took half." Box 9, MS 142, EPB Papers.

8 EPB to Mrs. M. H. Torres McCullough, January 24, 1861, Box 8, MS 142, EPB Papers.

9 Multi-color journal, 1809–1819, Box 13A, MS 142, EPB Papers and annotation in EPB's hand to a letter from James McElhiney to her, April 16, 1816, in ibid.

10 "I have the pleasure of acknowledging receipt of your favor of March [blank] by which was glad to see you had received the Documents I had sent you for my claims on the french Government, to amounts of 9384..19..9 pounds and 9069..2..0 pounds for supplies furnished the Colony of St. Domingo, and that you had put them in proper train for settlement which is perfectly satisfactory. This is intended to go by my Daughter Madam Elizabeth Bonaparte, who is to embark shortly with her husband for France, where they will probably remain for some time, and being desirous of establishing a credit at Paris for the use of my Daughter, I have to request you will pay her at the rate of five thousand Francs per annum." William Patterson to J. C. Hollinger Esq. Banker in Paris, June 6, 1804, MS 145, William Patterson Papers, MdHS.

11 Noted in an undated summary of money EPB received from France written in her own hand, Box 9, MS 142, EPB Papers.

12 EPB to Prince Gorchakov, 1858, Box 7, MS 142, EPB Papers.

13 Folder of 12 Receipts of William Patterson 1805–1809, MS 145, EPB Papers. "Recd the 6 June 1807 of Wm Patterson one hundred and fifty three Dollars & seventy five cents in full for Doctors Bills as follows for the year 1806/For His own Family $87.50 Madam Bonaparte $44.75. . . ."

14 Burn, *Betsy Bonaparte,* 134–35.

15 Noted in an undated summary of money EPB received from France, written in her own hand, Box 9, MS 142, EPB Papers. That amount was approximately

one hundred times an average American family's annual income.

16 Burn, *Betsy Bonaparte*, 146. This is substantiated by Elizabeth's notebook found in Box 9, MS 142, EPB Papers.

17 Eugene L. Didier. *The Life and Letters of Madame Bonaparte* (New York: Charles Scribner's Sons, 1879), 45.

18 A copy of a letter sent to Mrs. M. H. Torrens McCullugh written in EPB's hand, January 24, 1861, Box 8, MS 142, EPB Papers.

19 Annotation in *Memoirs of Princess Frederique*, Tome Premier, 339.

20 Burn, *Betsy Bonaparte*, 41. Louis André Pichon, Jérôme's banker, "estimated that young Bonaparte was spending a stunning thousand dollars a week."

21 This is perhaps one of the most frequently quoted remarks EPB ever made and appears in numerous publications, including Burn, *Betsy Bonaparte*, 138.

22 Undated journal with miscellaneous financial records from 1809 to 1819, pages unnumbered, Box 13A, MS 142, EPB Papers.

23 Nancy Spear continued to play a central role in Elizabeth's finances until the 1830s, guiding her investments as well as maintaining them during Elizabeth's frequent trips abroad.

24 R[obert] Patterson to EPB, Receipt, Baltimore February 25, 1811, Box 2, MS 142, EPB Papers. The receipt also records: "By balance due you as [?] acct./rendered 12th day Jany 1811 $7.675.98/By balance rec'd from you this date 1.324.02/R Patterson."

25 Robert Patterson to EPB, November 8, 1811, Box 2, MS 142, EPB Papers.

26 For additional information about the formation of Baltimore's water company, see Sherry H. Olson, *Baltimore: The Building of an American City* (Baltimore: The Johns Hopkins University Press, 1980), 48–49.

27 Probate Records of Elizabeth Patterson Bonaparte, October 1, 1879, Administration Accounts, Box 92, MSA T627-66, MSA. Elizabeth left $1,177.50 or 785 shares in the Reisterstown Turnpike Company.

28 Jerome Napoleon Bonaparte to EPB, March 5, 1813, Box 1, MS 144, EPB Papers.

29 Multi-color journal, 1809–1819, Box 13A, MS 142, EPB Papers.

30 Burn, *Betsy Bonaparte*, 64.

31 Ibid., 156.

32 See annotation in various journals.

33 The silver pitchers and gown both survive at the MdHS. The gown is on page 5 of Chapter 1.

34 Copy of a letter to Prince Alexandre Gorchakov, written in EPB's hand, February 19, 1861, Box 8, MS 142, EPB Papers. Elizabeth went on to say "that the restoration of the Bonaparte Dynasty has

neither caused his uncle's promises to myself to be carried out."

35 Nancy Spear to EPB, December 1, 1815, Box 2, MS 142, EPB Papers.

36 Mary Caton Patterson to EPB, December 18, 1815, in ibid.

37 Nancy Spear to EPB, 1815, "Your father appears to be making another fortune." In ibid.

38 Burn, *Betsy Bonaparte*, 169.

39 Although Elizabeth had entrusted the care of her son to Mary and Robert, she carried a lifelong resentment toward Mary and her sisters.

40 1809–1812—EPB about Pension from French Govt (stack of receipts for payments with this note attached to the front of it), Box 9, MS 142, EPB Papers. "It follows that if the franc is noted as in the Louisiana Convention 5000 francs will be worth Dolls. 937.50. If rated at its intrinsic value, or ascertained at the Mint 5000 francs will be worth Dolls. 931.50."

41 Berkin, *Wondrous Beauty*, 91–92.

42 Calculations are quoted from Burn, *Betsy Bonaparte*, 170. Her friend Lydia Russell's husband had warned Elizabeth of the expense of living abroad. Box 2, MS 142, EPB Papers, as quoted in Burn, *Betsy Bonaparte*, 168.

43 Nancy Spear to EPB, December 1, 1815, Box 3, MS 142, EPB Papers.

44 Nancy Spear to EPB, 1815, Box 3, MS 142, EPB Papers.

45 James McElhiney to EPB, April 16, 1816 including a transcription of William Patterson's letter to EPB of March 8, 1815, Box 2, MS 142, EPB Papers.

46 Nancy Spear to EPB, 1815, Box 3, MS 142, EPB Papers.

47 Burn, *Betsy Bonaparte*, 201.

48 Nancy Spear to EPB, May 5, 1816, Box 2, MS 142, EPB Papers.

49 Nancy Spear to EPB, 1816. Beside the date, EPB wrote, "I suppose." Box 3, MS 142, EPB Papers.

50 EPB to John Spear Smith, Esq., August 22, 1816, ibid.

51 Edward Patterson to EPB, January 3, 1817, ibid.

52 Edward Patterson to EPB, January 11, 1817, ibid.

53 Account book, Box 14, MS 142, EPB Papers.

54 Multi-color journal, 1809–1819, Box 13A, MS 142, EPB Papers.

55 The House of Willink was owned by Jan and Wilhelm Willink, who had ties to the United States dating back to the American Revolution. For additional information about the banking firm, see Gregg L. Lint, C. James Taylor, Margaret A. Hogan, Jessie May Rodrique, Mary T. Claffey, and Hobson Woodward, eds., *The Adams Papers: Papers of John Adams*, volume 13 (Boston: The Belknap Press of Harvard University Press, 2006), ix. Bills of Exchange are defined as "an

unconditional order in writing, addressed by one person to another, signed by the person giving it, requiring the person to whom it is addressed to pay on demand or at a fixed or determined future time a sum certain in money to or to the order of a specified person, or to the bearer." *The Encyclopedia Britannica: A Dictionary of Arts, Sciences, Literature and General Information,* Eleventh Edition, Volume III (New York: The Encyclopædia Britannica Company, 1910): 940.

56 Didier, *Life and Letters of Madame Bonaparte,* 66.

57 Burn and Berkin both note the story of Bo's request for a horse from his mother who could, at that time, ill afford it. Instead she is said to have bought the boy a dog. See Burn, *Betsy Bonaparte,* 187 and Berkin, *Wondrous Beauty,* 104.

58 Didier, *Life and Letters of Madame Bonaparte,* 64.

59 Burn, *Betsy Bonaparte,* 187.

60 Didier, *Life and Letters of Madame Bonaparte,* 150.

61 EPB to William Patterson, June 23, 1820, Bonaparte Vertical File, MdHS.

62 Burn, *Betsy Bonaparte,* 188. Burn also notes that Elizabeth preferred not to be isolated outside of town, away from her friends.

63 Burn, *Betsy Bonaparte,* 189.

64 Berkin, *Wondrous Beauty,* 121.

65 Jerome Napoleon Bonaparte to William Patterson, March 3, 1824 in Didier, *Life and Letters of Madame Bonaparte,* 154.

66 Lewis, *Elizabeth Patterson Bonaparte,* 204.

67 Daily Accounts, 1826–32, Box 13A, MS 142, EPB Papers.

68 EPB to William Patterson, as quoted in Lewis, *Elizabeth Patterson Bonaparte,* 120.

69 Solid red journal, Box 13A, MS 142, EPB Papers.

70 William Patterson to EPB, August 15, 1831, MS 145, William Patterson Papers, MdHS.

71 John White to EPB, April 14, 1833 and copied verbatim on April 27, 1833, Box 6, MS 142, EPB Papers.

72 Nancy Spear to EPB, August 4, 1833, ibid.

73 William Patterson to EPB, March 10, 1834 and annotated by EPB in 1867, ibid. Among the many affronts Elizabeth felt her father inflicted upon her was his refusal to give her the money her mother left to her.

74 Fragment of an account book, undated, Box 13A, MS 142, EPB Papers.

75 Notes on William Patterson's Last Will and Testament, undated, Box 11, MS 142, EPB Papers.

76 William Patterson, Will, August 20, 1827, MS 145, William Patterson Papers.

77 Box 10, MS 142, EPB Papers.

78 Notes on letter wrappers, Box 11, MS 142, EPB Papers.

79 Carter, Diaries.

80 Solid red journal, Box 13A, MS 142, EPB Papers.

81 William Patterson to EPB, September 14, 1824, MS 145, William Patterson Papers.

82 Taken from fragment of an account book, Box 10, MS 142, EPB Papers.

83 Box 10, MS 142, EPB Papers. Statement made by EPB on August 8, 1838 concerning her income:

3 Houses Market St. at $400 each	$1200
South Street Duncan	$ 400
Watts, water St called Lombard Street	$ 300
Daley House, $300 & story across yard 50	$ 350
2 granite front at $400 of each	$ 800
Two granite fronts (without tenants) Balt Street	
of rents 4014	

Yearly income of EP alias	
Rent aforementioned—per year 1838	$4014
$10,000 Lent to Durham at 6 per cent per annum	$600
$5,000 Lent to George Hughes at 6 per cent	$300
$10,098 Lent to Elizabeth Edwards at 6 per cent	$606..88
$37,000 in City 5 per cent	$1850
$12,000 in Ste. Maryland 6 per cents	$720
$8,000 in ditto 5 per cent	$400
18,000 in ditto 4 ½ percent	$810
Shares in Reister T. Pike Road (187 shares)	$ .94..20
9 shares of Frederick ditto	$..3..60
40 shares Merchant Bank of Baltimore, at 6 percent	$240
42 ditto in Bank of United States at 8 per cent per annum	$336
3 Ditto in Bank of Baltimore	$63
2 Bonds (1 & three) of Baltimore & this R.R. Comp 7	
40 shares water stocks	
30 ditto Union Cotton Factory	
43 ditto in Baltimore & Ohio R&R	
2 empty granite fronts in Market Street	
Certificate $261..29. Indemnity to water,	
French 5 per cents in Paris	
Account taken august 8th year 1838	
amount total	$10,717.76

84 EPB to Alexander Yearly, July 2, 1839, Box 10, MS 142, EPB Papers.

85 Didier, *The Life and Letters of Madame Bonaparte,* 248.

86 Both calculations are found written on fragments of an account book, Box 13A, MS 142, EPB Papers.

87 Solid red journal, ibid.

88 Didier, *The Life and Letters of Madame Bonaparte,* 252–53.

89 Harriet Stewart to EPB, March 20, 1849, Box 7, MS 142, EPB Papers.

90 Solid red journal, Box 13A, MS 142, EPB Papers.

91 Burn, *Betsy Bonaparte*, 226.

92 Solid red journal, Box 13A, MS 142, EPB Papers.

93 Ibid.

94 Burn, *Betsy Bonaparte*, 176, 222–23.

95 Lewis, *Elizabeth Patterson Bonaparte*, 225. Numerous scholars have stated that EPB collected her own rents. I have yet to see evidence of it. There is no question that Elizabeth put agents in charge of collecting her rents when she was in Europe, but how they were collected while she was in Baltimore, I cannot state with any certainty.

96 EPB to Jerome Napoleon Bonaparte, her grandson, September 2, 1858, Box 7, MS 142, EPB Papers.

97 Solid green journal, Box 13A, MS 142, EPB Papers.

98 William Mentzel to EPB, December 28, 1860, May 14, 1861, October 11, 1862, and December 8, 1863, Box 7, MS 142, EPB Papers.

99 Solid green journal, Box 12A, MS 142, EPB Papers.

100 Small green journal, 1863, Box 13A, MS 142, EPB Papers.

101 Probate Inventory of Elizabeth Patterson, April 23, 1879. Maryland State Archives, Baltimore City, Inventories, original.

102 The most informative source of information for the growth in Elizabeth's wealth during the war is the solid green journal, Box 13A, MS 142, EPB Papers.

103 EPB to Charles Joseph Bonaparte, September 24, 1869, MS 2978, EPB Papers.

104 In several letters to her grandson, Jerome, Elizabeth tried to use money to manipulate his decisions. She had hoped that her gift of $5,000 when he was in France would compel him to follow her advice and make a match in Europe. When he chose to marry Caroline LeRoy Appleton Edgar, a widow with three children, Elizabeth wrote, "Those $5,000, which misplaced affection had contributed to the support of high Position for yourself will cease with the defeat of my object." EPB to Jerome Napoleon Bonaparte, August 18, 1871, Box 8, MS 142, EPB Papers.

105 EPB to Charles Joseph Bonaparte, September 24, 1869, MS 2978, EPB Papers.

106 Composition book, 1871, Box 13A, MS 142, EPB Papers. In 1871, after her grandson Jerome Jr.'s marriage to a widow, she ended his allowance and became more generous with Charles.

107 EPB to Charles Joseph Bonaparte, October 6, 1873, MS 2978, Charles Joseph Bonaparte Papers, MdHS. The financial panic of 1873 led to a four-year depression, until then the most severe in American history.

108 Solid red journal, Box 13A, MS 142, EPB Papers.

109 Ibid.

110 Frances Scott and Anne Cipriani Webb, *Who is Markie? The Life of Martha Custis Williams Carter, Cousin and Confidante of Robert E. Lee* (Westminster, Md.: Heritage Books, Inc., 2007), 54.

CHAPTER 3
"O, for Celebrity . . ."

1 EPB draft of a letter to an unknown person, August 12, 1864, Box 8, MS 142, EPB Papers.

2 Lewis, *Elizabeth Patterson Bonaparte*.

3 Obituary of Elizabeth Patterson Bonaparte entitled, "Death of a Celebrated Personage," *Baltimore Sun*, April 5, 1879.

4 EPB to Charles Joseph Bonaparte, October 24, 1870, Box 2, MS 2978, Bonaparte Papers, MdHS.

5 Carter, Diaries, entry dated May 1, 1876.

6 W. T. R. Saffell, *The Bonaparte-Patterson Marriage in 1803 and the Secret Correspondence on the Subject Never Before Made Public* (Philadelphia: by the Proprietor, 1873), vii–viii. According to Saffell, he copied the letters, then "returned them to Mr. Patterson's grandson." Who that was remains unclear. In a letter to his mother, Susan May Williams, dated February 15, 1873, Charles Bonaparte wrote, "I understand that Edward Patterson has recovered the original of Saffell's letters. Is this what you meant to say?" Box 1, MS 141, Charles Joseph Bonaparte Papers. Charles was referring to Edward Patterson Jr. (1825–1886), William Patterson's grandson, born to Elizabeth's brother Edward Patterson and his wife Sidney Smith Patterson. The letters that Saffell borrowed are not in the collection of the Maryland Historical Society.

7 Saffell, *The Bonaparte-Patterson Marriage*, v.

8 Solid red journal, 1858–59, Box 13A, MS 142, EPB Papers.

9 Frédérique Sophie Wilhelmine de Prusse, *Mémoires de Frédérique Sophie Wilhelmine . . . Soeur de Frederic-Le-Grand: Ecrits de sa Main, Tome I and II* (Paris, 1811), 2:240, Book Collection 1741–1928, MS 3134, Bonaparte Book Collection. EPB bought this book in 1840 and later gave it to her grandson, Charles Joseph. The margins contain her thoughts, most of which relate to her ex-husband and her father.

10 Solid red journal, Box 13A, MS 142, EPB Papers.

11 Ibid.

12 Ibid. Elizabeth recorded this thought among many comments about the 1861 lawsuit she and Bo pressed in the French courts to gain acknowledgment of Bo's right to the French throne.

13 Ibid.

14 Ibid.

15 Scott and Webb, *Who is Markie?*, 56.

16 EPB to Charles Joseph Bonaparte, October 24, 1870, Box 2, MS 2978, Charles Joseph Bonaparte Papers, MdHS.

17 Burn, Lewis, and Berkin all discuss Elizabeth's European friendships. Her longtime friendship with Lady Sydney Morgan was the most intimate and lasting female relationship in her life, from the 1820s until Morgan's death in 1859. Elizabeth's trip to Europe in 1849 was in large part motivated by her desire to see Lady Morgan. Numerous letters from Morgan to EPB survive in MS 142, EPB Papers.

18 Nancy Spear to EPB, undated, Box 9, MS 142, EPB Papers.

19 Grey-green journal, 1873–75, Box 13A, MS 142, EPB Papers.

20 "Death of a Celebrated Personage," *Baltimore Sun*, April 5, 1879.

21 Last Will and Testament of Elizabeth Patterson Bonaparte, September 2, 1871, Box 12, MS 142, EPB Papers.

22 Carter, Diaries, entry dated May 1, 1876.

23 Burn, *Betsy Bonaparte*, 252.

24 The letter from James McElhiney to EPB dated April 16, 1816 also bears EPB's annotation, which reads, "Note made 16 January 1867—His [William Patterson's] Mistress Nancy Todd was in his house when his wife was on her death bed & expelled by Edward Patterson. [She] was succeeded in the same capacity by Somers by whom he had in old age a bastard daughter—the Wheelers succeeded the Somers." See Box 2, MS 142, EPB Papers.

25 As quoted in Lewis, *Elizabeth Patterson Bonaparte*, 220.

26 The cartoon is found in an undated scrapbook in Box 14, MS 142, EPB Papers.

27 Elizabeth's inventories repeatedly note both the portrait of Jérôme by Stuart and her husband's wedding suit.

28 Solid red journal, Box 13A, MS 142, EPB Papers.

29 Blue marbled journal, ibid., records: "August 9 1860/ Mme Bonaparte has placed in the Gallery of M Historical Society four Paintings to be returned at any time on her orders A M Rogers/No 1 Portrait of Mme Bonaparte/No 2 ditto by Stewart/No 3 of King Jérôme Bonaparte/No 4 Crayon of Grandson/No. 5 & 6 Engraving of Nap. & Empress."

30 Journal, "Mme Bonaparte née Patterson Memorial of Personal Effects year 1875 Jewelry included," Box 13A, MS 142, EPB Papers. "1 April 1875 at the Mercantile Library: Stewards [*sic*] 3 views of my Face on 1 Canvas/Stewards Portrait of the late King Jérôme/Dalmaines Pastel Portrait of My Grand Son JNB/Kinsons Portrait of Myself; painted year 1817/Engraving of Empress Eugenie/Engraving of Emperor Louis Napoleon." The Mercantile Library Association was founded in 1839 and was located at the corner of St. Paul and Saratoga Streets in Baltimore.

31 Greenish-red marbled journal labeled, "Account of jewelry this book year 187_, Years 71-72-73" notes that the painting of "ex-husband J.B." was at the "Library corner of St. Paul & Saratoga Street." EPB Papers.

32 Last Will and Testament of Elizabeth Patterson Bonaparte, September 2, 1871, Box 12, MS 142, EPB Papers.

33 Jill Lepore, *Book of Ages: The Life and Opinions of Jane Franklin* (New York: Alfred A. Knopf, 2013), 114.

34 Solid red journal, Box 13A, MS 142, EPB Papers.

35 Lewis provides the most compelling discussion of Elizabeth as a "new" aristocrat. See Lewis, *Elizabeth Patterson Bonaparte*.

36 "Death of a Celebrated Personage," *Baltimore Sun*, April 5, 1879.

37 Entries dated between 1874 and 1876, Carter, Diaries, "Memorial of Personal Effects, 1875," MS 142, Box 13A, EPB Papers.

38 Grey-green journal, 1875, Box 13A, MS 142, EPB Papers.

39 Charles's wife, Ellen Channing Day Bonaparte, gave the armoire and Elizabeth's books to the Maryland Historical Society in 1921.

40 Mary Wollstonecraft Godwin, *Maria or, the Wrongs of Woman: A Posthumous Fragment* (Philadelphia, 1799). MS 3134, Bonaparte Book Collection, MdHS. "Miss Spear" is on the title page in handwriting that does not appear to be Elizabeth's, suggesting it may have been a gift to Elizabeth from her aunt, Nancy Spear. On page 24, Elizabeth wrote, "Eliza Patterson 1801." Wollstonecraft's "feminist" writing would have appealed to Elizabeth's independent-minded aunt, who did not conform to the model of female behavior prescribed by society. Spear's choice to remain unmarried, maintain a keen interest in politics, and manage her finances as well as those of her niece, were atypical for a woman of the nineteenth century. A note card in the library's collection records indicates that the book traveled with Elizabeth on her 1804 voyage that ended in a shipwreck off the coast of Long Island. Several pages are water-stained, confirmation that the book was aboard that ship.

41 Wilhelmine, *Mémoires de Frédérique Sophie Wilhelmine de Prusse*.

42 Ibid., 1:190.

43 Marginalia in *Mémoires de Frédérique Sophie Wilhelmine de Prusse*, 2:405.

44 Solid red journal, Box 13A, MS 142, EPB Papers.

45 Madame de Staal, *Memoires de Madame de Staal, Tome Premier* (London, 1755), 62, Bonaparte Book Collection, MS 3134, MdHS.

46 Didier, *The Life and Letters of Madame Bonaparte*, 45.

47 Lady Sydney Morgan, *Lady Morgan's Memoirs in Three Volumes in Collection of British Authors, Tauchnitz Edition* (Leipzig: B. Tauchnitz, 1863), 2:180.

48 In the preface to the *Lady Morgan's Memoirs*, her "literary executor," W. Hepworth Dixon, recounted

that Morgan left all her writings to him and his role in assembling her memoir was only to record Morgan's own thoughts. If his assertion is accepted as fact, the descriptions of Elizabeth in the *Memoirs* reflect Morgan's true opinions of her friend. Based on surviving letters between the two women at the Maryland Historical Society, Morgan's feelings toward Elizabeth were warmer and more genuine than the narrative in her *Memoirs* suggests.

49 *Lady Morgan's Memoirs*, 2:205.

50 Ibid., 2:204.

51 Ibid., 3:210.

52 Solid red journal, Box 13A, MS 142, EPB Papers.

53 From a list of possessions "left at the bank" in 1825, Box 9, MS 142, EPB Papers.

54 In 1935, Laura Patterson Swan, a descendant of Elizabeth's brother, Edward, presented a large group of French ceramics to the Maryland Historical Society. Included in the gift is a plate with an image of Napoléon and another with an image of King Jérôme. These plates may be part of a set Elizabeth sold to her brother Edward in 1815 for $600.

55 Greenish-red marbled journal, Box 13A, MS 142, EPB Papers.

56 Reference to the gift of the watch found in John White to EPB, January 23, 1833, Box 6, MS 142, EPB Papers, and reference to the gift of a ring to Gallatin in 1875, Box 13A, MS 142, EPB Papers.

57 Memorial of Personal Effects, 1875, Box 13A, MS 142, EPB Papers.

58 Ibid.

59 Elizabeth Patterson Bonaparte to William Patterson, September 9, 1829, Box 5, MS 142, EPB Papers.

60 *Baltimore Sun*, Sunday morning, June 30, 1907.

61 Elizabeth gave her grandson Jerome gifts of jewelry prior to her death in 1879, but the most significant collection went to Charles. In 1979, a theft at the Maryland Historical Society led to the unfortunate loss of some of the most valuable Bonaparte jewelry in the collection. To date, those pieces have not been recovered.

62 Entry dated December 5, 1876, Carter, Diaries.

63 Last Will and Testament of Elizabeth Patterson Bonaparte, September 2, 1871, Box 12, MS 142, EPB Papers.

64 Carter, Diaries, December 28, 1876.

65 Ibid., December 19, 1876.

66 Ibid., November 1876 [no date].

67 Burn, *Betsy Bonaparte*, 207.

68 Carter, Diaries, December 1877, [no date].

69 Helen Jean Burn suggests that Gorchakov may have been the one man to whom Elizabeth genuinely

became emotionally attached. For more information about their friendship see, Burn, *Betsy Bonaparte*, 205–8.

70 EPB to Prince Alexandre Gorchakov, February 19, 1861, Box 8, MS 142, EPB Papers.

71 Carter, Diaries, undated.

72 Clipping in Box 1, MS 141, Charles Joseph Bonaparte Papers.

73 EPB to Charles Joseph Bonaparte, May 16, 1872, Box 2, MS 2978, Charles Joseph Bonaparte Papers.

CHAPTER 4
"Mésalliances are Fatal in Most Families"

1 The verb mésallier is defined as, "to marry beneath one." Here, Elizabeth probably means "a bad match."

2 Wilhelmine, *Mémoires de Frédérique Sophie Wilhelmine*, 1:330.

3 Birth Certificate of Jerome Napoleon Bonaparte, July 7, 1805, copy, Box 12, MS 144, Jerome Napoleon Bonaparte Papers, MdHS.

4 Bishop John Carroll to EPB, May 3, 1809, Box 2, MS 142, EPB Papers.

5 Scott and Webb, *Who is Markie?*, 55. Carter wrote, "She [Elizabeth] refused to allow me to read the Bible to her—said she hated the mention of religion."

6 Jérôme Napoléon Bonaparte to EPB, May 23, 1806, MS 143, Jérôme Bonaparte, King of Westphalia Papers, MdHS.

7 Jérôme Napoléon Bonaparte to EPB, April 26, 1806, ibid.

8 Bo to EPB, January 14 and April 4, 1814, and December 18 and 26, 1813, Box 1, MS 144, JNB Papers.

9 Bo to William Patterson, February 1, 1817, Box 1, MS 144, and Bonaparte Commonplace Book, Box 5, MS 144, JNB Papers.

10 Bo to EPB, March 5, 1813, Box 1, MS 144, JNB Papers.

11 Bo to EPB, March 5, 1814, Box 1, MS 144, ibid.

12 Mary Caton Patterson to EPB, July 15, 1815, Box 2, MS 142, EPB Papers.

13 Jérôme Napoléon Bonaparte to EPB to Bo, May 16, 1808, MS 143, Jérôme Bonaparte, King of Westphalia Papers, MdHS.

14 Jérôme Napoléon Bonaparte to EPB, November 22 and May 16, 1808, MS 143, ibid.

15 Bo to EPB, January 14, 1814 and February 9, 1814, Box 1, MS 144, JNB Papers.

16 Jérôme Napoléon Bonaparte was driven out of Cassel, Germany, on September 30, 1813. For a history of Jérôme's life see Philip Walsingham Sergeant, *The Burlesque Napoleon: Being the Story of the Life and the Kingship of Jerome Napoleon Bonaparte, Youngest Brother of Napoleon the Great* (London: T. W. Laurie, 1905).

17 Notebook of EPB, Box 9, MS 142, EPB Papers, as noted by Helen Jean Burn, *Betsy Bonaparte*, 132.

18 Translation of a letter from Jérôme Bonaparte to EPB ("ma chère Eliza"), February 20, 1812, MS 143, Jérôme Bonaparte, King of Westphalia Papers. MdHS. See Burn, *Betsy Bonaparte*, 152.

19 Bo to EPB, December 18, 1813, Box 1, MS 144, JNB Papers.

20 Bo to EPB, December 26, 1813 and March 28, 1814, ibid.

21 Bo to EPB, December 7, 1813, ibid.; Elbridge Gerry to EPB, April 22, 1814, Box 2, MS 142, EPB Papers.

22 Between 1813 and 1815, all of Bo's letters to his mother were addressed to her in Washington, D.C. On March 30, 1815, shortly before she sailed for Europe, he wrote to her in Boston. See MS 142, EPB Papers; Bo to EPB, March 30, 1815, MS 144, Box 1, JNB Papers.

23 Mary Caton Patterson to EPB, July 15, 1815, Box 2, MS 142, EPB Papers.

24 EPB to John Spear Smith, August 22 1816, ibid.

25 William Patterson to EPB, June 12, 1826, Box 1, MS 145, William Patterson Papers, MdHS.

26 Edward Patterson to EPB, March 25, 1816, Box 2, MS 142, EPB Papers.

27 Burn, *Betsy Bonaparte*, 186, taken from a letter from EPB to WP, April 25, 1820, in Didier. *Life and Letters of Madame Bonaparte*.

28 Lewis, *Elizabeth Patterson Bonaparte*, 208.

29 All these documents survive in MS 142, EPB Papers.

30 Bo to William Patterson, May 5, 1819, MS 144, Box 1, JNB Papers.

31 Didier, *Life and Letters of Madame Bonaparte*, 56.

32 Ibid., 55, 56.

33 Ibid., 74.

34 Draft of a letter from Bo to Prince Jérôme Bonaparte, May 22, 1821, Box 1, MS 144, JNB Papers.

35 Bonaparte Commonplace Book, Blue and Red Marbled Book, undated, Box 5, MS 144, JNB Papers.

36 Ibid.

37 EPB to William Patterson, April 25 and May 8, 1820, Didier, *Life and Letters of Madame Bonaparte*, 63, 64, 68.

38 EPB to William Patterson, December 21, 1821, in Didier, *The Life and Letters of Madame Bonaparte*, 96.

39 EPB to William Patterson, January 29–30, 1822, in Didier, *The Life and Letters of Madame Bonaparte*, 104.

40 Bonaparte Commonplace Book, Box 1, MS 144, JNB Papers.

41 Diary of James Gallatin, August 11 and 18, 1816 as quoted in Burn, *Betsy Bonaparte*, 180.

42 Madame Mère to Joseph Bonaparte, January 25, 1822 as quoted by Didier, *Life and Letters of Madame Bonaparte* and referenced by Burn, *Betsy Bonaparte*, 189; William Patterson to EPB, June 12, 1826, MS 145, William Patterson Papers; EPB to William Patterson, November 28, 1821, in Didier, *The Life and Letters of Madame Bonaparte*, 94.

43 Red and blue marbled notebook, undated, pages unnumbered, Box 1, MS 144, JNB Papers.

44 Solid red journal, Box 13, MS 142, EPB Papers. Elizabeth wrote, "Malaparte [Jérôme] did not give words to what mentally he had determined on. The words would have been as follow. . ." above this verse.

45 EPB to William Patterson, July 7, 1822, in Didier, *Life and Letters of Madame Bonaparte*, 102.

46 Bo to William Patterson, December 7, 1822; EPB to William Patterson, January 29–30, 1822 in Didier, *Life and Letters of Madame Bonaparte*, 87, 90.

47 Didier, *Life and Letters of Madame Bonaparte*, 110.

48 EPB to William Patterson, October 15, 1822, in Didier, *Life and Letters of Madame Bonaparte*, 112. Within the Jerome Bonaparte Papers, Box 5 MS 144, are various notebooks Bo used while at Harvard.

49 Jérôme Bonaparte to Bo, Box 1, MS 143, Jérôme Bonaparte, King of Westphalia Papers, MdHS.

50 Bo to William Patterson, July 28, 1822, Box 1, MS 144, JNB Papers.

51 EPB to William Patterson, September 23, 1824 and June 4, 1825, in Didier, *Life and Letters of Madame Bonaparte*, 158, 161.

52 EPB to William Patterson, September 23, 1824 and June 4, 1825; William Patterson to Bo, August 14, 1825, Didier, *Life and Letters of Madame Bonaparte*, 158, 161, 164–65.

53 Didier, *Life and Letters of Madame Bonaparte*, 162; Prince Jérôme Bonaparte to Bo, March 6, 1826 as cited by Burn, *Betsy Bonaparte*, 196; EPB to John Spear Smith, August 22, 1816, Box 2, MS 142, EPB Papers.

54 Bo to William Patterson, January 7 and 25, 1827, and EPB to William Patterson, December 18, 1826; Didier, *The Life and Letters of Madame Bonaparte*, 193, 199, 200; EPB to John Spear Smith, August 22, 1816, Box 2, MS 142, EPB Papers.

55 Helen Jean Burn points out that Bo's response to his visit was mercenary in tone when he remarked, "I see no possibility of his doing anything for me." *Betsy Bonaparte*, 198; Bo to William Patterson, January 7, 1827; Didier, *Life and Letters of Madame Bonaparte*, 198.

56 William Patterson to EPB, April 23, 1827, MS 145, William Patterson Papers.

57 Jérôme Bonaparte to Bo, April 14, 1827, Box 8, MS 144, JNB Papers.

58 William Patterson to EPB, July 24, 1829, MS 145, William Patterson Papers.

59 EPB to William Patterson, September 29, 1829, MS 142, Box 5, EPB Papers; EPB to William Patterson, September 29, 1829, Box 5, MS 142, EPB Papers; EPB to William Patterson, September 5, 1829, letter in the collection of Mark B. Letzer; EPB to William Patterson, 1829, as quoted in Lewis, *Elizabeth Patterson Bonaparte*, 209; EPB to William Patterson, October 17, 1828, Box 5, MS 142, EPB Papers.

60 Letizia Romolino to Bo, November 10, 1829, Box 1, MS 144, JNB Papers.

61 William Patterson to EPB, November 4, 1829, MS 145, William Patterson Papers.

62 Lewis, *An American Aristocrat*, 210–11.

63 EPB to William Patterson, November 4, 1829, in Didier, *Life and Letters of Madame Bonaparte*, 218–20; Bonaparte Commonplace Book, Box 5, MS 144, JNB Papers; Edward Patterson to EPB, March 5, 1830, Box 5, MS 142, EPB Papers; Nancy Spear to EPB, August 20, 1830, Box 6, MS 142, EPB Papers, quoted in Lewis, *An American Aristocrat*, 211.

64 William Patterson to EPB, November 4, 1829, MS 145, William Patterson Papers.

65 Edward Patterson to EPB, March 5, 1830, Box 5, MS 142, EPB Papers.

66 Spear to EPB, August 29, 1830, Box 5, MS 142, EPB Papers.

67 For a discussion of Elizabeth's actions after Bo's marriage, see Burn, *Betsy Bonaparte*, 202–3.

68 EPB to William Patterson, September 29, 1829, Box 5, MS 142, EPB Papers.

69 Bonaparte Commonplace Book, Box 5, MS 144, JNB Papers; Lewis, *An American Aristocrat*, 143.

70 Drawing of coat of arms, n.d., Box 11, MS 142, EPB Papers.

71 On March 3, 1824, Bo wrote to his grandfather: "Mamma complains of my expenses a great deal and says that she will allow in future eleven hundred dollars per annum for my expenses . . . however advantageous I may conceive a college education to be for me, I should prefer giving it up too, rather than to hear these continual and uninterrupted complaints about my expenses." See Bo to William Patterson, March 3, 1824, in Didier, *Life and Letters of Madame Bonaparte*, 154. On August 22, 1859, he wrote to Susan, "I have ordered a leopard carpet without the red stripes" (Box 3, MS 2978, JNB Papers). That same year, he acquired numerous household goods for an apparent redecoration of the Park Avenue house. See also Invoices, Box 5, MS 144, JNB Papers and Jerome Napoleon Bonaparte Probate Inventory, 1870, Maryland State Archives.

72 Burn, *Betsy Bonaparte*, 209.

73 Burn writes, "Betsy visited there, but rarely. Susan never forgave the original opposition to her marriage. It was clear Betsy wasn't welcome." Evidence for this is scant, but given Elizabeth's tendency to bear grudges, it would not be out of character for her to have scorned her daughter-in-law. See Burn, *Betsy Bonaparte*, 209.

74 Carter, Diaries, entry dated 1876, pages unnumbered. See Box 7, MS 142, EPB Papers.

75 Numerous publications provide detailed information about William Patterson's will. Recent publications include Lewis, *An American Aristocrat*, 188–92, 226; Burn, *Betsy Bonaparte*, 210–11, 212–14; and Berkin, *Wondrous Beauty*, 149–59, 161, 162, 163, 166, 174.

76 Bo to EPB, March 31, 1835, Box 2, MS 144, JNB Papers.

77 William Patterson Will, MS 145, William Patterson Papers.

78 Burn, *Betsy Bonaparte*, 213–15.

79 Solid red journal, Box 13A, MS 142, EPB Papers.

80 Burn, *Betsy Bonaparte*, 212–16.

81 Solid red journal, Box 13A, MS 142, EPB Papers. "He never says . . ." written on Bo's letter to EPB, March 31, 1835, as quoted in Burn, *Betsy Bonaparte*, 217.

82 Solid red journal, Box 13A, MS 142, EPB Papers. "John" is crossed out in the original. George is not mentioned because of his kindness to her during the lawsuit. John, her brother who lived in Virginia, did not involve himself in the suit. At the time of Patterson's death, John, who had already received property from his father during his lifetime, only inherited a portion of the household goods and the wine cellar. See Burn, *Betsy Bonaparte*, 212.

83 Solid red journal, Box 13A, MS 142, dated by EPB, "22 April 1857," EPB Papers.

84 Bo to Louis-Napoléon Bonaparte, April, [no date] 1837, and Louis-Napoléon Bonaparte to Bo, April 18, 1837, Letterbook Volume II, p. 20, Box 8, MS 144, JNB Papers.

85 Fenton Bressler, *Napoleon III: A Life* (New York: Carroll & Graf Publishers, 1999). Bo to Lewis Cass, October 20, 1838, Letterbook III, p. 4, Box 8, MS 144, JNB Papers.

86 Lewis Cass to Bo, October 25, 1838, and Bo to Cass, December 9, 1838, Letterbook III, pp. 5–6, Box 8, MS 144, JNB Papers.

87 Lewis Cass to Bo, December 7, 1838, and September 3, 1839; Bo to Henry Muhlenberg, November 14, 1839, Letterbook III, Box 8, MS 144, JNB Papers.

88 J. R. Clay to Bo, October 30, 1839, Letterbook III, Box 7, MS 144, JNB Papers.

89 Bo to Lewis Cass, August 26, 1839, Letterbook III, Box 8, MS 144, JNB Papers.

90 Bo to Messrs. Fenzi & Co., September 8, 1845, Letterbook III, Box 8, MS 144, JNB Papers.

91 Bo to Berryer, May 28, 1857, ibid.

92 Jerome Jr. to EPB, August 18, 1849, Box 2, MS 144, JNB Papers.

93 Burn, *Betsy Bonaparte,* 224. Robert E. Lee, then a brevet-colonel in the U.S. Army, moved to Baltimore in 1847 to oversee the construction of Fort Carroll, which he designed. He established his residence on Madison Avenue not far from the Bonapartes, and was a close friend of the family even through the Civil War, despite their differing loyalties.

94 General George Cadwalader to Bo, June 18, 1851, Letterbook I, Box 7, MS 144, JNB Papers. Cadwalader had retired to Philadelphia after the Mexican War but would resume his military career during the Civil War and command Fort McHenry in 1861.

95 Jerome Jr. to Bo, December 7, 1850, Box 2, MS 2978, Bonaparte Papers, MdHS.

96 Jerome Jr. to Bo, February 8, 1850, ibid.

97 Solid red journal, Box 13A, MS 142, EPB Papers.

98 Jerome Jr. to Bo, February 8, 1850, Box 2, MS 2978, Bonaparte Papers, MdHS.

99 Jerome Jr. to Bo, June 22, 1851, ibid.

100 Jerome Jr. to Bo, February 1, 1851, ibid.

101 Bo to Captain Breverton, January 14, 1852, Letterbook I, Box 8, MS 144, JNB Papers.

102 Jerome Jr. to Bo, January 11, 1852, Box 2, MS 2978, Bonaparte Papers, MdHS.

103 Carter, Diaries.

104 Edwards Lester and Edwin Williams to Jerome Jr., April 29, 1852, Letterbook II, Box 8, MS 144, JNB Papers.

105 Jerome Jr. to Edward Lester, undated, Letterbook II, Box 8, MS 144, JNB Papers; Bo to Lester & Williams, May 6, 1852, Letterbook I, Box 7, MS 144, ibid. "When I executed a Portrait of yourself for Madame Bonaparte in 1856 . . . ," George D'Almaine to Col. Jerome N. Bonaparte Jr., May 23, 1879, Box 4, MS 144, ibid.

106 Jerome Jr. to Bo, January 11, 1852, Box 2, MS 2978, Bonaparte Papers, MdHS.

107 Jerome Jr. to Bo, January 22, 1850, "I might make a very good cavalry or Artillery officer. . ."; Jerome Jr. to Bo, January 11, and February 8, 1852, Box, 2, MS 2978, Bonaparte Papers, MdHS.

108 Jerome Jr. to Susan, February 2, 1853; Jerome Jr. to Bo, February 2 and December 31, 1853, ibid.

109 Jerome Jr. to Secretary of War Jefferson Davis, April 7, 1854, and Robert E. Lee to Bo, May 30, 1854, Box 1, MS 144, JNB Papers.

110 Sergeant, *The Burlesque Napoleon,* 371.

111 Bo to Susan, June 18 and 21, 1854; Jerome Jr. to Susan, June 21, 1854, Box 2, MS 2978, Bonaparte Papers, MdHS.

112 Bo to Susan with additions by Jerome Jr., June 21, 1854, ibid. Bo referred to his half-brother as Plomplon. Jerome Jr. referred to him as Plonplon. Napoleon Joseph Charles Paul Bonaparte is now most commonly referred to as "Plon Plon."

113 Bo to Susan, June 25, 1854, Box 2, MS 2978, Bonaparte Papers, MdHS.

114 Ibid.

115 Bo to Susan, June 30 1854, ibid.

116 Bo to Susan, July 16, 1854, ibid.

117 Bo to Susan, July 16 and 22, 1854, ibid.

118 Ibid.

119 Bo to Susan, July 22 and September 12, 1854, ibid.

120 Jerome Jr. to Susan, July 18, 1854, ibid. Joachim Murat (1834–1901) was the son of Lucien Murat, who married Caroline, Napoléon's sister. Bo and Jerome Jr. socialized extensively with the Murats. Bo commissioned a bust of Lucien in New York; the whereabouts are now unknown.

121 Bo explained this to Susan in a letter of July 28, 1854, Box 2, MS 2978, Bonaparte Papers, MdHS.

122 Bo to Susan, September 3, 1854, ibid.

123 Bo to Susan, September 4, 1854, ibid.

124 Jerome Jr. to Bo, July 2, 1855, Box 3, MS 2978, Bonaparte Papers, MdHS.

125 Bo to Susan, June 18 and July 16, 1855, Letterbook V, Box 8, MS 144, JNB Papers.

126 Jerome Jr. to Bo, February 25, 1855, ibid.

127 Memorial of Personal Effects, 1875, Box 13A, MS 142, EPB Papers. Elizabeth notes a miniature of Plon Plon. The miniature passed to Charles and is now in the collections of the Maryland Historical Society.

128 EPB to Mrs. M. H. Torres McCullough, January 24, 1861, Box 8, MS 142, EPB Papers.

129 Bo to Susan, June 23, 1855, Box 2, MS 2978, Bonaparte Papers; Bo to Susan, July 22, 1855, Letterbook V, Box 8, MS 144, JNB Papers. For more information about Jerome Jr.'s military career, see Clarence Edward Noble Macartney and John Gordon Dorrance, *The Bonapartes in America* (Philadelphia: Dorrance & Co., 1939).

130 Bo to Susan, September 13, 1855, Letterbook, V, Box 8, MS 144, JNB Papers; Jerome Jr. to Susan, February 14, 1856, Box 3, MS 2978, Bonaparte Papers, MdHS.

131 Jerome Jr. to Susan, April 24, May 28, and July 14, 1856; Jerome Jr. to Bo, June 4, 1856, Box 3, MS 2978, Bonaparte Papers, MdHS.

132 For a concise discussion of the Council of Family case, see Burn, *Betsy Bonaparte,* 231–33. Jerome Jr. to Bo, August 4, 1856, in ibid.

133 Jerome Jr. to Bo, July 17, 1856, ibid.

134 Jerome Jr. to Bo, July 21 and August 4, 1856, ibid.

135 Solid red journal, Box 13A, MS 142, EPB Papers; Jerome Jr. to Susan, September 4, 1856, Box 3, MS 2978, Bonaparte Papers, MdHS.

136 Bo to Napoléon III, July 28, 1856, Box 8, MS 144, JNB Papers; Jerome Jr. to Bo, October 20, 1856, Box 3, MS 2978, Bonaparte Papers, MdHS.

137 Jerome Jr. to Bo, June 25 and 26, 1859, Box 3, MS 2978, Bonaparte Papers, MdHS.

138 Bo to Susan, July 6 and 30, and August 15, 1859, ibid.

139 Bo to Susan, June 28, 1859, ibid.

140 Bo to Susan, July 18, 1859, ibid. Bo added, "The name of the Sculptor is Iselin, he is a young man has taken the last three gold medals at each exposition. He gave me twenty two days work to make the clay model. I had a large party of ladies & gentleman to see it broken up, when the mould was made. They all consider the model a perfect reproduction of the original, the bust will be done in three months, price 3000 frs. ($600)."

141 Jerome Jr. to Susan, August 22, 1859, Box 3, MS 2978, Bonaparte Papers, MdHS.

142 Letters from this period are found in Box 4, MS 2978, Bonaparte Papers. These detail Jerome Jr.'s finding his apartment in Paris and later wanting to offer it to his father because his duties took him away from it too often, as he found himself mostly in Tours. See specifically Jerome Jr. to Bo, Paris, March 14, 1860, Box 4, MS 2978, Bonaparte Papers, MdHS.

143 Bo to Susan, August 22, 1859, Box 3, MS 2978, Bonaparte Papers, MdHS. The Christofle silver company was founded by Charles Christofle in Paris in 1830. In the 1850s, the company undertook important commissions for Napoléon III.

144 Bo to Susan, August 29, 1859, ibid.

145 Jerome Jr. to Bo, February 8, 1860, Letterbook III, Box 8, MS 144, JNB Papers; Jerome Jr. to Bo, June 26, 1860, Box 4, MS 2978, Bonaparte Papers, MdHS.

146 Jerome Jr. sent a copy of his letter to the emperor to his father on June 26, 1860. It reads, "Il m'a été interdit de m'approcher de mon Grand père pendant sa maladie et à ses derniers moments. Je désire du moins lui rendre les derniers devoirs, et occuper au jour de ses funerailles la place que doit avoir son petit-fils. Craignant de ne recevoir aucun avis à cet effet, je viens prier Votre Majesté de vouloir bien donner ses ordres pour que cette légitime satisfaction ne me soit pas refusée. J'ose espèrer que votre Majesté voudra bien acceuillir favorablement ma prière..." [I have been forbidden to come near my grandfather during his illness and at his last moments. I desire to pay one's last respects, and, on the day of his funeral, to occupy the place that his grandson must have. Fearing not to receive any judgment on this matters, I come to beg your Majesty to be willing to give his orders that his legitimate satisfaction not be rejected. I dare to hope that your Highness will receive my plea favorably.] Jerome Jr. to Bo, June 26, 1860, Letterbook III, Box 8, MS 144, JNB Papers.

147 Jerome Jr. to Bo, June 28, 1860, Volume III, Box 8, MS 144, JNB Papers.

148 Jerome Jr. to Susan, July 4, 1860, ibid.

149 Jerome Jr. to Bo, July 4, 1860, ibid.

150 Jerome Jr. to Bo, July 4, 1860, ibid.

151 Solid red journal, Box 13A, MS 142, EPB Papers.

152 Jerome Jr. to Bo, April 18, 1860, Box 3, MS 2978, Bonaparte Papers, MdHS.

153 Jerome Jr. to Bo, April 18, 1860, Letterbook III, Box 8, MS 144, JNB Papers.

154 For a discussion of the lawsuit see Burn, *Betsy Bonaparte,* 236–37.

155 Most of the articles pasted into Elizabeth's scrapbooks do not include dates or the source of the article. These quotes are taken from undated clippings. The scrapbooks are found in Box 15, MS 142, EPB Papers.

156 The Cour de cassation is the highest court in France. It considers decisions generated by lower courts and determines whether the law was applied correctly in a specific case.

157 EPB to Bo, July 18, 1861, Box 8, MS 142, EPB Papers.

158 A copy of a letter from EPB to Bo, July 18, 1861, Box 8, MS 142, EPB Papers.

159 Jerome Jr. to Bo, June 11 and September 9, 1861, Box 4, MS 2978, Bonaparte Papers, MdHS.

160 John Thomas Scharf, *Chronicles of Baltimore, Being a Compete history of "Baltimore Town" and Baltimore City from the Earliest Period to the Present* (1874; repr., Port Washington, N.Y.: Kennikat Press, 1972), 652–53.

161 Scrapbook, Box 15, MS 142, EPB Papers.

162 Jerome Jr. to Bo, February 8, 1865, Box 4, MS 2978, Bonaparte Papers; Bonaparte Book Collection, MS 3134, MdHS.

163 Jerome Jr. to Susan, November 10, 1863, Box 4, MS 2978, Bonaparte Papers, MdHS.

164 Carter, Diaries.

165 EPB to Charles, March 18, 1870, Box 1, MS 2978, Bonaparte Papers, MdHS.

166 "Death of Jerome Napoleon Bonaparte," *Baltimore Sun,* June 18, 1870.

167 A draft of the wording on Bo's gravestone and its translation are found in Box 4, MS 144, JNB Papers. In the draft, "King of Westphalia" is crossed out in favor of "son of Jerome Napoleon Bonaparte" which ultimately was the Latin inscription on the stone.

168 EPB to William Patterson, September 9, 1829, Box 5, MS 142, EPB Papers. "I feel that when I gave

birth to a child I incurred the charge of maintaining him & I prefer doing it to allowing him to be paid by the Williams for ennobling their dirty blood—Let them marry their daughter to one of her equals."

169 Charles to Susan, Cambridge, February 25, 1871, Box 4, MS 2978, Bonaparte Papers, MdHS; "A Bonaparte Among Us: Arrival of Col. Jerome Napoleon Bonaparte," *New York Times*, April 14, 1871.

170 Jerome Jr. to Bo, February 8, 1850 and February 1, 1851, Box 2, MS 2978, Bonaparte Papers, MdHS.

171 EPB to Bo, July 1, 1861, Box 8, MS 142, EPB Papers.

172 Charles to Susan, January 21, 1871, Box 4, MS 2978, Bonaparte Papers, MdHS. During the war, Dix was responsible for arresting pro-Southern Maryland legislators and working to ensure Maryland would remain in the Union. He gave Bo an inkwell in the form of a sarcophagus.

173 Charles to Susan, February 25, 1871, ibid.

174 "Marriage of Jerome Napoleon Bonaparte to Boston Lady," *Baltimore Sun*, September 11, 1871.

175 Jerome Jr. to EPB, July, 1871, Box 4, MS 144, JNB Papers.

176 EPB to Jerome Jr., August 18, 1871, Box 8, MS 142, EPB Papers.

177 EPB to Charles, May 27, 1872, MS 2978, Bonaparte Papers, MdHS.

178 Cameron Allen, *The History of the American Pro-Cathedral of the Holy Trinity, Paris (1815–1980)* (iUniverse.com, 2013): 504.

179 Carter, Diaries, entry dated 1876. Obituary of Elizabeth Patterson Bonaparte, "Death of a Celebrated Personage," *Baltimore Sun*, April 5, 1879.

180 EPB to Charles, June 3, 1872, Box 1, MS 2978, Bonaparte Papers, MdHS. Although Charles inherited all of his grandmother's material possessions, some of her objects were later owned by Jerome Jr., some of which passed to his daughter, Louise Eugenie.

181 I am indebted to the Newport Preservation Society for assisting me with my research into the history of Harrison House.

182 Charles to Susan, Box 1, MS 141, Charles Joseph Bonaparte Papers, MdHS [hereinafter CJB Papers]; "Mme. Bonaparte Dead," *Baltimore Sun*, November 20, 1911.

183 Charles to Susan, February 15, 1873, Box 1, MS 141, CJB Papers.

184 Charles Bonaparte to Susan, February 22, 1873, Box 1, MS 141, CJB Papers.

185 "Simple Funeral for Mrs. Bonaparte," *Baltimore Sun*, November 20, 1911.

186 Charles to Susan, February 15, 1873, MS 141, CJB Papers.

187 Charles always called his brother, "The Major" and his nickname for his mother, begun by his father,

188 EPB to Charles, January 3, 1873. Box 4, MS 2978, and EPB to Charles, October 16, 1873, Box 1, MS 2978, Bonaparte Papers, MdHS.

189 Charles to Susan, March 22, 1873, Box 1, MS 141, CJB Papers.

190 EPB to Charles, February 15, 1872, Box 1, MS 2978, Bonaparte Papers, MdHS.

191 Charles to Susan, March 22, 1873, Box 1, MS 141, CJB Papers.

192 W. T. R. Saffell, "The Baltimore Bonapartes: Views of Madame Patterson and Col. Jerome Bonaparte on the French Situation," in Saffell, *Bonaparte-Patterson Marriage*, 233-42.

193 EPB to Charles, January 3, 1873, Box 4, MS 2978, Bonaparte Papers, MdHS.

194 Saffell, *The Baltimore Bonapartes*, 237.

195 "Mme. Bonaparte's Illness: Her Condition Extremely Critical," *New York Times*, March 31, 1879.

196 Scrapbook of Mr. and Mrs. W. Hall Harris Jr., MS 2008, Archives of the Maryland Historical Society.

197 Carter, Diaries

198 "Death of a Celebrated Personage," *Baltimore Sun*, April 5, 1879.

199 "Col. Bonaparte's Washington Residence," *New York Times*, July 17, 1881.

200 This description of Chateau Bonaparte can be found at http://ghostsofdc.org/2012/04/09/if-walls-could-talk-chateau-bonaparte-on-k-street/.

201 Charles to Susan, February 25, 1871 and May 16, 1873, Box 4, MS 2978, Bonaparte Papers, MdHS.

202 Joseph Bucklin Bishop, *Charles Joseph Bonaparte: His Life and Public Services* (New York: C. Scribner's Sons, 1922), 24.

203 Ellen Channing Day to her mother, October 27, 1875, MS 3152, Charles Joseph and Ellen Bonaparte Papers, MdHS.

204 Obituary, *Chicago Daily Tribune*, September 5, 1893; "Col. Bonaparte Is Dead," *Washington Post*, September 5, 1893.

205 "The Bride of a Count," *Washington Post*, December 30, 1896.

206 *Baltimore American*, January 27, 1897.

207 Caroline Bonaparte to Ellen Bonaparte, May 20, 1905, Box 3, MS 141, CJB Papers.

208 A detailed inventory of Louise Eugenie's jewelry is now in a private archive in Denmark. It lists several pieces of jewelry given to her by the empress, including a black pearl and diamond brooch and the crescent-shaped pearl hair ornament seen in a miniature of

remained "Miss Susan." Even in adulthood, he occasionally referred to himself as "The Child," the name his parents used when they spoke of him.

Louise Eugenie, as well as in a photograph taken shortly after her marriage.

209 *Washington Post*, January 20, 1912.

210 Finn Pedersen and Adam C. Moltke-Huitfeldt, *Espe: fra landsby til herregård* (Næstved, 2010), 206–10.

211 Maurice Francis Egan, *Ten Years Near the German Frontier: A Retrospect and a Warning* (Charleston, S.C.: George H. Doran Company, 1918; repr., Charleston, S.C.: Bibliolife, 2009), 22.

212 Ibid.

213 "Jerome Bonaparte Wed. . . . She Got a Divorce on April 3," *New York Herald*, April 9, 1914.

214 "Mrs. Jerome Bonaparte Meets Alfonso in Palace by Chance," *Baltimore Sun*, May 6, 1924.

215 Letters from Charles to Susan, dating to his undergraduate days at Harvard can be found in Box 4, MS 144, JNB Papers.

216 Bishop, *Charles Joseph Bonaparte,* 92–93, 103.

217 Ibid.

218 "New Head of the Navy," *Washington Post*, June 1, 1905; "Charles Joseph Bonaparte, Head of the Navy, Totally Unlike the Corsican Man of Destiny," *Washington Post*, December 9, 1906.

219 Caroline Bonaparte to Charles, June 1, 1905, Box 3, MS 141, CJB Papers.

220 Ellen Bonaparte to Mabel Whitney Wheeler, May 24, 1905, Box 1, MS 3152, Charles Joseph and Ellen Bonaparte Papers, MdHS.

221 Joseph Bucklin Bishop, *Theodore Roosevelt's Letters to His Children* (New York: Charles Scribner's Sons, 1919), 145.

222 Bishop, *Charles Joseph Bonaparte,* 159–60.

223 "The Bonaparte Home," [Baltimore] *Sunday Evening News*, January 28, 1912.

224 Although this inventory refers to these particular chairs as "Napoleon II's," it is possible this may be a typographical error and may, in fact, have been chairs associated with Napoléon III.

225 "Inventory of Chattels and Personal Estate of Charles J. Bonaparte," June 28, 1921, Box 8, MS 141, CJB Papers.

226 "Charles Joseph Bonaparte, 1851–1921, An Appreciation," Box 1, MS 3152, Charles Joseph and Ellen Bonaparte Papers, MdHS.

227 *Maryland Historical Magazine*, 17 (1922): 94–97; Ellen Bonaparte to J. Appleton Wilson, January 16, 1922, Bonaparte donor file, MdHS.

BIBLIOGRAPHY

PRIMARY

Baltimore American, Baltimore, Md.

Baltimore City Directories. *Matchett's Baltimore Directory*. Baltimore: Richard J. Matchett, 1842, 1847–1848, 1849–1850 and *Baltimore Directory for 1845, the City Register*. Baltimore: John Murphy, 1845.

Bishop, Joseph Bucklin. *Theodore Roosevelt's Letters to His Children*. New York: Charles Scribner's Sons, 1919.

Bonaparte, Elizabeth Patterson. Administration Account. Register of Wills, Baltimore City, Administration Accounts, Original. Box 92. MSA T627-66, Maryland State Archives.

Bonaparte, Elizabeth Patterson. Inventory, 23 April 1879. Register of Wills, Baltimore City, Inventories. MSA T643, 1789–1927. Maryland State Archives.

Bonaparte, Elizabeth Patterson. Will, September 2, 1871. Register of Wills, Baltimore City, Wills. MSA T597, Maryland State Archives.

Bonaparte Vertical File, Maryland Historical Society.

Callcott, Margaret Law, ed. *Mistress of Riversdale: The Plantation Letters of Rosalie Stier Calvert, 1795–1821*. Baltimore: The Johns Hopkins University Press, 1991.

Carter, Martha Custis Williams. Conversations or notations from Madame Bonaparts [*sic*] conversations: Miss Gwinn's, 84 Cathedral St., Baltimore: autograph manuscript diary, 1875–1877. Department of Literary and Historical Manuscripts, Pierpont Morgan Library, New York, N.Y.

Carter, Martha Custis Williams. Letters Concerning Elizabeth Patterson Bonaparte. 1805–1893. Micro 3504. Maryland Historical Society.

Evening News, Sunday, Baltimore, Md.

Lint, Gregg L., and C. James Taylor, Margaret A. Hogan, Jessie May Rodrique, Mary T. Claffey, and Hobson Woodward, eds. *The Adams Papers: Papers of John Adams*, vol. 13. Boston: The Belknap Press of Harvard University Press, 2006.

Madison, Dolley. Dolley Madison Papers. University of Virginia Digital Library. http://rotunda.upress. virginia.edu/dmde/.

[Maryland Historical Society.] "Proceedings of the Society," *Maryland Historical Magazine* 17 (1922): 89–113.

MS 141. Charles Joseph Bonaparte Collection, 1851–1921. [CJP Papers] Maryland Historical Society.

MS 142. Elizabeth Patterson Bonaparte Papers, 1802–1879. [EPB Papers] Maryland Historical Society.

MS 143. Papers, 1801–1852 [Jérôme Bonaparte, King of Westphalia, 1784-1860]. Maryland Historical Society.

MS 144. Jerome Napoleon Bonaparte Papers, 1805–1893. [JNB Papers] Maryland Historical Society.

MS 145. [William Patterson]Collection, 1798–1835 [William Patterson, 1752-1835]. Maryland Historical Society.

MS 2978. Bonaparte Papers, 1805-1890. Maryland Historical Society.

MS 3134. Bonaparte Book Collection, 1741-1928. Maryland Historical Society.

MS 3152. Charles J. and Ellen C. Bonaparte Collection, 1852-1925. Maryland Historical Society.

Morgan, Lady Sydney. *Lady Morgan's memoirs: autobiography, diaries, and correspondence*, vol. II. In *Collection of British Authors*. Leipzig: B. Tauchnitz, 1863.

National Intelligencer, Washington, D.C.

New York Times, New York, N.Y.

Shippen, Rebecca Lloyd Post. "Mrs. B. I. Cohen's Fancy Dress Party," *Maryland Historical Magazine* 14 (1919): 348–58.

Sun, Baltimore, Md.

Sunday Herald, Baltimore, Md.

Washington Post, Washington, D.C.

Wilhelmine, Frédérique Sophie. *Mémoires de Frédérique Sophie Wilhelmine de Prusse…Soeur de Frederic-Le-Grand: Ecrits de sa Main, Tome I and II.* Paris, 1811.

SECONDARY

Allen, Cameron. *The History of the American Pro-Cathedral of the Holy Trinity, Paris (1815-1980).* iUniverse.com, 2013.

Berkin, Carol. *Wondrous Beauty: The Life and Adventures of Elizabeth Patterson Bonaparte.* New York: Alfred A. Knopf, 2013.

Bishop, Joseph Bucklin. *Charles Joseph Bonaparte: His Life and Public Services.* New York: C. Scribner's Sons, 1922.

Bressler, Fenton. *Napoleon III: A Life.* New York: Carroll & Graf Publishers, 1999.

Burn, Helen Jean. *Betsy Bonaparte.* Baltimore: Maryland Historical Society, 2010.

Didier, Eugene L. *The Life and Letters of Madame Bonaparte.* New York: Charles Scribner's Sons, 1879.

Earman, Cynthia D. "Remember the Ladies: Women, Etiquette, and Diversions in Washington City, 1800–1814." In Bowling, Kenneth R., "Coming into the City: Essays on Early Washington, D.C.," *Washington History,* 2000.

Egan, Maurice Francis. *Ten Years Near the German Frontier: A Retrospect and a Warning.* New York: George H. Duran Company, 1918; Charleston, S.C.: Bibliolife, 2009.

Lepore, Jill. *Book of Ages: The Life and Opinions of Jane Franklin.* New York: Alfred A. Knopf, 2013.

Lewis, Charlene M. Boyer. *Elizabeth Patterson Bonaparte: An American Aristocrat in the Early Republic.* Philadelphia: University of Pennsylvania Press, 2012.

Macartney, Clarence Edward Noble and John Gordon Dorrance. *The Bonapartes in America.* Philadelphia: Dorrance & Co., 1939.

Olson, Sherry H. *Baltimore: The Building of an American City.* Baltimore: The Johns Hopkins University Press, 1980.

Robbins, Jane. *The Trial of Queen Caroline: The Scandalous Affair that Nearly Ended a Monarchy.* New York: Free Press, 2006.

Saffell, W. T. R. *The Bonaparte-Patterson Marriage in 1803 and the Secret Correspondence on the Subject Never Before Made Public.* Philadelphia: The Proprietor, 1873.

Scharf, John Thomas. *Chronicles of Baltimore, Being a Complete history of "Baltimore Town" and Baltimore City from the Earliest Period to the Present.* Baltimore: Turnbull Bros., 1874; Port Washington, N.Y.: Kennikat Press, 1972.

Scott, Frances and Anne Cipriani Webb. *Who is Markie? The Life of Martha Custis Williams Carter, Cousin and Confidante of Robert E. Lee.* Westminster, Md.: Heritage Books, Inc., 2007.

Sergeant, Philip Walsingham. *The Burlesque Napoleon: Being the Story of the Life and the Kingship of Jerome Napoleon Bonaparte, Youngest Brother of Napoleon the Great.* London: T. W. Laurie, 1905.

Wass, Ann Buermann and Michelle Webb Fandrich. *Clothing through American History: The Federal Era through the Antebellum, 1786–1860.* Santa Barbara, Cal.: ABC-CLIO, LLC, 2010.

INDEX

Page numbers in italics refer to illustrations.